T0299012

The first revolution in the Chinese countryside was the land reform implemented in the 'liberated areas' and extended throughout China after the proclamation of the People's Republic of China in 1949. This was important in the consolidation of the Communist Party's political power.

The second revolution was the decollectivisation of agriculture and the shift to the household responsibility system as a basis for agricultural production. The phenomenal increase in Chinese agricultural output from 1978 to 1984 resulted partly from the new system of production and with a resulting explosion of farm incomes.

The second revolution in the Chinese countryside from the late 1970s set the scene for the third revolution: the freeing of markets for farm products and the linking of domestic markets and international markets. The third revolution is still in progress and this book explores its beginnings.

Initially, the book covers the issues of poverty in China and feeding the population. The second section describes the agricultural markets in China and the price reform of agricultural products. The next two parts discuss international and regional issues of China's agricultural economy. Finally, there are contributions on what institutional changes have been associated with the third agricultural revolution. The contributions are from a team of experts on the Chinese economy from inside and outside China led by Professor Garnaut.

The third revolution in
the Chinese countryside

Trade and Development

A series of books in international economic relations and economic issues in development

Edited from the National Centre for Development Studies, The Australian National University.

Academic editor
Ron Duncan, *National Centre for Development Studies, The Australian National University*

Advisory editors
Ross Garnaut, *The Australian National University*
Reuven Glick, *Federal Reserve Bank of San Francisco*
Enzo R. Grilli, *The World Bank*
Mario B. Lamberte, *Philippine Institute for Development Studies*

Executive editor
Maree Tait, *National Centre for Development Studies, The Australian National University*

Other titles in the series
Helen Hughes (ed.), *Achieving industrialization in East Asia*
Yun-Wing Sung, *The China-Hong Kong connection: The key to China's open door policy*
Kym Anderson (ed.), *New silk roads: East Asia and world textile markets*
Rod Tyers and Kym Anderson, *Disarray in world food markets: a quantitative assessment*
Enzo R. Grilli, *The European Community and developing countries*
Peter Warr (ed.), *The Thai economy in transition*
Ross Garnaut, Enzo Grilli and James Riedel (eds.), *Sustaining export-oriented development: ideas from East Asia*

The third revolution in the Chinese countryside

Ross Garnaut
Division of Economics Research School of Pacific and Asian
Studies, The Australian National University, Canberra,
Australia.

Guo Shutian
PRC Ministry of Agriculture, China.

Ma Guonan
Department of Economics and Finance, City University of
Hong Kong and
The Australian National University, Canberra, Australia.

CAMBRIDGE
UNIVERSITY PRESS

CAMBRIDGE UNIVERSITY PRESS
Cambridge, New York, Melbourne, Madrid, Cape Town,
Singapore, São Paulo, Delhi, Mexico City

Cambridge University Press
The Edinburgh Building, Cambridge CB2 8RU, UK

Published in the United States of America
by Cambridge University Press, New York

www.cambridge.org
Information on this title: www.cambridge.org/9780521554091

© Cambridge University Press 1996

This publication is in copyright. Subject to statutory exception
and to the provisions of relevant collective licensing agreements,
no reproduction of any part may take place without the written
permission of Cambridge University Press.

First published 1996

A catalogue record for this publication is available from the British Library

Library of Congress Cataloguing in Publication Data
The third revolution in the Chinese countryside / [edited by] Ross
   Garnaut, Guo Shutian, Ma Guonan.
      p.   cm. – (Trade and development)
   Includes bibliographical references.
   ISBN 0 521 55409 8 (hc)
      1. Agriculture – Economic aspects – China.   2. Agriculture and
   state – China.   I. Garnaut, Ross.   II. Guo Shutian.   III. Ma
   Guonan.   IV. Series: Trade and development (Cambridge, England)
   HD2097.T48   1996
   338.1′851–dc20   95-31548   CIP

ISBN 978-0-521-55409-1 Hardback

Cambridge University Press has no responsibility for the persistence or
accuracy of URLs for external or third-party internet websites referred to in
this publication, and does not guarantee that any content on such websites is,
or will remain, accurate or appropriate. Information regarding prices, travel
timetables, and other factual information given in this work is correct at
the time of first printing but Cambridge University Press does not guarantee
the accuracy of such information thereafter.

Contents

Figures

Maps

Tables

Symbols

..	not available
-	zero
n.a.	not applicable
.	insignificant

Contributors

Chen Chunlai
Economist
Department of Economics
University of Adelaide, Adelaide
Australia

Chen Fan
Deputy Director
Research Institute for Agricultural Economics
Chinese Academy of Agricultural Science, Beijing
People's Republic of China

Dan Etherington
Fellow
Economics Division
Research School of Pacific and Asian Studies
The Australian National University, Canberra
Australia

Fang Cai
Research Fellow
Population Research Institute
Chinese Academy of Social Sciences, Beijing
People's Republic of China

Christopher Findlay
Co-Director
Chinese Economy Research Unit
University of Adelaide, Adelaide
Australia

Keith Forster
Senior Lecturer
Faculty of Arts
Southern Cross University, Lismore
Australia

Ross Garnaut
Professor of Economics
Research School of Pacific and Asian Studies
The Australian National University, Canberra
Australia

Ke Bingsheng
Dean
School of Economic Management
Beijing Agricultural University, Beijing
People's Republic of China

Li Bingkun
Director
Research Department for the Rural Economy
Research Office of the State Council, Beijing
People's Republic of China

Li Qingzeng
Visiting Fellow
Centre for Asian Studies
University of Adelaide, Adelaide
Australia

Justin Yifu Lin
Director
China Center for Economic Research, Peking University
Department of Rural Economic Development, Beijing
People's Republic of China
Adjunct Professor of Economics
The Australian National University, Canberra
Australia

Lu Weiguo
Postdoctoral Fellow
Australia–Japan Research Centre
The Australian National University, Canberra
Australia

Ma Guonan
Lecturer of Economics
Department of Economics and Finance
City University of Hong Kong
Hong Kong
Formerly Postdoctoral Fellow
The Australian National University, Canberra
Australia

Ma Xiaohe
Associate Research Fellow
Economic Research Institute
State Planning Commission, Beijing
People's Republic of China

Carl Riskin
Adjunct Professor of Economics
Columbia University, New York
United States of America
Formerly Visiting Fellow
The Australian National University, Canberra
Australia

Sun Keliang
Economist
Australia–Japan Research Centre
The Australian National University, Canberra
Australia

Tang Renjian
Deputy Director
Minister's Office
Ministry of Agriculture, Beijing
People's Republic of China

Xu Boyuan
Associate Research Fellow
Research Centre for the Rural Economy
Ministry of Agriculture, Beijing
People's Republic of China

Andrew Watson
Co-Director
Chinese Economy Research Unit
University of Adelaide, Adelaide
Australia

Zhang Wenbao
Economist
Policy and Regulation Department
Ministry of Agriculture, Beijing
People's Republic of China

Zhang Xiaohe
Economist
Economics Department, School of Business
Hong Kong Baptist College
Kowloon, Hong Kong

Zuo Chang Sheng
Economist
Policy and Regulation Department
Ministry of Agriculture, Beijing
People's Republic of China

Preface

Reform and development in the Chinese countryside contains some of the most important and interesting economic and political challenges of modern times. This book brings together the results of recent research into reform and development in the Chinese countryside.

There has been a major Australian research effort into the Chinese reforms and economy in recent years, at The Australian National University and the University of Adelaide. Scholars of these two Universities have worked closely together. The rural economy had been one of the foci of research, including recently within a major project sponsored by the Australian Centre for International Agricultural Research. Important contributions have been made to the research by Chinese Ph.D. students, several of whom have now been appointed to the staff of the two Universities. The Australian contributions to this book are part of the output and continuing research effort and collaboration in and between the two Universities.

The rural economy has been a major focus of research in a wide range of institutions within China throughout the reform period. Guo Shutian, Secretary General of the Policy Research Institute of China's Ministry of Agriculture, has brought together recent work from a number of the most highly reputed Chinese agricultural economists from the key rural research institutions in China.

The editors are grateful to The Australian National University and Policy Research Institute of the Chinese Ministry of Agriculture for providing the base for this collaborative effort.

The idea of a book grew out of a conference on China's Reform and Economic Growth hosted by The Australian National University's Research School of Pacific and Asian Studies, which owed much to the organisational skills of Carol Kavanagh, Hilda Heidemanns, Sonya Bodger and Jesmin Fernando. A grant from the Ford Foundation facilitated international participation in the conference.

We are particularly grateful to Maree Tait, Lou Will and Debia Grogan at The Australian National University's National Centre for Development Studies, and to Gary Anson, for excellent editorial work on the manuscript. We acknowledge as well the good work of Amanda Jacobsen and Karen Haines in producing the quality typescript.

Canberra and Beijing
1 January, 1995

1 The third revolution

Ross Garnaut and Ma Guonan

Mao Zedong's successful strategy for the Chinese Communist Party in the civil war was based on the building of political support and strength in rural China – on 'surrounding the cities from the countryside'.

The first revolution in the Chinese countryside was the land reform implemented in the 'liberated areas' and extended throughout China after the proclamation of the People's Republic in 1949. This was important in the consolidation of the Communist Party's political power. It was associated with early gains in agricultural production as order was restored to a war-torn economy, but these were swallowed up by the effects of the forced collectivisation of agriculture that gathered pace through the late 1950s.

The second revolution was the decollectivisation of agriculture and the shift to the household responsibility system as a basis for agricultural production. This was initiated locally in poorer provinces (Anhui and Sichuan), and generally sanctioned by the Central Committee from 1981. The household responsibility system spread rapidly throughout China as its success in raising productivity was demonstrated in the early 1980s.

The phenomenal increase in Chinese agricultural output from 1978 to 1984 resulted partly from the new system of production and partly from large increases in the relative price of grain and other food at this time. The growth in farm incomes was encouraged by the expansion of opportunities to sell a proportion of output at higher prices on local markets rather than to the state, as well as by opportunities to specialise and diversify production according to local comparative advantage.

The resulting explosion of farm incomes between 1978 and 1984 promoted further structural change as farmers sought outlets for their increased savings, and their surplus labour, in the new activities that were opening up in the more market-oriented rural economy. Rural non-farm economic activity expanded rapidly, in commercial services and manufacturing. The township and village enterprises in rural China became the most dynamic component of the national economy through the reform

1

period. They absorbed large amounts of labour freed by rising productivity on the farms, and by the second half of the 1980s they had made the non-farm contribution to output and incomes in rural China greater than the farm contribution.

The second revolution in the Chinese countryside from the late 1970s set the scene for the third revolution: the freeing of markets for farm products, and the linking of domestic markets to international markets. The third revolution was always a necessary element of the 'socialist market economy' towards which China was groping from 1978, and which became explicitly the objective of the reforms at the Chinese Communist Party's National Congress in 1992; but it was always recognised to be politically difficult. The movement away from rations of grain and some other foods made available to urban residents at prices fixed by the state, and from large-scale purchases of farm products by the state at fixed prices, after four decades, increased uncertainty and was bound to be contentious.

In the event, the major progress on breaking the back of the old system of planned procurement and distribution, and on establishing a relatively free national market for almost all farm products for the first time in the history of the People's Republic, was made quickly between mid-1991 and mid-1993. This was rather earlier than anticipated by Chinese and foreign observers alike.

The third revolution is still in progress. It is inevitable that this profound transformation has teething problems. The expansion of the role of markets and market prices in domestic distribution was challenged severely in December 1993 and through 1994, when huge increases in domestic incomes and demand, and associated speculation, led to sharp and large increases in food prices. The knee-jerk reaction of some provincial and central officials was to re-impose controls, although this response was constrained by the absence or weakening of old mechanisms for state procurement and distribution.

One important element of the third revolution – the linking of domestic to international markets – has barely begun. The unification of the swap and official foreign exchange markets in January 1994 was an important precondition for effective integration into world markets. State approval is still required for most international trade in agricultural products, notably for grains. The centralised controls on trade have been so far relaxed only at the margins: for some transactions of foreign joint ventures, and in a limited way for some grain-deficit provinces in coastal areas. Chinese membership of the World Trade Organization (WTO) will require replacement of these controls by tariffs, and significant reductions of tariffs on commodities where they turn out to be relatively high.

Issues and controversies

The third revolution in the Chinese countryside has spurred large changes
in food and other rural output, consumption and trade. Already the
markets are reflecting consumer preference for high quality produce with
markedly higher prices, while low quality items are now sometimes difficult to sell. There are already signs of greater regional specialisation within
China, with provinces or localities concentrating more on activities in
which they are relatively efficient, and becoming less self-sufficient in other
items. There are localised signs, too, of greater international specialisation
– most notably in Guangdong province, where the extraordinary boom in
economic activity in the early 1990s was associated with significantly
reduced plantings and output of grain, accompanied by increased imports
from other Chinese provinces and overseas.

The structural change and uncertainty of outcomes associated with the
integration of domestic markets, and their linkage to international
markets, have inevitably generated tension, debate and controversy. It is a
particular source of unhappiness that growth in farmers' incomes has been
slow in recent years. Grain prices have been rising – notably when inter-
provincial sales have increased from grain surplus regions, and, pending
further and deeper reform, this has sometimes increased fiscal burdens on
local governments. Greater inter-regional specialisation requires freedom
of inter-regional trade, and is the source of anxiety until confidence grows
in the reliability of inter-regional trade. Free domestic prices seem to be
less predictable, generating anxiety about food security. Linkage to international markets is widely felt to exacerbate price instability and supply
uncertainty.

Few of these anxieties are justified by the underlying realities. For some
of those anxieties that have some justification in reality – for example, the
fear that inter-regional specialisation is risky in the absence of reliably free
inter-regional trade – the superior solution is invariably deeper reform,
sometimes associated with the building of new institutions. Still others –
for example, the anxieties about widening disparity in income distribution
as development proceeds in a market framework – require new fiscal policies as well as the deepening of market-oriented reform.

Feeding the people

It is remarkable that China has been able to feed, at standards that are
comfortable compared with other developing economies, over one-fifth of
the world's population with only one-fifteenth of the world's useable land
(Lin, chapter 2). A crucial contribution to the extraordinary expansion of

agricultural output in the reform period has been made by the change in the incentive structure facing farm households. Many weaknesses in the system of Chinese agriculture remain, including in price formation, and institutions for domestic and foreign trade. Further reform – the completion of the third revolution – is a necessary part of the solution to many remaining problems and weaknesses in the Chinese farm sector. This will lead to various regions in China specialising more in production of those agricultural commodities for which their economic capacities are best suited. For China as a whole, this is likely to lead to larger exports of labour-intensive products, and increases in grain imports (Huang, chapter 3). But while achievement of the 'Third Revolution' is necessary for continued progress in Chinese agriculture, there is no doubting the difficulty of moving ahead.

Trends in demand in the reform period show large increases in expenditure on food, in line with rising incomes (Garnaut and Ma, chapter 4). Since the mid-1980s, rising living standards have been associated with an overall fall in per capita consumption of grain directly by people, but a huge increase in indirect consumption of grain in such high-value foods as meat, eggs, dairy products and alcoholic beverages. The levels and pattern of Chinese food demand through the reform period have tracked closely those of Taiwan through the 1960s and early 1970s, when its per capita income in today's dollars was almost three times that recorded officially for mainland China now. These trends are likely to continue with rising incomes through the 1990s. Rising domestic demand has underwritten the expansion of production in an agricultural economy in which international trade remains of marginal importance. The domestic supply of grain is unlikely to increase in line with demand in the future, in the absence of large price increases (supported by protection against imported food) or large subsidies to production. It would probably require both protection and production subsidies. China faces a crucial public choice dilemma in the course of the third revolution: whether to integrate fully into international markets, and accept large increases in imports of grain in one form or another; or to follow the precedents of Japan, Taiwan and Korea, into high protection for agriculture, high prices and heavy fiscal burdens (Ma, chapter 12 and Fang, chapter 13). Garnaut, Fang and Huang (chapter 14) show that these are now urgent issues. After suppressing agriculture in most of the years since the founding of the People's Republic, Chinese domestic prices rose above world prices for several major food commodities. China has reached a crucial turning point, at which it must choose between protection and free trade. Choice will become harder, and the costs of change will rise considerably if internationalisation is delayed.

The critical question of whether economic growth has been associated with the alleviation of poverty provokes a mixed conclusion: there was a large and rapid reduction in the number of people living in poverty in rural China in the period to the mid-1980s; but the rate of reduction slowed after that, and in some periods may have reversed (Riskin, chapter 5). There have been large regional variations in the rate of reduction of poverty. Location in western provinces is associated with higher probabilities of living in poverty, principally because of the scarcity of income opportunities off the farm. A majority of the poor are scattered through the population and not concentrated into officially designated poverty areas. Riskin draws an important conclusion that the effective transfer to the poor of a relatively small proportion of the incomes of people who are not poor would remove poverty from China.

Marketing and price reform

China faces dilemmas in price reforms (Li, chapter 6). There have been three phases of price reform. The latest, since 1991, has seen rapid movement towards determination of agricultural prices in markets, even for commodities like grain and cotton, the prices of which have been the focus of high political sensitivity. Many problems of China in the reform period have derived from weaknesses in the price structure, including irrational relativities between the prices of farm output and inputs. There is a considerable challenge in finding the right paths to market determination of prices, alongside effective regulation to make markets work better. The role of buffer stocks in generating price stability, and achievement of consistency between domestic and international prices as China enters the WTO, are aspects of this search. There are problems in the market system that have emerged since 1988 in the 'third revolution', the solution to which requires further reform. Many Chinese are anxious about price stability as the old state controls are withdrawn, and seek greater stability than seems to be ensured when prices are set in markets (Tang, chapter 7). this raises questions about the appropriate role of regulation in a market economy. Tang discusses the case for a continuing state role in stabilisation, through the maintenance of buffer stocks, as well as through a range of regulatory arrangements.

The prices of inputs – and in particular the price of fertiliser – can be as important to agricultural output as product prices (Zhang and Zuo, chapter 8). Past policies and contemporary reforms affecting fertiliser prices show that direct subsidy has been large, with much being spent to encourage the production of fertiliser, rather than of agricultural goods. A first requirement of an efficient fertiliser price regime is that any subsidy reaches its desired target – presumably the stimulation of agriculture rather than fertiliser output. A number of other distortions result from the remaining controls on fertiliser prices: excessive use in high-yield areas and deficient use in low-yield areas; irrational relative prices across different chemical fertilisers; and distorted choices between importing fertiliser and importing food. Price subsidies for fertiliser still remain a major burden on central and local government budgets. The solution to all of these problems is market-based reform. Some of the fiscal savings from reform could usefully be applied to assisting agriculture in more productive ways. Other important issues, such as the environmental consequence of using fertiliser excessively, have not yet become part of the agenda for discussion.

The growth of new wholesale markets during the reform period has been spectacular, especially when they have grown spontaneously, without government promotion (Xu, chapter 9). But once they have become important, their presence raises questions about appropriate forms and levels of government intervention. Where they are functioning well, they help to stabilise prices and widen the seasonal and geographic spread of consumption and production. Much can be learned from the successful operating markets.

The rural economy has experienced problems characteristic of partial reform over the past decade (Zhang et al., chapter 10). Commodity 'war' or 'chaos' has emerged when local governments have had fiscal or other incentives to block the free inter-regional movement of commodities. Each case of chaos has its own fascinating features, but each has a similar cause, to which the solution is deeper reform to establish an integrated domestic market.

Vegetable marketing presents a remarkable case of institutional development, free of the political sensitivity of grain and oil markets, and therefore of tendencies for the state to apply pervasive controls. A highly sophisticated and differentiated national market for vegetables has developed. The result is fine regional specialisation according to climate, seasons and the value of land in alternative uses, all co-ordinated through markets with dispersed and rapidly changing and expanding consumer demand. Prices are free to rise, attracting produce from more distant places as demand increases, and as old supply sources lose their competitiveness with the rising value in other uses of land adjacent to the large cities. In the vegetable markets, problems of regulation remain, but the overall tendency has been towards rapid and productive institutional change. The scale of the trade in high-value fruit and vegetable products confirms the argument that we have made elsewhere (Garnaut and Ma 1993a) that China's consumption patterns are those of an economy with substantially higher per capita income than is presented in the official data of China.

Internationalisation

The international dimension of establishing a market framework for Chinese agriculture introduces difficult issues for China, as for many countries whose resource endowments tend to generate increasing food imports in the process of economic growth. For China, the early revolutionary leaders' strong commitment to 'self-sufficiency', supported by memories of difficulties in obtaining access to world markets against the American embargo in the famine of the early 1960s, makes the internationalisation of grain markets particularly sensitive. While the 'self-sufficiency' reflex from Maoist days is weakening, there are still anxieties about food security and price stability. In reality, once China sought grain from international markets, it was able to obtain supplies from non-American sources; but the memories and associated anxieties are nevertheless important to Chinese discussion. Feelings of these kinds are now being challenged by the undoubted gains to efficiency and economic growth, and to productive international trade relations within the World Trade Organization (WTO), from maintaining open grain markets.

China's entry into the WTO will provide some opportunities to expand exports and the production of those agricultural products whose prices in China are now below world prices (Ma, chapter 12 and Fang, chapter 13). But economic growth, acting on China's low per capita endowment of agricultural land, will cause fewer and fewer commodities to be in this category, as both domestic demand for these products and the opportunity costs of producing more of them increase. Increasingly, open trade in agricultural products will force adjustment in Chinese agriculture, and contraction in production of some, perhaps many, items.

It is desirable that China expands imports and undergoes substantial structural change in its agricultural sector in the process of general trade liberalisation. It will be costly for Chinese development if this path is avoided. But there will undoubtedly be political pressures for resisting structural change, as there have been in other countries with low per capita endowments of agricultural land as their incomes have grown.

Regional issues

Guangdong, now together with Shanghai, is in the forefront of economic reform, internationalisation and economic growth in China. Some of the trends identified in Guangdong can be expected to emerge later elsewhere, at least in densely populated coastal provinces (Garnaut and Ma, chapter 15). The powerful tendency for rising incomes to raise demand for high-value food, and to encourage re-specialisation in high-value production in response to new market opportunities, has led to large reductions in grain acreage and output and large increases in flows of grain into Guangdong from other provinces and abroad. This has generated some protectionist responses, suggesting that China's eventual choice between open grain trade and Northeast Asian-style protectionism will face the usual range of political pressures.

There is a tendency for coastal provinces to reduce concentration on grain production as markets become more important in distributing output and allocating resources (Li, Watson and Findlay, chapter 16). There is also a tendency in those provinces towards net grain imports, while larger levels of inter-regional trade within China raise prices in provinces with comparative advantage in grain production and lead them to retain a net surplus for longer. There are large efficiency gains from inter-regional specialisation in production, and the resulting higher levels of trade in grain. But the realisation of these opportunities requires substantial reform of and investment in domestic trade and transportation, and recognition at the provincial level of the advantages of free movement of agricultural produce within China.

Rural incomes per person are much lower and growing more slowly in the central and western provinces than in the coastal (eastern) provinces (Ke, chapter 17). A striking conclusion is that the clear superiority of the coastal provinces over the rest is overwhelmingly associated with differences in off-farm economic activities rather than in agricultural performance. The cause is to be found in the proximity to and the close links with dynamic urban economies – a deficiency which will not easily be remedied in the Chinese inland.

Institutional change

Ambiguities now associated with property rights, especially in relation to ownership of township and village enterprises, are damaging performance. A response is to convert the various supposed rights that individuals in rural areas have in collective entities into shares in incorporated enterprises (Chen, chapter 18).

The fiscal arrangements between the various levels of government have created powerful incentives for local governments to encourage the growth of township enterprises. Some of these incentives complicate the process of efficiency-raising reform (Watson, Findlay and Chen, chapter 20).

At first sight, the household responsibility system has not served as well for tea as for other rural industries. Acreage, planting and production of tea have grown more slowly than during the Cultural Revolution. Closer examination reveals economic reasons why this might be expected. Tea requires good local 'public goods' to maintain quality and efficiency in processing and some other activities. There have been deficiencies in the supply of agricultural public goods under the reformed system, and this is an issue of general relevance. In the case of tea, however, part of the decline in plantings and output growth is the result of *increased* efficiency: tea was boosted artificially in the Cultural Revolution, with unsuitable land being brought into production (Etherington and Forster, chapter 19). It is economically efficient for some of this now to be left minimally attended.

Surrounding the cities from the countryside

The first and second revolutions in the Chinese countryside were carried along with widespread popular support. They were associated with large and rapid expansion in agricultural production, and helped to entrench the political position of the Communist Party.

It was later, when the first revolution was extrapolated beyond the initial program of land reform into compulsory collectivisation, that production and associated political problems emerged. It fell to the second revolution to restore incentives for high levels of agricultural output, yielding a spectacular response.

The third revolution is as important for long-term development in the Chinese countryside as the first and second. It is necessary for the supply of food and fibre to keep pace with the rising incomes associated with reform and growth beyond the farm. But it is more complex, more problematical, more politically contentious than the first and second. In its early stages it has thrown up contradictions and dilemmas, the resolution of which requires careful observation and analysis. The following chapters contribute to that observation and analysis.

Feeding the people

2 Success in early reform: setting the stage

Justin Yifu Lin

One of China's most remarkable achievements in the reform era has been its rapid agricultural growth. The initial success of reforms in agriculture, especially the remarkable growth of grain output, greatly encouraged China's political leaders. As a result, a series of more far-reaching reforms was initiated in 1984 in both urban and rural areas. Between 1978 and 1984 the value of agricultural output grew at a rate of 7.4 per cent annually, and grain output at 4.8 per cent. Both rates exceeded by a wide margin those achieved in the previous 26 years, 2.9 and 2.4 per cent, respectively. Compared with the era preceeding reform, the growth in the availability of agricultural products in the early 1980s was truly exceptional. Meanwhile, the population growth rate dropped from an average of 2.0 per cent per year before reform to 1.4 per cent in the 1980s.

Agriculture as a whole continued to grow at a respectable average rate of 4 per cent per year but grain production stagnated after reaching a peak of 407 million tons in 1984, and did not again reach this level until 1989. As grain production is given strategic importance in China's politics, the optimism that robust agricultural development generated during the first five years of rural reforms was swiftly replaced by pessimism. The desirability of instituting the household-based farming system was questioned by some in government and academic circles, and a call even emerged for re-collectivisation. The direction of China's agricultural development again became a much discussed issue.

Development strategy and agricultural collectivisation

After recovering from wartime destruction, China adopted in 1952 a Stalin-type heavy industry oriented development strategy. The goal was to build as rapidly as possible the capacity to produce capital goods and military materials. Capital was extremely scarce at that time and the voluntary saving rate was far too low to finance the high rate of investment in heavy industry sought by the development strategy. To facilitate rapid capital expansion a policy of low wages for industrial workers evolved alongside the heavy industry oriented development strategy. It was assumed that through low wages state-owned enterprises would be able to achieve large profits which they could reinvest. The practice of establishing low prices for energy, transportation and other raw materials such as cotton was instituted for the same reason. To implement the policy of low wages the government provided urban dwellers with inexpensive food and other necessities, including housing, medical care and clothing. A strict food rationing system was instituted in 1953 and continued into the 1990s.[1] Meanwhile, in order to secure the food supply for rationing, a compulsory grain procurement policy was imposed in rural areas in 1953.

The industrial development strategy also resulted in a great demand for agricultural products. First, the urban population increased dramatically from 58 million in 1949 to 72 million in 1952, and to 99 million in 1957 (SSB, *Zhougguo tongji nianjin* (ZTN) 1988: 97). As the industrial strategy did not permit the use of large amounts of scarce foreign reserves to import food for urban consumption, satisfying the increasing food demand in urban areas hinged on the growth of domestic grain production. Second, as the bulk of China's exports consisted of agricultural products, the country's capacity to import capital goods for industrialisation depended on agriculture's growth.[2] Third, agriculture was the main source of raw materials for many industries, such as textiles and food processing. Agriculture, therefore, was clearly viewed as the bottleneck and the major point of intervention in pursuing the overall economic development strategy in China in the early 1950s.

Under these conditions, agricultural stagnation and poor harvests not only affected food supply but also had an almost immediate adverse impact on industrial expansion.[3] As the government was reluctant to divert resources from industry to agriculture, a new agricultural development strategy was adopted that permitted and fostered the simultaneous development of agriculture alongside the development of industry. The core of this strategy involved mass mobilisation of rural labour to work on labour-intensive investment projects, such as irrigation, flood control and land reclamation, and to raise unit yields in agriculture through traditional methods and inputs, such as closer planting, more careful weeding and the use of more organic fertiliser. Collectivisation of agriculture was viewed by the government as the institutional innovation to perform these functions. Moreover, collectivisation was also regarded as a convenient vehicle for effecting the procurement of grain and other agricultural products to carry out the industrial development strategy (Luo 1985: 53).

The independent family farm was the traditional farming institution in rural China for thousands of years prior to the founding of the People's Republic. Experiments with various forms of co-operatives began even before the adoption of the heavy industry oriented development strategy. The official approach to collectivisation was initially cautious and gradualist. Peasants were encouraged and induced to join the different forms of co-operatives on a voluntary basis.

Proponents for accelerating the pace of collectivisation in the summer of 1955 won the debate within the Party. Collectivisation was surprisingly successful in the initial stage. It encountered no active resistance from the peasantry and was carried out relatively smoothly. Between 1952 and 1958 the gross value of agriculture (measured at constant prices in 1952) increased 27.8 per cent and grain output increased 21.9 per cent (table 2.1). This experience greatly encouraged the leadership within the Party and led it to take a bolder approach. The 'people's commune', which consisted of about 30 collectives of 150 households, was forced on farmers in 1958. From the end of August to the beginning of November, 753 thousand collective farms were transformed into 24 thousand communes, consisting of 120 million households, or over 99 per cent of total rural households in China at the time. The average size of a commune was about 5 thousand households, with 10 thousand labourers and 10 thousand acres of cultivated land. Payments in the commune were made according to subsistence needs and partly according to the work performed. Work on private plots was prohibited.

Billions of work-days were mobilised as expected. The communal movement ended up facing a profound agricultural crisis, however, between 1959 and 1961. The gross value of agricultural output measured at constant 1952 prices dropped 14 per cent in 1959, 12 per cent in 1960, and by another 2.5 per cent in 1961. Most importantly, grain output declined by 15 per cent in 1959, and another 16 per cent in 1960, then slowly began to rise. The dramatic reduction in grain output resulted in a widespread and severe famine, estimated to have resulted in 30 million deaths (Aston *et al.* 1988).

Communes were not abolished after the great crisis. From 1962, however, the agricultural operation was divided and management was delegated to a much smaller unit, the 'production team', which consisted of about twenty to thirty neighbouring households. In this new system, land was jointly owned by the commune, brigade and production team. The production team was treated as the basic operating and accounting unit. Income distribution, based on work points earned by each member, was undertaken within the production team. After 1962 many attempts to improve the grading of work points were made. Nevertheless, the production team remained the basic farming institution until the household responsibility system reform began in 1979.

16   Justin Yifu Lin

Table 2.1 *Population, agricultural output and grain output in China, 1952–90*

	Population (million)	Agri. output (1952=100)	Grain output (million tonnes)	Grain trade[a] (million tonnes)
1952	574.8	100.0	163.9	1.5
1953	588.0	103.1	166.8	1.8
1954	602.7	106.6	169.5	1.7
1955	614.7	114.7	184.0	2.1
1956	628.3	120.5	192.8	2.5
1957	646.5	124.8	195.1	1.9
1958	659.9	127.8	200.0	2.7
1959	672.1	110.4	170.0	4.2
1960	662.1	96.4	143.5	2.7
1961	658.6	94.1	147.5	−4.5
1962	673.0	99.9	160.0	−3.9
1963	691.7	111.5	170.0	−4.5
1964	705.0	126.7	187.5	−4.7
1965	725.4	137.1	194.6	−4.0
1966	745.2	149.0	214.0	−3.6
1967	763.7	151.3	217.8	−1.7
1968	785.3	147.6	209.1	−2.0
1969	806.7	149.2	211.0	−1.5
1970	829.9	157.8	240.0	−3.2
1971	852.3	162.9	250.0	−0.6
1972	871.8	161.1	240.0	−1.8
1973	892.1	174.5	265.0	−4.2
1974	908.6	180.7	275.3	−4.5
1975	924.2	186.3	284.5	−0.9
1976	937.2	185.5	286.3	−0.6
1977	949.7	184.8	282.8	−5.7
1978	962.6	199.0	304.8	−7.0
1979	975.4	214.8	332.1	−10.7
1980	987.1	217.9	320.6	−11.8
1981	1,000.7	230.5	325.0	−13.6
1982	1,016.5	256.5	354.5	−14.9
1983	1,030.1	276.5	387.3	−11.5
1984	1,043.6	310.4	407.3	−7.2
1985	1,058.5	321.0	379.1	1.2
1986	1,075.1	331.8	391.5	−0.1
1987	1,093.0	351.1	403.0	8.9
1988	1,110.3	364.9	349.1	−8.2
1989	127.0	376.2	407.6	−10.0
1990	1,143.3	404.8	446.2	−7.9

Note:
[a] Positive figures indicates net exports and negative figures indicates net imports.
Sources: SSB, *ZTN*, (1990: 647, 650; 1991: 55, 79, 623, 726); Ministry of Agriculture, Planning Bureau (1989d: 147–9, 520–2, 534–5).

A more realistic approach towards agricultural development was adopted after the 1959–61 crisis. The mobilisation of rural labour for public irrigation projects continued and greater emphasis was given to modern inputs. Irrigated acreage increased gradually after 1962. Additional acreage was brought into production from more effective irrigation rather than the construction of labour-intensive canals and dams. The utilisation of chemical fertiliser was accelerated after 1962, accompanied by the promotion of modern fertiliser-responsive varieties with high yields. Dwarf varieties of rice and wheat were introduced in the early 1960s. By the end of the 1970s, about 80 per cent of the traditional varieties of rice and wheat had been replaced by the modern dwarf varieties. After 1976 dwarf varieties of rice were replaced by higher-yielding hybrid rice. Modern varieties of corn, cotton and other crops were also introduced and promoted in the 1960s and 1970s. The pace of mechanisation also accelerated after 1965, especially during the 1970s.

Rural reform in China

Despite dramatic increases in modern inputs in the 1960s and 1970s, agricultural output growth continued to be low. Although great emphasis was given to self-sufficiency, China changed from being a net grain exporter in the 1950s to a grain importer after 1961. The discouraging conditions of Chinese agriculture came to an end in 1978 when China started a series of fundamental reforms in the rural sector. Output growth accelerated to a rate several times the long-term average in the previous period. The annual growth rates of the three most important crops – grain, cotton and oil-bearing seeds – averaged 4.8 per cent, 17.7 per cent and 13.8 per cent respectively between 1978 and 1984, compared with their corresponding rates of 2.4 per cent, 1.0 per cent and 0.8 per cent per year in the preceding 26 years. For crops generally and agriculture as a whole, growth was equally impressive: average annual growth rates rose respectively from 2.5 per cent and 2.9 per cent in 1952–78 to 5.9 per cent and 7.4 per cent in 1978–84 (table 2.2). In 1985, for the first time in a quarter of a century, China again became a net grain exporter (table 2.1).

The dramatic output growth was a result of a package of reforms that reduced the functions of plans and gave priority to the roles of individual incentives and markets. Broad changes in rural policy began at the end of 1978. It was recognised that, in order to break the bottleneck of agricultural production, farmers needed sufficient incentives. The original intention of the government, however, was to achieve this goal through raising the long-depressed state procurement prices for major crops, modifying

Table 2.2 *Average annual growth rates of agricultural output, 1952–87 (per cent)*

	Agric. output value	Crop output value	Grain output	Cotton output	Oil crops output	Population
1952–78	2.9	2.5	2.4	2.0	0.8	2.0
1978–84	7.4	5.9	4.8	17.7	13.8	1.3
1984–87	4.1	1.4	–0.2	–12.9	8.3	1.3

Sources: Ministry of Agriculture, Planning Bureau (1989: 112–15, 146–9, 189–92); Ministry of Agriculture (1989d: 28–34); SSB, ZTN (1988: 97).

management methods within the context of the collective system and increasing budgetary expenditure on agricultural investment.

Price reform

The most important policy change intended by the government at the beginning of the reforms was the adjustment of procurement prices for major crops. Before the reforms two distinct prices – quota prices and above-quota prices – existed in the state commercial system. Quota prices applied to crops sold in fulfilment of procurement obligations; above-quota prices to crops sold in excess of the obligation. Announced at the end of 1978 and effective from 1979, quota prices increased 20.9 per cent for grain, 23.9 per cent for oil crops, 17 per cent for cotton, 21.9 per cent for sugar crops and 24.3 per cent for pork. The average increase for the quota prices was 17.1 per cent (SSB, Trade and Price Statistical Division 1986: 404–6). In addition, the premium paid for the above-quota delivery of grain and oil crops was raised from 30 per cent to 50 per cent of the quota prices, and a 30 per cent bonus was instituted for above-quota delivery of cotton (see Sicular 1988a). The average increase for the state procurement prices was 22.1 per cent (SSB, Trade and Price Statistical Division 1986: 401). If only the marginal prices (the above-quota prices) are considered, however, the increase in the state procurement prices was 40.7 per cent (table 2.3).

Corresponding to the increase in procurement prices, retail prices were raised 33 per cent for pork, 32 per cent for eggs and 33 per cent for fish in 1979 but retail prices for basic necessities such as grain and edible oils were not changed. To compensate for the rise in retail prices each urban dweller received 5 to 8 yuan a month (SSB 1988b: 8–14). Government subsidies to

Table 2.3 *Price, crop pattern and cropping intensity, 1965–87 (per cent)*

| | State above-quota contract price (1978=100) | Household responsibility system | Sown area | | | Multiple cropping index |
			Grain crops	Cash crops	Other	
1965	84.1	–	83.5	8.5	8.0	138.3
1970	97.2	–	83.1	8.2	8.7	141.9
1971	98.4	–	83.1	8.2	8.7	144.7
1972	98.4	–	81.9	8.5	9.6	147.0
1973	98.1	–	81.6	8.6	9.8	148.2
1974	98.4	–	81.4	8.7	9.9	148.7
1975	98.7	–	81.0	9.0	10.0	150.0
1976	99.4	–	80.6	9.2	10.2	150.6
1977	100.0	–	80.6	9.1	10.3	150.5
1978	100.0	–	80.4	9.6	10.0	151.0
1979	140.7	1	80.3	10.0	8.7	149.2
1980	140.4	14	80.1	10.9	9.0	147.4
1981	145.1	45	79.2	12.1	8.7	146.6
1982	144.3	80	78.4	13.0	8.6	146.7
1983	144.9	98	79.2	12.3	8.5	146.4
1984	142.5	99	78.3	13.4	8.3	146.9
1985	129.4	99	75.8	15.6	8.6	148.4
1986	130.1	99	76.9	14.1	9.0	150.0
1987	130.2	99	76.8	14.3	8.9	151.3

Sources: Column (1) is from Lin (1992a). Column (2) indicates the percentage of production teams in China that had adopted the household responsibility system. the data for 1978–81 are from *Jingjixue zhoubao* [Economic Weekly], 11 January 1982. Figures for 1982–4 are from Editorial Board of China Agriculture Yearbook (1984: 69; 1985: 120). Figures for 1985–7 are inferred from the fact that no major change occurred in the farming institution after 1984. Columns (3) to (7) are taken from Ministry of Agriculture, Planning Bureau (1989: 130–1, 355–7); SSB, ZTN (1988: 224, 243, 276).

prices increased as a result. The financial burden became especially heavy when unexpected output growth started to emerge in 1982. Price subsidies increased from 9.4 billion yuan in 1982 (8.4 per cent of the state budget) to 37 billion yuan (24.6 per cent of the state budget) in 1984 (SSB, ZTN 1988: 747, 763). To reduce the state's burden and to increase the role of markets, mandatory procurement quotas were abolished for cotton in 1984 and for grain in 1985, and replaced by procurement contracts which were supposed to be negotiated and agreed by the government and farmers. The contract price was a weighted average of the basic quota and above-quota prices. This change resulted in a 9.2 per cent decline in the margin paid to farmers (table 2.3). Following the decline of grain and cotton production in 1985 and stagnation thereafter, the contracts were made mandatory again in 1986.

Institutional reform

Unlike the price reforms, the change in farming institutions from the collective system to the household-based system, now called the household responsibility system, was not intended by the government at the beginning of the reforms. Although it had been recognised in 1978 that solving the managerial problems within the production team system was the key to raising incentives, the official position at that time maintained that the production team was to remain the basic unit of production management and accounting. Subdivision of collectively-owned land and delegation of production management down to individual households were prohibited. Nevertheless, a small number of production teams, first secretly and later with the blessing of local authorities, began to try out the system of contracting land, other resources and output quotas to individual households towards the end of 1978. A year later these teams brought in yields far larger than those of other teams.

The central authorities later conceded the existence of the new form of farming but required that this practice be restricted to the poor agricultural regions, mainly to the hilly and mountainous areas and to poor teams in which people had lost confidence in the collective. This restriction was ignored by most regions. Full official recognition of the household responsibility system as a universally acceptable mode of farming was eventually given in late 1981, three years after the initial price increases. By that time, 45 per cent of production teams in China had been dismantled and had instituted the household responsibility system. By the end of 1983, 98 per cent of production teams in China had adopted this new system (table 2.3). It is worth emphasising that the household responsibility system was worked out among farmers themselves, initially without the knowledge and approval of the central government, and spread to other areas because of its merits (see Ash 1988; Kueh 1985; Kojima 1988).

When the household responsibility system was originally introduced, collectively owned land was leased to each household in a team for one to three years. Along with the land lease was a contract between the household and the team specifying the household's obligations to fulfil state procurement quotas and to pay various forms of local taxes (see Crook

1985). A household could retain any product above the stated obligations. In the distribution of land leases, egalitarianism was in general the guiding principle. Therefore, collective land in most cases was leased to a household strictly in proportion to the size of the household, without taking inter-family differences in the size of the labour force into consideration (Kojima 1988). This manner of allocation inhibited efficient land use. Moreover, at the initial distribution, land was first classified into several different grades and a household then obtained a parcel from each grade. As a result, a typical household's holding on average was fragmented into nine tracts in a holding of only about 1.2 acres. The one to three-year short contract was also found to have detrimental effects on the incentives to invest in land improvement and soil fertility conservation (Wen 1989).

These problems led to the introduction of several new policies: from 1983 a household was allowed to exchange its labour with other households and to employ a limited amount of labour for farm work; from 1984 a leasehold was allowed to be extended to 15 years so as to provide better incentives for soil conservation and investment; and from 1984, to make land consolidation possible and to prevent land being left idle when a household engaged in non-farm business, subleasing one's land holding to other households with compensation was sanctioned. These policy reforms seem likely eventually to revive labour and land markets in rural China (Lin 1989b).

National policy has continued to stress the importance of maintaining stability in the newly established household farming institutions. There is still a deeply rooted tendency in China, however, to equate the big tractor to advanced technology, and the large farm size to efficiency (Ash 1988; Schultz 1964). In this context, the increasing discontent with the stagnation of grain production after 1984 led to a re-emergence of calls for enlarging operational size to exploit returns to scale. In some localities, this call resulted in contract disruption before expiration without the consent of farmers (Jiang 1988).

Market and planning reform

The prevalence of planning in agriculture before the reforms was associated with the objective of grain self-sufficiency, a component of the Stalinist heavy industry oriented development strategy that the Chinese government pursued from 1952. Because state grain procurement prices were artificially depressed, areas with comparative advantage in grain production were reluctant to raise grain output levels. Consequently, grain-deficit areas had to increase grain production if demand increased due to growth in population or income. National self-sufficiency thus degenerated into local self-sufficiency. In order to guarantee that each region would produce enough grain for its needs, planning of agricultural production was extensive.

Mandatory targets often specified yields and levels of inputs as well as sown acreage of each crop. Grain was given priority in planning, independently of economic considerations. Local governments were often forced to expand grain sown area at the expense of cash crops, and to increase cropping intensity so as to raise grain output to meet state procurement quotas and local demands, even though these practices often resulted in a net loss to farmers. Such measures caused the allocation of land to diverge from the principle of comparative advantage. The loss of regional comparative advantage was especially serious in areas which traditionally depended on inter-regional trade in grain to facilitate specialisation in cash crops.[4]

The loss of allocative efficiency caused by the self-sufficiency policy was conceded at the beginning of the reforms. Although planning was still deemed essential, more weight was given to market considerations. The decision to increase grain imports, cut the grain procurement quota and reduce the number of products covered by plan control reflected such an intention.[5] Moreover, restrictions on inter-regional trade in agricultural products by private traders were gradually loosened. Special measures were also taken to encourage areas that traditionally had comparative advantage in cotton production to expand cotton sown acreage.[6]

As a result of these policy changes, cropping patterns and intensity changed substantially between 1978 and 1984. Cash crops increased from 9.6 per cent of total sown acreage in 1978 to 13.4 per cent in 1984. Meanwhile, the multiple cropping index declined from 151.0 to 146.9 (table 2.3).[7] Much of the change in crop pattern was in conformity with regional comparative advantage. For example, between 1978 and 1984 the seven provinces traditionally specialising in cotton production increased cotton acreage by 2.3 million hectares while the other provinces reduced cotton acreage by 1.2 million hectares.[8] The cotton sown acreage nationally increased only 25 per cent between 1978 and 1984, but the yield increased 189 per cent. A substantial portion of this dramatic output surge was attributable to more effective use of regional comparative advantage.[9]

The climax of this stage of market reform was the declaration at the beginning of 1985 that the state would no longer set any mandatory production plans in agriculture, and that obligatory procurement quotas were to be replaced by purchasing contracts between the state and farmers.[10] The restoration of household farming and the increase in market freedom prompted farmers to adjust their production activities in accordance with profit margins. The acreage sown to cash crops further expanded from 13.4 per cent of the total sown acreage in 1984 to 15.6 per cent in 1985, while the grain sown acreage declined from 78.3 to 75.8 per cent in the same period (table 2.3). The expansion in animal husbandry, fisheries and subsidiary production was even faster. Total agricultural output grew at a respectable rate of 3.4 per cent in 1985, while the aggregate output of the cropping sector declined 1.9 per cent. Among the three most important crops in 1985, the output of grain declined 6.9 per cent and of cotton 33.7, per cent. Only oil crops registered an increase (33.3 per cent). The stagnation of the cropping sector lingered after 1985. In response to stagnation in grain production, in 1989 the state restored the monopoly in regional grain trade and in marketing chemical inputs.

A careful econometric analysis, using province-level input–output data covering the period 1970 to 1987 and employing the production function approach, found that of the remarkable 42.2 per cent output growth in the cropping sector in 1978–84, about 54 per cent was attributable to productivity growth due to reforms. Of the productivity growth, 97 per cent was attributable to the change in farming institutions from the production team system to the household responsibility system, and the remaining 3 per cent to changes in cropping patterns and intensity. The latter two items are related to reforms in the role of markets and planning. The change in state procurement prices is also found to have had significant effects on agricultural production. Its effect was derived indirectly through input uses: the state procurement price increase was estimated to contribute about 16 per cent to output growth in 1978–84 (Lin 1992a).[11]

Farming institutions and agricultural performance

In addition to farming institutions, the performance of agriculture reflects the reliability of supplies of modern varieties, chemical fertilisers, pesticides, irrigation, tractors and other inputs. It follows that the best way to measure the impact of farming institutions on agricultural performance is to compare total factor productivity in each institutional regime. The approach adopted here first uses factor shares as weights to compile individual input series into a total input series, and then divides the aggregate output series by the total input series to obtain the total factor productivity index. Wen (1989) calculates the gross value of agricultural output from grains, cash crops and livestock. Inputs (and weights) include labour (0.50), land (0.25), capital (0.10) and current inputs (0.15).

Total factor productivity indices for 1952 to 1988 can be divided into four periods: 1952–8, 1959–78, 1979–83 and 1985–8 (figure 2.1). In 1952–8 total factor productivity shows a rising trend, although the increments are

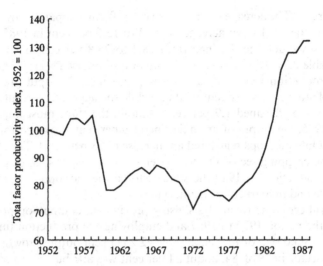

Figure 2.1   Total factor productivity index, 1952–1988 (1952 = 100)

very small. Total factor productivity declined dramatically in 1959–60, when compulsory collectivisation was first imposed, and throughout 1961–78 stayed at a level about 20 per cent below the level reached in 1952. Total factor productivity improved dramatically after 1978 in the period of decollectivisation: by 1983 had regained its 1952 level. In 1985–8, the post-reform period, total factor productivity remained about 30 per cent higher than the 1952 level, though the rate of increase slowed.

Among the significant causes of the collapse of agriculture in 1959–61, and the dismal agricultural performance up to 1978, are the abolition of the right to withdraw from the collectives in 1958, and the continuation of collectivisation as an imposed institution until 1978. Total factor productivity improved in 1952–8 because collectivisation was voluntary, and in 1978–84 because incentives to work were improved with the elimination of imposed collectivisation. Farmers' commitment to good performance in a collective is stronger when participation is voluntary, since each individual is aware that the survival of mutually beneficial activities (such public goods as irrigation facilities) depends on each member being convinced that others are pulling their weight.[12]

An unfinished agenda

The individual household-based farming system reform in 1979 greatly improved peasants' work incentives. Grain production and the agricultural sector as a whole registered unprecedented growth between 1979 and 1984.

While the average annual growth rate of 4 per cent for Chinese agriculture from 1984 to 1989 was high compared to the agricultural growth rates of other industrialised and developing economies, grain production in China stagnated after reaching its peak in 1984 and did not recover this level until 1989. Partly due to extremely good weather and partly due to the government's stress on grain production, grain output in 1990 registered a new record of 435 million tonnes. Farmers had difficulties in selling their grain to the state, due to the state's lack of storage facilities and procurement funds. Moreover, farmers' real incomes ceased to increase in 1990, for the first time since the commencement of rural reform in 1978.

Further reforms were required for sustained agricultural growth. The direction of future agricultural reform, however, was a much debated topic. By 1990 the 'easy' steps in reform had been completed, and an uncomfortable mix of central planning and market activity continued to hinder performance and efficiency in the grain sector: China's agriculture needed a third revolution.

Notes

1 In addition to grain, edible oils, pork and sugar are included under rationing.
2 In 1953 agricultural products alone represented 55.7 per cent of the total value of China's exports, with another 25.9 per cent consisting of processed agricultural products. Up to the mid-1970s, agricultural and processed agricultural products represented over 70 per cent of the total value of exports (Editorial Board of the Almanac of China's Foreign Economic Relations and Trade 1986: 954).
3 This argument is clearly supported by the fact that the heavy industry oriented development strategy had to temporarily give way to the 'agriculture first strategy' after the harvest failures caused by the collectivisation in the late 1950s.
4 Cotton sown area dropped 16 per cent nationally between 1957 and 1977–8. Production declined proportionately more in the northern provinces that initially had substantial comparative advantage in cotton production. For example, the cotton sown area in Hebei, the province initially with the strongest comparative advantage, fell 58 per cent between 1957 and 1977. Consequently, north China ceased to export cotton in the late 1970s (Lardy 1983b: 62–3).
5 Net grain imports increased from 7.0 million tonnes in 1978 to 14.9 million tonnes in 1982 (Ministry of Agriculture, Planning Bureau 1989: 522, 535). Grain purchase quotas were reduced 2.5 million tonnes in 1979 (Ash 1988). For example, the number of planned product categories and obligatory targets were reduced from 21 and 31 respectively in 1978 to 16 and 20 in 1981, and further to only 13 categories in 1982 (Kueh 1985).
6 In 1979 a policy that awarded above-quota delivery of cotton with low-priced grain was instituted. This policy made a huge expansion of cotton areas possible in the traditional cotton producing areas.

7 Reduction in the multiple cropping index may increase the net revenue to farmers, while the gross output declines.

8 The seven provinces traditionally specialising in cotton production are Hebei, Shanxi, Jiangsu, Shandong, Henan, Hubei, Xinjiang (Lardy 1983b: 58). The cotton sown acreage data are taken from SSB (1984: 78), and Editorial Board of China Agriculture Yearbook (1985: 150).

9 Another reason for the rapid growth was the introduction and diffusion of a new high-yield variety called *lurnian yihao* in the early 1980s.

10 'Zhonggong zhongyang guowuyuan guanyu jinyibu huoyue nongcun jingji de shixiang zhengce' [Ten policies of the CCP Central Committee and the State Council for the further invigoration of the rural economy] in Editorial Board of China Agriculture Yearbook (1985: 1–3).

11 Estimations, using Solow–Denison-type growth accounting, by McMillan, Whalley and Zhu (1989) and Wen (1989) also find that the household responsibility system reform was the main source of productivity growth in 1978–84. The institutional change may also have had a dynamic impact on productivity, which is not measured in the studies mentioned above. The shift to the household system also changed the incentive structure, increasing adoption of new technology. A study based on the adoption of hybrid rice before and after the household responsibility system reform confirms that the household system has been more responsive to the profitability of new technology (Lin 1991b). Therefore, the shift from the collective system to the household system may have speeded up the diffusion of new technology.

12 Income may not be the only objective for voluntarily joining a collective and that reorganisation is cost free. If a collective also provides services like risk-sharing and if reorganisation is costly, the productivity of a collective is allowed to be somewhat lower than the sum of the household farms. Moreover, if moral suasion is used in forming a collective, a member will also accept a somewhat lower income in the collective for fear of social opprobrium.

3   Completing the third revolution

Yiping Huang

The successful Chinese agricultural reforms from the late 1970s included decollectivisation and price increases (McMillan, Whalley and Zhu 1989, Fan 1991, Lin 1992a, Huang Yiping 1993).[1]

The household responsibility system reform is very important for the agricultural sector and is now regarded by farmers as the 'second revolution' (Garnaut and Ma, chapter 1).[2] Decollectivisation produced great productivity growth and output gains and also encouraged and called for further reforms in both the agricultural and non-agricultural sectors.[3]

Because the government did not change significantly the mechanisms determining prices and production structure (which remained important parts of economic plans) when it de-collectivised the farming institutions and increased procurement prices, significant diversification of agricultural production did not happen during 1978–84. Productivity gains and efficiency improvements from institutional reform were therefore reflected in the rapid output growth of a narrow range of agricultural products. Grain output, for instance, grew by 7.8 per cent per annum during 1981–4, leading to a temporary grain surplus (Gao and Xiang 1992, Huang Yiping 1993). In many grain-producing regions in 1983 and 1984, market prices for grain fell to levels very close to or even lower than state procurement prices and many farmers found it difficult to sell grain.[4] Gains from the institutional change had been fully exploited and farmers could benefit no more from the 'second revolution' if they continued to concentrate on a small group of agricultural commodities.

The successful institutional reforms in the early 1980s, therefore, called for the 'third revolution' in the Chinese countryside – introducing free markets and linking domestic and international markets. The aim of the third revolution is to accommodate agriculture within a broad, economy-wide market. In fact, Huang Yiping (1993) finds that agricultural performance in China since the mid-1980s has been determined by changes in economy-wide policies as well as by changes in sector-specific policies.[5] From the mid-1980s, increasingly, farmers were able to adjust their resource allocation and production structure to achieve maximum income (Lin 1992a).

Farmers now take 1992 – when the government unified the state purchase and marketing prices for grain – as the starting point of the third revolution. The origins, however, can be traced back to as early as the beginning of 1985 when the government first tried to abolish the central planning system in the rural economy and to introduce market mechanisms for all agricultural products such as grains and cotton. This third revolution, is a less clear-cut event than the second revolution: it takes much longer, follows a more difficult path, and is still far from accomplished.

The period 1985–94 was, in fact full of policy oscillations relating to free markets in agriculture. It can be divided into three sub-periods according to major policy changes. The first, between 1985 and 1988, was a period of comprehensive market reform in the rural economy, although some measures failed and, in some cases, planning measures were restored. The second stage in 1989–90 was dominated by an austerity program targeted at cooling-down the overheated economy and increasing agricultural output. And in the third stage, from 1991, significant progress was made in domestic market reforms for a number of important agricultural products, such as grains and oilseeds.

This chapter reviews major policy changes in the Chinese rural economy after 1985, following the reform scene in the earlier period laid out in the previous chapter, and examines the impact of these policy changes on agricultural production and farmers' income. It then analyses why the third revolution is more difficult to achieve than the second.

The first attempt of market reform: 1985–8

The temporary surpluses and the price falls in markets for major agricultural products, especially grain, in 1982–4, affected growth of agricultural output and farmers' incomes. The only feasible way for further development of agriculture appeared to be diversification of rural production. This was also based on the expectation that demand for, and so prices of, non-grain commodities, such as meat, poultry, fruit and vegetables, would rise as income continued to grow rapidly. Free markets were seen as the only mechanism that could successfully guide the transition of the production structure in directions required from forum prosperity in the new Chinese economy.

At the beginning of 1985, a package of reform policies was implemented to replace the unified purchase and marketing system for agricultural products by free markets. For grain and cotton, mandatory purchase quotas were to be eliminated and replaced by a combination of contract and market purchases. The state would sign contracts with farmers voluntarily before planting seasons (Sicular 1988a). The contract procurement level was about 70.5 million tonnes for grain in 1985 (Huang Yiping 1993). For other products, such as vegetables, fish and meat, government regulations were abolished and the state department would buy and sell in the markets.

The ending of the unified purchase and marketing system allowed Chinese farmers, for the first time in more than thirty years, to make their own decisions on what and how much to produce, given price signals in the markets.

The government also designed a set of related policy adjustments to promote diversification of the rural economic structure and to maintain rapid growth of rural production and farmers' income. First, private commercial agents were allowed to enter the urban markets for meat, poultry, vegetable and fruits, with prices determined in the markets.[6] Second, within the agricultural sector, livestock production was seen as an important activity to absorb domestic grain surplus and to increase value-added in agricultural production. In 1984 and 1985, a large amount of grain was sold to farmers at subsidised prices for feed grain use.[7] And, third, as the agricultural sector was unable to accommodate all the surplus labour in rural areas, the government encouraged the development of the rural township, village and private enterprises. These rural enterprises, from 1984 and 1985, enjoyed preferential policies including tax exemptions and subsidised bank loans.

Some of the policies did not last long. The government purchase contracts for grains and cotton, for instance, were quickly made mandatory in 1985 and 1986 after significant production falls. One reason was because, when the government tried to liberalise grain purchase through a designated contract system, it did not at the same time liberalise the marketing of grain to urban residents. The widening gap between the rising purchase and stagnant retail prices had to be financed by the government, which placed increasingly heavy pressure on the state budget.

The first attempt was made to reform the marketing policy for food (excluding grains and edible oils) in 1988.[8] In May 1988 in all cities, food retail prices were raised to levels similar to market prices and urban residents were given a fixed lump-sum subsidy ranging between 5 to 10 yuan per month. By so doing, the government attempted to de-link the price changes and government subsidy, which was a necessary condition for further reform of agricultural prices.[9]

In 1988, there was also a set of important grain policy reforms introduced in some regions. Guangdong and Fujian provinces, for example, abolished the consumption rations for grain. They were also assigned by the central government the autonomy to import grains for their own use. Various reforms to grain purchase and marketing policies were tried in Xinxian municipality of Henan province, Yulin municipality of Guangxi autonomous region and Zhuozhi county of Inner Mongolia autonomous region, approved by the central and the provincial governments. Although some of these experiments caused some short-term problems,[10] they did provide valuable experiences for nationwide reforms in the early 1990s.

There was much discussion of agricultural reforms during 1985–8 (Niu and Calkins 1986, Gunasekera *et al.* 1991, Lin 1992a, Huang Yiping 1993). Many agricultural economists criticise the policy changes because of the observed drop in output of major agricultural products (Niu and Calkins 1986, Gunasekera *et al.* 1991). Grain output fell by 6.9 per cent in 1985 and did not recover to the 1984 record level (407 million tonnes) until 1989 (408 million tonnes).[11]

However, reforms introduced in 1985 and in the following few years, targeting at a greater role for free markets, were largely successful. The most important contribution of the 1985 reform was that it expanded dramatically farmers' feasible choices from production of a small group of agricultural products to a wide range of agricultural and non-agricultural activities (Huang Yiping 1993). After the reform, farmers could choose to participate in some of the opportunities that were previously unavailable to them. The rural township, village and private enterprises grew rapidly from the mid-1980s. The number of such enterprises increased from 6.1 million in 1984 to 18.9 million in 1988, while the number of employees rose from 52.1 million in 1984 to 95.5 million in 1988. The growth rate of rural industry's output value was 47.2 per cent in 1985, 22.5 per cent in 1986, 25.4 per cent in 1987 and 15 per cent in 1988. As a result, farmers' real per capita income increased by 4.6 per cent in 1985 and continued to rise in the following years until 1989 when farmers' real income fell by 6.8 per cent.

Falls in some major agricultural outputs were, however, predictable and normal responses to the new opportunities (Huang Yiping 1993). First, for grain, the prices at the margin in 1985 were designed to be lower than in 1984.[12] It could be expected that farmers would reduce their use of inputs in grain production. Second, as resources were attracted to activities with higher returns, agricultural inputs decreased, which further reduced agricultural output. Lin (1992a) finds that the growth rate of chemical fertiliser inputs dropped from 8.9 per cent per year in 1978–84 to 3.7 per cent in 1984–7 and the annual growth rate of the agricultural labour force declined from 2.3 per cent to -8.6 per cent in the same period. Moreover, the agricultural sector as a whole still maintained a growth rate of above 4 per cent during this period, which is much higher than the world average, or China's average in the pre-reform period.

Policy adjustment: 1989–90

Despite the rapid expansion of the rural economy and the sharp increase in farmers' real income, falls in agricultural output placed the government under heavy pressure. Starting from 1989, to cool down the overheated economy,[13] an austerity programme was introduced. The importance of maintaining stable growth of agricultural production, especially of grain production, was re-iterated by the government. The government raised significantly grain purchase prices in 1989, and also increased budget spending on agriculture. The contract purchase of grain was termed 'the state purchase quota' to avoid the confusion caused by the form of contract.[14] The more important impact of the policy adjustment in 1989 came from the effects of the austerity program on the development of the township, village and private enterprises (Huang Yiping 1993). Because the policy adjustment sought particularly to restrict bank loans to rural industry, there was a significant contraction of the township, village and private sectors in 1989 and 1990. Part of the resources freed were channelled back into agricultural production.

The number of township, village and private enterprises fell from 18.9 million in 1988 to 18.7 million in 1989 and to 18.5 million in 1990, and the number of employees decreased from 95.5 million in 1988 to 93.7 million in 1989 and to 92.6 million in 1990. [15] The agricultural labour force showed a significant rise in 1989 and 1990.[16] Starting from 1988, more investment was directed to agricultural production, and investment in non-agricultural production dropped in 1989 in particular. Real output of the township, village and private sector declined in 1989 by 2.9 per cent. At the same time, their total profits in nominal terms dropped from 25.9 billion yuan in 1988 to 24 billion in 1989 and to 23.3 billion yuan in 1990.

Agricultural production grew more strongly. Grain output reached the 1984 record level for the first time in five years. Good harvests continued in the following four years, helped by favourable weather conditions. But farmers real income fell in 1989 and 1990.

Agricultural policy changes associated with the austerity programme were an important setback in the process of introducing free markets to Chinese agriculture (Huang Yiping 1993).

Establishing an integrated domestic market: 1991–4

Good grain harvests did not remove the fundamental dilemma: the rising demand for grain due to rapid increases in income and the decreasing resources for grain production because of competition from other (high-return) production activities. One important constraint on grain production was still the increasing gap between the rising purchase prices and the fixed marketing prices in the urban areas.[17] In an effort eventually to introduce the market mechanism for grain, the government first raised the marketing prices significantly at the beginning of 1991 and then brought the marketing prices into line with the purchase prices in April 1992.[18] By the end of 1993, only 25 counties out of 2,000 had not introduced market-based grain distribution systems.[19]

This last step of reform to the grain marketing policy was particularly important because it removed constraints on the movement of purchase prices in line with changes in the markets for the most important agricultural products. The government finally faced up to the long-lasting policy dilemma: on the one hand, it wanted to marketise the rural economy so that prices reflected true demand/supply relations; and, on the other hand, it always found it difficult to fund sufficient rises in purchase prices because marketing prices remained steady.

After the 1992 reform, rises and falls in prices of grain would be absorbed by producers and consumers in the markets, which would have no further implication for the government budget.[20] Farmers expected that, over the longer term, prices would rise faster than under the previous system. Farmers, therefore, regarded the 1992 reform as the 'third revolution'.

But the 'third revolution' was not a clear-cut success, as was the 'second revolution', and it caused new problems to the Chinese economy. The effort of introducing free markets in agriculture after 1985, most significantly marked by the 1992 reform, was, in fact, only half of the 'third revolution'. It did not touch the other half – linking domestic markets to international markets. Trade in some important agricultural products remained monopolised by the state. The consequence of liberalising only domestic markets in a densely populated large country like China is that prices for agricultural products would rise quickly when income grew strongly, as a result of increasing demand and the limited ability of production expansion. This is clearly evidenced by changes in food markets in 1993 and 1994 (Garnaut, Fang and Huang, chapter 14).

The sharp rise of grain market prices at the end of 1993 as a result of grain shortage in some southern provinces, although stabilised in ten days through the sale of some grain stocks and the establishment of an upper limit for grain sale prices, caused several policy changes in 1994. First, grain purchase prices under the state contract were raised further, on average by 20 per cent, to encourage grain production. Second, the government reiterated the importance of maintaining self-sufficiency in grain for each region, especially for the relatively developed regions.[21] Third, some administrative measures regulating grain markets were re-introduced. Private grain traders, for instance, were banned from having grain

from farmers in villages before the fulfilment of the state purchase contract. At the end of 1994, grain coupons were partially re-introduced to
employees of large-scale state enterprises due to rapidly rising food
prices.[22]

The attempt to introduce a free market for agricultural products within
the domestic economy without establishing effective linkage between
domestic and international markets has also brought some serious macro-
economic problems. In 1994, not only have domestic prices for many grain
products, such as wheat, maize and rice, exceeded international prices
marking a turning point in China's agricultural development, but the
increase in food prices has also become one of the most important contributors to the overall inflation (Garnaut, Fang and Huang, chapter 14).[23]

Why is the 'third revolution' so difficult to implement?

After one decade (1985–94) and surprisingly rapid progress for a while in
the early 1990s, the 'third revolution' is only half-way through. It has been
a much more difficult experience for agricultural reforms in these recent
ten years, especially in contrast to the clear-cut and rapidly wide-spreading
'second revolution'. Why is it much more difficult to give birth to the 'third
revolution'?

One important distinction between the second and the third revolution
lies in the different institutional problems they intended to correct. The
second revolution aimed at getting institutions right for the efficient use of
a certain amount of capital, labour, land and other inputs, through more
direct linkage between efforts and incentive. The third revolution, on the
other hand, intended to get institutions right to achieve maximum income
(welfare) through changes in the output structure. The gains from the
former were larger and more obvious, and so were associated with larger
political support.

The second revolution, or the implementation of the household responsibility system reform, was smooth or, incurring less resistance (except for
ideological resistance in early stage of the reform) because it had lower,
almost no, adjustment costs. The implementation of the second reform led
to a significant rise in total output (whatever the production structure)
through improved input efficiency and benefited almost everyone in
society (with farmers the biggest winners).

On the other hand, the third revolution, or the introduction of free
markets into the domestic economy and the linkage of domestic to international markets, involves more or less adjustment in production structure. After abolishing central planning over rural economic activities and
letting market prices guide farmers' production decision, it is natural that

farmers would choose to expand production of items generating higher returns. But every price change is a cost to someone at the same time as it is a gain to another.

The adjustments in the third revolution were associated with three types of problems.

First, if the government is not able to change low grain prices for urban marketing and is not able to subsidise increases in purchase prices, producer prices for grain will not be able to rise to market levels. Introducing markets to the other parts of the rural economy would lead to a significant fall in grain output and cause worries about a sufficient grain supply for domestic consumption (if international trade in grain is not liberalised). This generates pressures for the reversal of market reform, based on appeal to anxiety about the domestic food supply. This could be observed in the second half of the 1980s.

Second, if the government is able to liberalise the grain marketing system but insulates the domestic economy from international markets, domestic demand and supply can be balanced but market prices are expected rise dramatically (Garnaut and Ma, chapter 1, Garnaut, Fang and Huang, chapter 14). In a relatively less-developed country with food a high share of expenditure, this rise in food prices could cause macro-economic problems and adverse effects on welfare for many consumers, leading to pressures for the re-introduction of some administrative controls. These affects could be observed in China in 1993 and 1994.

Fortunately, both of the above two problems can be solved if China links its domestic markets to the international agricultural markets. If, at the margin, China does not have a comparative advantage in grain production, it can export other products, such as labour-intensive manufactured goods, to exchange for grains in the international markets. Reduction in domestic grain production following changes in relative prices, therefore, would not lead to a shortage of the domestic grain supply. On the other hand, as a part of the integrated world agricultural market, rapid increase in domestic demand induced by a sharp rise in income and by the stable growth of the population would not cause dramatic inflation in food prices. The successful completion of the third revolution will largely depend on the success of the internationalisation of domestic agricultural markets.

Internationalisation of the agricultural sector, of course, would introduce a third concern about the 'third revolution': national food security. The Chinese government has deep concern over national food security when introducing further agricultural reforms, especially when introducing a free trade regime for agriculture. Worries are expressed that not only would a wider world market transmit more fluctuations to the Chinese economy, national food security would be vulnerable to embargo by grain exporting countries in the case of political conflicts. These are reasonable concerns, for which there are answers if China and the international community work together co-operatively (Garnaut, Fang and Huang, chapter 14).

Notes

1 Agricultural price reform in those studies refers mainly to increases in the state purchase prices for agricultural products before 1985.
2 In a study on agricultural growth between 1978 and 1984, McMillan, Whalley and Zhu (1989) find that 78 per cent of the increase in productivity in Chinese agriculture was due to changes in the incentive scheme. In addition, they suggest that the incentive effects of the de-collectivisation resulted in a 32 per cent increase in total factor productivity in agriculture. Similarly, Fan (1991) finds that institutional change contributed 27 per cent to agricultural growth during 1965–85. Lin (1992a), using a production function approach, proposes that the institutional reform alone produced 49 per cent of the farming output growth during 1978–84.
3 Institutional reform in the agricultural sector encouraged further reform in at least two ways. First, rapid increase in agricultural output created a favourable food supply environment for other reforms. Second, the contracting system was important in providing experience for similar reforms in state industry, the trading sector and the fiscal system. Agricultural reform also called for further reform in the sense that the old state planning system was already unable to accommodate changes in the agricultural sector in 1982–4 when agricultural output rose sharply.
4 Before 1985, it was formal policy that the state grain departments had the responsibility to buy all the grain that farmers wanted to sell, on top of the quota purchase. In 1983 and 1984, however, because of shortage of storage capacity and heavy pressure on the state budget, the government was not able to purchase all the grain that farmers wanted to sell.
5 Those important economy-wide policies that have significantly affected agricultural growth in the second half of the 1980s include monetary and fiscal policies, trade policies and policies targeted at other sectors of the economy, especially the rural township, village and private enterprises.
6 For many years after 1985, the government stores remained in the urban areas, partly because the government wanted to use these stores to stabilise the markets when prices rose dramatically. Usually they sold products of low quality and at low prices.
7 Another motivation for the government for this feed grain sale was to solve the 'overcapacity storage' of grain accumulated in the previous years.
8 The products covered by the 1988 food policy reform programme included consumption rations on meat, egg and soybean products that were sold by the government stores at subsidised prices.

9 In theory, urban residents would have to face all the changes in market prices for major food products (excluding grains), though they would receive a fixed amount of subsidy each month. But, in many cities, local governments maintained the consumption ration, at higher prices, after the 1988 food policy reform. This was the reason for another round of subsidies when market prices continued to rise while the prices set by the government were fixed.

10 In 1988, after grain policy reforms, Guangdong and Fujian provinces sent agencies to their neighbouring grain producing provinces, such as Hunan and Jiangxi provinces, to buy grain at higher prices. This pushed up market prices in Hunan and Jiangxi and caused difficulties for local grain departments to fulfil purchase contracts because these grain-producing provinces did not have enough revenue to subsidise grain purchase. Receiving complaints from grain producing provinces, the central government issued a policy mid year prohibiting Guangdong and Fujian from buying grain from their neighbouring provinces, excepting those arranged between provincial governments.

11 In Chinese statistics, grain includes soybean and root products like potatoes as well as wheat, rice, maize and other cereals. Potatoes, for instance, are converted into the grain equivalent in statistics using a 4-to-1 conversion ratio.

12 In 1984, there were basically two types of purchase prices: one (lower) state purchase price and the other (higher) negotiated price. In 1985, the two prices were unified into one which was calculated according to 30 per cent of the state purchase price in the previous year and 70 per cent of the negotiated price in the pervious year. This new price in 1985 is lower than the negotiated price in 1984 according to the formula.

13 The inflation rate was as high as 18.5 per cent in 1988 and 17.8 per cent in 1989.

14 Many village and township leaders and the grain departments were actually often challenged by farmers during 1985–9 who asked why they did not have the negotiating power over prices and the right not to sign a contract.

15 This decline of the rural industry was mainly caused by reductions in bank loans. Because of the lack of an effective market in the rural economy, bank loans were the only source of capital investment in rural industry, apart from farmers' own savings. Without the facilitation of the bank loans, farmers' own savings cannot reach the minimum level for establishing an enterprise.

16 While the number of employees of the township, village and private enterprises fell, the total rural labour force increased by 2.2 per cent in 1989 and 2.6 per cent in 1990.

17 Free markets existed after 1985 in both urban and rural areas. But the state grain department still purchased more than half of farmers' total grain sale. In some cases, the government also had the power to close free markets for grain before it fulfilled the purchase quota.

18 As in the case of food policy reform in 1988, a lump-sum subsidy per month is paid to urban residents as a compensation.

19 Among these 25 counties, 13 are in Yunnan province and 12 are in Qinghai province.

20 The government spends a fixed amount of money on the lump-sum subsidy for each urban resident.

21 During a tour to Zhejiang province in early 1994, China's Vice Premier Zhu Rongji stressed that relatively developed regions (such as Guangdong, Fujian, Jiangsu and Zhejiang provinces) should not rely on purchases of grain from other regions or on imports to meet demand. More recently, Chen Junshen also pointed out that the sustainability of the rapid growth of the whole economy in the coastal developed region depends on their ability to balance grain demand and supply, and that realisation of national balance between grain demand and supply depends on the balance in the coastal region (*Economic Daily* 14 November 1994).

22 The grain coupon system was officially abolished in 1993. This partial re-introduction at the end of 1994 reflected partly the pressure of food price increases and partly the failure of the state sector in increasing their employees' income.

23 For the year to September 1994, food prices rose by 27.4 per cent which contributed 46.3 per cent to overall inflation.

4   China's grain demand: recent experience and prospects to the year 2000

Ross Garnaut and Ma Guonan

The massive structural reform of the Chinese grain sector through the 1980s and 1990s is continuing. The years 1991 and 1992 marked an historical turning point in China's market-oriented reform when for the first time the government removed the massive subsidy on urban grain supply and most of the controls on grain marketing. By the end of 1993 the mechanisms for state procurement and allocation by coupon had been removed in more than 90 per cent of mainland China's 30 provinces. For the first time in the PRC's history, government control over the grain sector, a core element of the old plan system, was broken.

The Chinese grain sector, like other parts of the national economy, has experienced various cycles of reform since 1978 (Li, Watson and Findlay, chapter 16). There has been inevitable pressure for re-control in response to market outcomes – for example, those generated by the sharp price increases from December 1993. The dismantling of some of the old institutions of control in 1991–3, however, places limits on the reversal of the recent reforms. More importantly, there is a logic to increased market orientation in the grain sector that becomes evident in practice and which therefore constrains the cycle of reform.

The deregulation of 1991–3 had profound implications for China's grain demand and supply. Direct per capita human consumption of food grain fell for a while, at least in volume, as consumers responded to higher prices and the removal of the psychological influence of valuable ration coupons. Consumption shifted to reflect consumer preferences for higher quality, leaving an unsaleable, almost valueless surplus of the high-yielding hybrid grains that were promoted in the drive to expand production volumes during 1989–92. Demand for animal products continued its strong growth, reflecting changing diet patterns as Chinese income levels rose. Through market forces, now given more scope, these changes in consumer demand will strongly influence the supply of grain.[1]

Past patterns of food consumption

There is a close association among living standards, food grain consumption and consumption of animal products in China from 1952 to 1992 (table 4.1). Two points stand out. First, since 1984 direct grain consumption has stagnated – indeed, declined somewhat – while consumption of animal products (which require grain as feed) has increased rapidly. Second, consumption of animal products has changed much more than food grain, following increases in the level of per capita real income.

Pork has represented the greater part of the consumption of meat (and fish) – about 60 per cent – although pork consumption fell sharply during the three-year famine of 1959–62. The relative importance of pork declined slightly in the 1980s and early 1990s, as that of other meat products increased, as well as that of fish.

In the 1980s and early 1990s average consumption of most food items grew rapidly. According to the official estimates, unmilled food grain consumption per capita rose from 245 kilograms in 1980 to a peak of 290 kilograms in 1986, but thereafter gradually fell to about 270 kilograms in 1990–2. By contrast, per capita pork, beef and mutton consumption increased steadily, by an accumulated total of 73 per cent between 1980 and 1992. Egg consumption more than trebled, and that of poultry and fish more than doubled in the same 12 years.

There have been important differences between rural and urban food consumption. Per capita consumption of food grain in cities in the 1980s declined: from more than 190 kilograms between 1981 and 1984 to about 175 kilograms during 1985–90 (Garnaut and Ma 1992a). Consumption of food grain is much higher in rural areas (about 260 kilograms per capita) than in the cities and was more stable in the 1980s, but also started to drop noticeably in the early 1990s.

The term 'staple supplements' is used to cover meat, eggs, fish and other items of mass consumption that become important when incomes rise. Average city residents consumed much more 'staple supplement' food than their rural counterparts. City consumption ranged between 33 and 44 kilograms per year whereas rural consumption increased steadily from 12 kilograms in 1981 to 17 kilograms in 1990.

The distinctive food consumption patterns of rural and city residents reflect two factors, one inherent in the economic circumstances of the two groups, the other attributable to policy distortions. The first is that higher living standards in urban areas tend to reduce the share of staples in total food consumption. The second is that basic food items in urban areas were heavily subsidised until 1992.

There have been some changes to these patterns following the major

Table 4.1 *Per capita annual food consumption in China, 1952–92 (kg)*

	National income (1952 yuan)	GDP per capita (1987 US$) (unadjusted official)	Food grain	Pork, beef & mutton	Pork	Beef & mutton	Poultry	Fresh eggs	Fish & shrimp	Sugar	Liquor	Milk
1952	102.5	–	227.2	6.8	5.9	0.9	0.4	1.0	2.7	0.9	1.1	–
1957	139.4	–	233.4	6.2	5.0	1.1	0.5	1.3	4.3	1.5	1.4	–
1965	160.3	83	210.2	7.3	6.3	1.0	0.4	1.4	3.3	1.7	1.3	–
1977	250.4	134	220.8	8.0	7.3	0.7	0.4	1.9	3.2	2.9	2.5	0.9
1978	277.4	149	224.7	8.4	7.7	0.8	0.4	2.0	3.5	3.4	2.6	1.0
1979	292.9	157	238.0	10.5	9.7	0.8	0.6	2.1	3.2	3.6	3.0	1.3
1980	308.1	165	245.8	12.0	11.2	0.8	0.8	2.3	3.4	3.8	3.4	1.4
1981	318.9	171	251.9	11.9	11.1	0.9	0.8	2.4	3.6	4.1	4.4	1.6
1982	339.4	182	250.0	12.8	11.8	1.0	0.8	2.5	3.9	4.4	5.2	1.9
1983	368.4	197	266.1	13.4	12.3	1.1	1.0	3.0	4.0	4.5	5.8	2.2
1984	413.1	221	287.0	14.2	12.9	1.2	1.2	3.9	4.3	4.9	6.6	2.5
1985	462.2	246	289.3	15.2	13.8	1.3	1.4	4.9	4.8	5.6	7.7	2.8
1986	490.1	262	290.4	15.5	14.2	1.3	1.6	5.2	5.3	6.0	9.0	3.2
1987	531.2	284	286.1	15.9	14.4	1.4	1.7	5.6	5.5	6.6	10.4	3.5
1988	582.1	308	282.9	16.3	14.7	1.6	1.7	5.7	5.7	6.2	11.4	3.9
1989	594.3	313	274.9	16.9	15.4	1.6	1.8	5.9	6.2	4.9	11.3	3.9
1990	613.9	325	274.5	18.4	16.6	1.7	1.8	6.3	6.5	5.0	11.6	4.2
1991	654.2	346	269.5	19.2	17.4	1.8	1.7	7.1	6.8	5.0	11.9	4.5
1992	732.7	386	271.2	20.7	18.2	2.1	2.0	7.8	7.3	5.4	12.9	4.8

Notes:
(1) National income is at 1952 constant prices. GDP is at 1987 constant prices.
(2) Food grain is unlimited grain based on Ministry of Commerce data, which is shown later to be overestimated.
(3) Food grain, sugar, meat and eggs include direct human consumption and part of the consumption of the food industry. Milk is measured as milk production per capita.

Sources: Garnaut and Ma (1992); SSB (1993).

price adjustments in 1991 and 1992. Available data do not yet permit definitive analysis of these effects, but there seems to have been a once-and-for-all downward adjustment in staple food consumption. Even in rural areas, the increased trading of grain combined with higher market prices probably reduced home consumption of food grains, especially in coastal provinces.

Some of the observed higher market prices of grain in late 1993 seem to have been caused by the increased demand for high quality grain associated with rising incomes, combined with the after-effects of the concentration on quantity rather than quality in the drive to expand grain production between 1990 and 1992.

Large regional differences in incomes and factor endowments in China, different dietary habits, high costs and limited capacity of inter-regional transport and the perishable nature of many fresh food items generated a wide spectrum of consumption and production patterns across regions. This became more evident following the decentralisation of economic decision-making associated with the reforms. Several important regional features emerge when national data are disaggregated (table 4.2).

The northeast has the highest GNP per capita, twice that of the southwest. The largest inter-regional gap in per capita total grain consumption is only about 30 per cent, less than the income gap. The south has the highest consumption of meat, eggs and fish (30 kilograms), while the north consumes only 54 per cent (16 kilograms) of the average level in the south.

A number of the more prosperous coastal cities and provinces, including Shanghai, Tianjin, Guangdong, Zhejiang and Fujian, had an especially high consumption of major non-grain foodstuffs, while several poorer inland provinces (Hebei, Gansu, Guizhou, Shanxi and Ningxia) consistently fell below the national average level. The differences in consumption between regions vary by factors from 7 to 20.

China's food consumption in an East Asian context

Rationing and price distortion in China make it difficult to use standard models of consumer behaviour based on historical data to estimate future patterns. Fortunately, these standard methods can be supplemented with comparisons of the effects of market influences in communities with similar basic consumer preferences to those in China, particularly Taiwan, Hong Kong and Singapore.

The application of insights from overseas Chinese communities is complicated by doubts about current official data on income levels in China. These doubts make it difficult to judge which historical periods in other

Table 4.2 Regional food consumption patterns, 1985–7 (average, per capita, annual)

	GNP (yuan)	Consump. (yuan)	Food expenditure share (%)	Total grain consump. (kg)	Meat, poultry fish & eggs (kg)	Of which, pork share (%)	Implied feed grain (kg)	Derived food grain (kg)
Northeast	1,255.6	612.8	54.1	324.0	26.0	47.3	88.0	236.0
North	928.3	409.1	52.6	305.0	16.3	54.0	60.0	245.0
Mid and Lower Yangtze Area	1,064.3	478.1	54.0	398.0	26.4	54.9	92.0	306.0
South	905.5	474.7	58.7	356.0	30.1	49.2	94.0	262.0
Southwest	587.9	357.0	54.8	370.0	24.0	77.1	104.0	266.0
West	827.7	440.7	53.2	311.0	16.9	55.0	68.0	243.0

Notes:
(1) The six regions are defined as follows: Northeast; Liaoning, Jilin, Heilongjiang. North: Beijing, Tanjing, Hebei, Shanxi, Shaanxi, Shandong, Henan. Mid and Lower Yangtze Area: Shanghai, Jiangsu, Zhejiang, Anhui, Jiangxi, Hubei, Hunan, South: Fujian, Guangdong, Guangxi, Hainan. Southwest: Sichuan, Guizhou, Yunnan. West: Inner Mongolia, Ningxia, Gansu, Qinghai, Xinjiang, Tibet.
(2) GNP is the 1986 figure.
(3) Grain is unmilled grain without adjustment. Total grain consumption includes feed grain. Different feed-meat conversion ratios apply to different regions.

Source: Food Study Group (1991), vol 1: 118–20.

Chinese communities are relevant to projections of Chinese food consumption on the mainland. Research has established that, for purposes of
international comparison, it is necessary to multiply official Chinese per
capita income figures of the early 1990s by a factor of around three
(Garnaut and Ma 1993a).

Income and food consumption levels in China during 1985–8 are compared with those of other 'Chinese communities' (Hong Kong, Singapore
and Taiwan) and other economies in East Asia (Korea and Japan) during
1961–5 (table 4.3).

Although China's GDP per capita in 1985–8 was officially less than
US$350 (at 1987 constant prices), or between 14 and 30 per cent of the
income per capita in other Chinese East Asian economies in 1961–5,
China's food consumption pattern was remarkably similar to that in the
other economies in the 1960s. If China's per capita income is considered as
being about US$1,000 in 1993 at 1987 constant prices – and varying from
the official data by a similar proportion in earlier years – the relationship
between income and food consumption in China is remarkably similar to
that in other East Asian economies when their incomes were similar to
China's 1993 level.

These East Asian comparisons suggest that in the 1990s China's consumption may follow a path similar to its neighbouring Chinese communities in the 1960s and 1970s. As it happens, the income elasticities of
demand for various foods in these economies when their per capita
incomes were similar to (adjusted) Chinese levels today, were similar to the
income elasticities that have been observed in China in the reform years.
The strong growth in high-value food consumption in these East Asian
economies suggests that in the 1990s China is likely to follow a similarly
strong growth path. This conclusion is strengthened by observation of
recent patterns of consumption growth in the higher-income provinces of
China.

Determinants of food demand: price and income effects

While improvements in living standards seems to have been the dominant
influence on changes in Chinese grain consumption in recent years, it is
nevertheless important to examine the interaction between changes in
incomes and in relative prices. Several reform-related factors are also
examined: major housing reforms, urbanisation and industrialisation,
regional transfers and trade, fiscal reform and reform of the foreign trade
system. All of these factors may be seen as affecting food demand primarily through prices and incomes.

Strong incomes growth has been largely responsible for the rapid

Table 4.3 *International comparison of income and food consumption, 1961–88 (per capita, annual)*

	Year (average)	GDP (US$)	Grain (kg)	Cereals (kg)	Pork, beef & mutton (kg)	Poultry (kg)	Fish (kg)	Eggs (kg)	Milk (kg)	Alcohol (kg)
China	1985–8	275.2	297.4	231.6	18.4	2.1	7.5	5.2	5.2	8.3
Taiwan	1961–5	962.2	181.1	157.4	17.4	1.8	26.9	1.9	6.7	–
Singapore	1961–5	1,650.2	177.6	155.3	19.9	9.7	33.6	5.3	32.1	17.0
Hong Kong	1961–5	1,914.4	174.4	147.0	33.6	5.4	34.4	9.0	22.9	9.7
Korea	1961–5	597.9	228.6	177.5	3.6	0.6	15.4	1.8	5.5	20.1
Japan	1961–5	5,908.0	243.1	172.8	8.0	1.7	50.3	10.8	22.8	32.9

Notes:
GDP is measured at 1987 US$ constant prices. China's GDP is the unadjusted official figure. Grain is FAO definition, which differs slightly from Chinese measures.
Source: Garnaut and Ma (1992a).

increases in the average consumption levels of animal products and the pronounced changes in the composition of food consumption through the reform period. The continuation of economic reforms can be expected to underwrite market-driven incomes growth in the 1990s, and with it increases in food consumption and changes in the composition of diets (Tang, chapter 7).

The relationship between rising incomes and food demand is far from straightforward in contemporary China, with huge changes in relative prices and the economic structure.

In China, within the old central planning system, prices did not reflect the underlying scarcity of resources and changing market conditions. Closely associated with state price control was the widespread rationing of subsidised consumer goods for urban residents.

The partial reforms of the 1980s resulted in a complicated multiple-pricing system and the pace of reform has been uneven. While market forces dominated the supply and demand for many foodstuffs by the mid-1980s, marketing of grain and edible oil mostly remained under strict central control until the early 1990s. Central government price controls and rations for these commodities ceased to be economically important only from 1991–2, and even then they were subject to pressures for their reinstatement at times of rising market prices, as in late 1993 and through 1994.

Overall, market forces gained a much wider role in price determination in the economy in the 1980s. By 1990, the shares of state pricing in both gross retail sales and farm procurement had fallen to about 30 per cent. In Guangdong, these shares were even lower, being only 15 per cent in 1990 (*China Price*, No.11, 1991: 27), and were far below 10 per cent by 1993.

The urban household survey data suggest that there were sizeable discrepancies between the state and free market prices for other major foodstuffs. The major cities continued to subsidise the supply of many staple supplements for urban consumers after the removal of most central government subsidies for grain in 1992.

Overall, a declining trend is observed in the relative grain price in the first half of the 1980s (Garnaut and Ma 1992a). The initial falling relative price of grain might have contributed to the increase in per capita food grain consumption from 1978 to 1986. The increase in the relative grain price in the second half of the 1980s helps to explain in part the decline in food grain consumption after 1987. The simultaneous increases in consumption and relative prices of meat in the 1980s are strong indications that income effects dominated price effects for these commodities over this period.

If these interpretations are sound, the large increases in relative prices of

grain in 1991 and 1992, and sharply from late 1993, can be expected to
have generated some reduction in food grain consumption.

Under the old central planning system there was little interest in the
relationship between Chinese domestic and world prices. As the Chinese
economy becomes more deeply integrated into the international economy,
and especially as it prepares for entry into the post-Uruguay Round World
Trade Organization, the importance of this comparison is being recognised. It is now clearer to more Chinese policymakers that it makes economic good sense to keep the divergence between domestic and
international prices within reasonable bounds (Garnaut, Fang and Huang,
chapter 14).

To appraise the effects of income and relative price changes on food
consumption, information on income (expenditure) and own price elasticities of demand for various foodstuffs is needed. Complications associated
with poor data and institutional change have made it difficult to obtain
reliable estimates of these elasticities. The following selective review of
recent major studies serves to highlight these difficulties.

Estimates of income elasticity of urban grain demand range from 0.024
to 0.46, and price elasticity from –0.06 to –0.37 (Garnaut and Ma 1992a).
The estimates for rural income (own-price) elasticities range from 0.20 to
0.39 (–0.14 to –0.62) (table 4.4). These diverse estimates of income and
price elasticities illustrate the frustration experienced by analysts in their
efforts to evaluate the relationship between these two key determinants
and the quantities of various foodstuffs demanded in China. They underline the inevitable uncertainty in the projection of future food consumption in China. In general, price elasticities are relatively low, while income
elasticities are low for food grain and higher for food products with higher
unit values. But very little is known about the price elasticity of overall
grain demand when consumer demand for animal products is included in
the analysis.

Structural change affecting grain demand: urban housing reform

Urban housing subsidies are massive. One Chinese study estimates that in
1988 the average rental rate of urban public housing was only 5 per cent of
the housing cost (Wang 1991). A high proportion of urban residents have
access to public housing.

The scheduled and seemingly inevitable nationwide urban housing
reform, starting in 1992, could affect not only relative prices but also the
budget of urban consumers. The main thrust of the recent housing reform
plan is to narrow the gap between the rent paid and the cost of housing.
There is likely to be some indirect income compensation, even if no direct

Table 4.4 *Income (expenditure) and own-price elasticities of grain demand*

Studies	Features	Income (expenditure) elasticities	Own-price elasticities
Pudney and Wang (1991)	Urban (1987)	0.024	−0.354
Wang (1989)	Urban (1981–7) at 1987	0.046	−1.475
Lewis and Andrews (1989)	Urban (1982–5)	0.31	−0.26
	Rural (1982–5)	0.22	−0.14
van der Gaag (1984)	Urban (1982)	0.114 to 0.117	−0.08
	Rural (1981–2)	0.207 to 0.217	
Chen and Buckwell (1991)	Urban (time-series)	−0.05	−0.58
	Rural (time-series)	0.16	−0.21
Kueh (1988)	Rural (1980–5)	0.36 to 0.07	
FAO (1991a)	Aggregate (1965–86)	0.18	−0.11
Food Study Group (1991)	Urban (1984–8)	0.34	−0.29
	Rural (1986–7)	0.39	−0.62
Zhu et al. (1991)	Rural (1988)	0.03	
Suzuki (1987)	Aggregate rice (1978–84)	0.27	−0.68
Ito et al. (1991)	Aggregate rice (1960–86), at 1986	−0.15	–
Ito et al. (1989)	Aggregate rice (1961–85), at 1985	0.13	–

Note:
All estimations are based on per capita level.

compensation is paid. If compensation were complete, housing reform would raise food demand, in response to the increase in the relative price of housing. Much depends on the precise ways in which the housing reforms are implemented.

Structural change: urbanisation and industrialisation

Two factors are responsible for the differentials between rural and urban food consumption patterns in the 1980s: relative prices and incomes. Chinese peasants choose their consumption bundles largely in response to market signals, while state controls are more influential in urban areas – although less so post-1992. As the rural and urban economies become more integrated, urban and rural consumers make consumption decisions on the basis of more similar sets of market prices. The substantial steps towards market determination of grain prices in 1991 and 1992 made rural and urban consumption patterns more similar. Rural consumption patterns have been becoming more sensitive to market prices, even for the diminishing proportion of food used for subsistence on the farm.

Rural income growth may induce convergence of future rural food consumption towards the current urban pattern. Urbanisation can also be expected to move a substantial number of people currently living in rural areas towards urban consumption patterns. This might support an expectation of declining per capita rural food grain consumption, alongside larger increases in indirect demand derived from animal products.

The remarkable progress of industrialisation in the countryside during the 1980s, and especially since the mid-1980s, has been a major source of strong growth in rural incomes. The share of agricultural production in total rural economic activity fell from 69 per cent in 1980 to 43 per cent in 1991.

The very low rates of growth in real farm incomes from 1989 to 1993 temporarily deferred growth in total rural consumption of grain and animal products. The stagnation of farm incomes is the source of some political tension and has generated considerable public comment. Market-oriented reformers favour greater emphasis on production of high-value, non-grain farm products, and on expansion of off-farm employment as a means of raising incomes of people who are now farmers. But support for the traditional tendency to rely on price protection and subsidising farm inputs is still strong.

Structural change: subsidies and fiscal reform

Fiscal subsidies on farm product prices have been large, accounting for 10 per cent of total fiscal outlays, and 80 per cent of total official fiscal price subsidies, in the late 1980s. The official data might substantially underestimate the magnitude of the overall fiscal subsidy to consumption as well as production of farm products (Tang, chapter 7).

One prominent feature of the decade-long fiscal reforms has been greater decentralisation of fiscal revenues and expenditures from the central government to various levels of local government (Garnaut and Ma 1993b, Watson, Findlay and Chen, chapter 20). Fiscal subsidies to reduce farm product prices have been provided by both central and local governments. By the late 1980s, the central government (the state) was committing itself only to a fixed amount of subsidy on grain, leaving an increasing portion of farm price subsidies to be shouldered by local governments. In 1990, of the 40 billion yuan of fiscal subsidies incurred in grain procurement and marketing, local governments paid 25 billion yuan, or more than 60 per cent (Shi 1990).

The larger burden for local government of subsidies eroded the local fiscal revenues available for the central government. As a result, both the localities and the state were under great pressure to keep the size of subsidies under control. This is one principal motive for the major hikes in the urban retail prices of grain and edible oil since 1991. The decisive movement towards market determination of grain prices in 1992 was accompanied by the removal of most state consumer and producer subsidies.

The decentralisation of the fiscal system may create strong incentives to expose and alleviate some of the price distortions associated with the massive subsidy for farm products, as it did with the far-reaching liberalisation of 1991 and 1992. But the absence of local government intervention in the grain market in response to the price rises in late 1993 prompted the central government to intervene.

Sources of grain demand

Food grain represents the major part of China's aggregate grain consumption. In 1990 per capita food grain consumption was estimated officially at 275 kilograms (unmilled grain). This translates into an aggregate of 314 million tonnes of unmilled grain, amounting to 70 per cent of current total grain production.

Despite population growth, the relative importance of food grain in total grain consumption has been declining rapidly in recent years, from 80 per cent in 1985 to 70 per cent by 1990.

There are strong reasons to suspect that these official data overestimate the average consumption of food grain, at least for the 1980s. First, there is an apparent inconsistency in the trends of rural and urban food grain consumption between the official estimates and the household survey estimates. Second, the official estimates suggest implausibly low grain use for animal feed. Third, China's food grain consumption in the 1980s, as measured by the official Ministry of Commerce data, is unusually high compared with neighbouring economies in earlier years, even when account has been taken of underestimation of Chinese GDP in the official data.

Estimates of direct human consumption of food grain are recalculated using the urban and rural survey data and allowing for changing milling intensity (table 4.5). Our revised estimate of food grain consumption per capita is 244 kilograms in 1987, 241 kilograms in 1990 and 223 kilograms in 1992 (unmilled grain), about 85 per cent of the official estimates. These revised estimates are referred to as the adjusted consumption levels of China. The movements in the adjusted data on per capita food grain consumption are smoother than in the official data.

The food grain share in total domestic grain consumption (or available

Table 4.5 *New estimates of food grain consumption, 1981–92 (kg per capita, per annum)*

	1981	1982	1983	1984	1985	1986	1987	1988	1989	1992
(a)	145.4	144.6	142.5	142.1	134.8	137.9	133.9	137.2	133.9	111.5
(b)	184.1	185.3	187.6	187.0	181.7	185.9	180.5	185.0	180.6	150.3
(c)	256.0	260.0	259.9	266.5	257.5	259.3	259.4	259.5	263.3	250.5
(d)	3.6	3.5	3.6	4.1	4.3	4.4	4.4	2.7	2.6	2.6
(e)	245.1	247.7	247.8	252.3	243.8	245.7	243.8	243.0	243.5	222.8
(f)	0.8	0.8	0.8	0.8	0.7	0.7	0.7	0.7	0.7	0.7

Notes:
All the figures in this table refer to unmilled grain except (a).
(a) is urban food grain consumption in processed form (survey data).
(b) is urban food grain consumption, computed by dividing (a) by (f).
(c) is rural food grain consumption (survey data).
(d) is grain related to cakes and sweets consumption, computed by assuming that
    1 kg of cakes and sweets requires 0.8 kg of unmilled grain.
(e) is national average food grain consumption.
(f) is the conversation factor from unlimited to processed grain. For instance, 1
    kg of unmilled grain can produce 0.7416 kg of processed grain. The changing
    milling intensity has been discussed in Food Study Group (1991a, Vol. 2).
Sources: Garnaut and Ma (1992a); SSB, ZTN (1993).

supply of grain) was significantly lower in the adjusted data (table 4.6): 76
per cent in 1987 and 69 per cent in 1990 by the official estimates and 65 per
cent in 1987, 61 per cent in 1990 and 59 per cent in 1992 by the new estimates.

The adjusted data on food grain consumption sit more easily in international comparisons and alongside Taiwan data. The new estimates suggest
that China's current food grain consumption per capita is not far from
Taiwan's in the late 1960s and early 1970s. The adjusted data look more
reasonable in the context of the total domestic grain balance sheet. They
also generate more likely and credible trends.

Feed grain demand, derived from demand for animal products, is likely
to account for most of the growth in China's future aggregate demand for
grain. The estimation of feed grain consumption is difficult, for a variety
of reasons, including lack of data and unreliable estimates of grain conversion coefficients (Garnaut and Ma 1992a).

Per capita consumption more than doubled for some items and quadru-
pled for others during 1977–92 (table 4.7). Garnaut and Ma (1992a)
survey a large body of existing studies on income and price elasticities of

Table 4.6 Apparent domestic grain consumption, 1987, 1990 and 1992

		1987 Aggregate (million tonnes)	1987 Per capita (kg)	1990 Aggregate (million tonnes)	1990 Per capita (kg)	1992 Aggregate (million tonnes)	1992 Per capita (kg)
Grain output	(1)	403.0	368.7	446.2	393.1	422.7	377.7
Net import	(2)	8.9	8.2	7.9	6.9	-0.1	0
Total domestic consumption	(3)	411.9	376.9	454.1	397.2	442.6	377.6
Food grain	(4)	266.5	243.8	275.8	241.2	261.1	222.8
Seed grain		21.5	19.7	21.6	18.9	18.5	15.8
Liquor production		13.2	12.1	15.3	13.4	17.5	14.9
Ethyl alcohol		3.0	2.8	4.2	3.7	4.7	4.0
Other industrial use		4.3	4.0	6.1	5.4	7.0	6.0
Wastes (state)		3.6	3.3	3.9	3.5	3.9	3.3
Wastes (private)		3.6	3.3	3.9	3.5	3.9	3.3
Stock change (state)		2.0	1.9	4.0	3.5	2.0	1.7
Stock change (private)		2.0	1.9	4.0	3.5	2.0	1.7
Sub-total	(5)	319.6	292.4	339.0	296.5	320.6	273.5
Feed use	(6)	92.3	84.4	115.2	100.7	122.0	104.1
Domestic consumption	(7) (%)	100.0	–	100.0	–	100.0	–
Food grain	(%)	64.7	–	60.7	–	59.0	–
Feed grain	(%)	22.4	–	25.4	–	27.6	–
Others	(%)	12.9	–	13.9	–	13.4	–

Notes:
All are in unmilled equivalent. (3)=(1)+(2). (6)=range listed (4) to (5). (7)=(3)−(6). Food grain is from (e) of Table 4.5. Seed grain is computed by multiplying the sown areas of grain crops with 12.9 kg per *mu* in 1987 and 12.7 kg per *mu* in 1990 (Food Study Group 1991, vol. 2). Grain uses for other industrial production in 1987 are based on Food Study Group (1991, vol. 2) and in 1990 are estimated by the industrial growth of 41.3 per cent between 1987–90. State wastes and stock changes are provided by Food Study Group 1991, vol. 2) for 1987, and for 1990, estimated by the growth factor of domestic consumption (10.26 per cent) for wastes and doubling for stock changes. We assume that private wastes are the same as the state wastes.
Sources: Garnaut and Ma (1992a); SSB, ZTN (1993).

Table 4.7 *Per capita annual consumption of animal products, 1987–92 (kg)*

Product	1977	1985	1992	Annual growth rate, % (1977–92 average)	Annual growth rate, % (1985–92 average)
Pork	7.3	13.8	18.2	6.3	4.0
Beef and mutton	0.7	1.3	2.1	7.3	6.6
Poultry	0.4	1.6	2.3	13.2	5.8
Eggs	1.9	4.9	7.8	10.0	6.7
Fish	3.2	4.8	7.3	5.6	6.0
Milk	0.9	2.8	4.8	11.6	8.2

Sources: Garnaut and Ma (1992a); SSB, ZTN (1993).

demand for animal products. In general, demand is quite elastic with respect to both price and income.

In response to deregulation, favourable market prices and strong consumer demand, total output of animal products increased strongly throughout the 1980s and early 1990s, despite stagnant grain output in the late 1980s. In particular, meat output grew at an average annual rate of more than 8 per cent between 1985 and 1992, reaching 34 million tonnes (table 4.8). Output of eggs, milk and fish increased at 10 and 14 per cent per annum respectively. Pork accounted for a dominant but declining share of meat production, falling from 86 per cent in 1985 to 78 per cent in 1992. Different meat products require different grain feeding intensities, so that the trajectory of demand for feed grain changes significantly with the composition of final demand for staple supplements.

There are two basic approaches adopted by analysts of China to analyse feed grain consumption. One is the demand approach based on estimated feed–meat conversion ratios and actual meat output to estimate the derived demand for feed grain. The other is the supply approach (or balance-sheet approach) deriving feed grain as a residual from the grain balance sheet. These two methods give vastly different estimates of total feed grain consumption (table 4.9).

The main source of uncertainty about feed grain consumption derives from the difficulty of distinguishing between human consumption and feed use of grain. Given the fact that 90 per cent of China's livestock raising activities were undertaken by non-specialised individual farm households, it is virtually impossible to demarcate clearly between food and feed uses of grain.

The same problems also affect the reliability of using estimated feed conversion factors. Various distinct feed conversion factors for the same

Table 4.8 *Aggregate annual production of animal products, 1985–92 (million tonnes)*

Products	1985	1987	1988	1989	1991	1992	Annual growth rate, % (1985–92 average)
Total meats	19.2	22.1	24.7	26.2	31.2	33.9	8.5
Pork	16.6	18.4	20.2	21.2	24.5	26.4	6.9
Beef	0.5	0.8	1.0	1.1	1.5	1.8	21.2
Mutton	0.6	0.7	0.8	1.0	1.2	1.3	11.3
Poultry	1.6	2.2	2.7	2.8	4.0	4.5	16.1
Eggs	5.4	5.9	7.0	7.2	9.2	10.2	9.7
Milk	2.9	3.8	4.2	4.4	5.2	5.6	10.0
Fish (1)	3.1	4.6	5.3	5.8	6.5	7.8	14.0
Fish (2)	7.1	9.6	10.6	11.5	13.5	15.5	12.0

Notes:
'Total meats' refers to the sum of pork, beef, mutton and poultry. 'Fish (1)' refers to the output of fish farming only, and 'fish (2)' is the total fishery output.
Sources: Garnaut and Ma (1992a); SSB, ZTN (1993).

Table 4.9 *Estimates of feed consumption, 1980–9 (million tonnes)*

	(i) Demand approach		(ii) Supply approach		
	Feed grain	Oilmeals	Feed grain	Oilmeals	Cereal-milling by-products
1980	–	–	68.2	1.7	20.1
1981	–	–	70.8	2.3	23.3
1985	48.7	5.3	82.2	3.6	40.9
1986	60.6	6.5	81.8	3.7	41.8
1987	73.8	7.8	86.0	5.2	44.3
1988	89.0	9.9	–	–	–
1989	105.2	11.4	–	–	–
1985–87 average growth rate (%)	23.2	20.8	2.3	20.1	4.0

Note:
'Feed grain' is unmilled grain.
Sources: Garnaut and Ma (1992a).

product have been used in estimating feed requirements (Garnaut and Ma 1992a). Multiplying the minimum grain–meat conversion factors by production and consumption quantity of animal products should yield estimates of about 100 and 89 million tonnes for feed use of unmilled grain in 1987, substantially higher than both of the estimates from official sources (table 4.9).

Pork is the most grain-intensive meat product. The declining pork share in total meat output, and possible technological improvements, imply that with the demand approach, the growth rate of tot l feed grain use should be somewhat lower than of livestock output in the late 1980s. The demand-approach estimate (table 4.9) produces an implausibly high growth rate of feed use of grain between 1985 and 1989, when compared with the growth rates of animal products (table 4.7).

Here, actual feed grain use for 1987–90 is estimated using a modified balance-sheet approach, and the demand approach based on the minimum conversion factors is then used to project the growth rate of total feed grain demand. Grain use in livestock feed is estimated to be 92 million tonnes in 1987, 115 million tonnes in 1990, and 122 million tonnes in 1992 (table 4.6), substantially higher than the data presented in table 4.9. The main difference between earlier estimates and the adjusted data lies in the different estimations of direct human consumption of food grain. The lower estimate of food grain consumption naturally provides a higher estimate of feed grain consumption.

Adjusted estimates show the share of feed use in total grain absorption rising to 22 per cent in 1987, 25 per cent in 1990 and 28 per cent in 1992 (table 4.6). The average annual growth rate of feed grain use was 8.6 per cent between 1987 and 1992, consistent with the growth rate of the output of animal products. The supply approach estimate of 94 million tonnes of feed grain for 1987 lies between the two illustrative demand approach estimates given above (89 and 100 million tonnes, respectively). Hence these estimates achieve greater consistency between the demand and supply methods, permitting the use of the demand approach in projecting future demand for feed grain.

Grain consumption in alcohol production

In 1988 total grain used in alcohol production reached 17 million tonnes (unmilled form), or 4.3 per cent of grain output. Between 1984 and 1992 liquor sales increased 11 per cent annually on a compound basis. By 1992 they reached the per capita level of 13 kilograms, which translates into aggregate consumption of 15 million tonnes (SSB, ZTN 1993). Meanwhile, there was a significant shift in consumption from high-alcohol spirits to lower alcohol beer. By 1991 beer dominated city alcohol demand volumes, its share in total liquor consumption by volume having risen from 45 per cent in 1984 to 60 per cent in 1989 (Garnaut and Ma 1992a).

Demand for liquor is quite sensitive to changes in income and prices. From 1987 to 1991 average liquor consumption growth was considerably slower, averaging only 5 per cent annually. The steep rises in liquor prices with price reform in 1988 and slower income growth in 1989 and 1990 would seem to be the main contributing factors. Strong economic growth in 1992 lifted the growth rate of per capita liquor consumption by 8.5 per cent (SSB, ZTN 1993).

This changing demand pattern is mirrored on the production side. There have been spectacular increases in total output and remarkable changes in product mix (table 4.10). Between 1978 and 1991, total liquor supply increased more than six-fold (registering an annual growth rate of about 16 per cent), reaching 15.4 million tonnes in 1991. Beer output registered the fastest growth: from 0.4 million tonnes in 1978 to 8.4 million tonnes in 1991. This is an eighteen-fold increase or an average annual compound growth rate of 27 per cent. As a result, the beer share in total volume of liquor output surged from 16 to 50 per cent between 1978 and 1991.

The rapid change in output mixes has important implications for grain demand derived from liquor production, because of the varying grain requirements of different beverages. In 1990 the total implied grain consumption in liquor production reached 15.3 million tonnes (in unmilled form). But, due to changes in product mix, the overall average grain to liquor conversion ratio dropped from 1.63 in 1978 to 1.22 in 1985, and further to around 1.1 in 1988–90.

Other uses of grain

Seed grain use reportedly fell from 24 million tonnes in 1980 to 22 million tonnes in 1986–7, due to declining sown areas and improvement in seed quality during the 1980s. It is expected that seed requirements per unit of sown area will decline further because of technological progress, and that sown areas of grain may not increase very much.

Other established industrial uses of grain include production of seasonings, medicines and textiles. Total demand from these sources was around 4.5 million tonnes during 1986–7. This component of grain demand may grow quite rapidly with industrial output. But it will remain relatively small and influence the aggregate demand for grain only in a limited way.

In sum, changing food consumption in China has induced marked shifts in the sources of grain demand growth during the 1980s and early 1990s.

Table 4.10 *Alcohol production, 1978–90 (million tonnes and per cent)*

	1978	1980	1981	1982	1983	1984	1985	1986	1987	1988	1989	1990
All alcoholic drink (million tonnes), of which	2.5	3.7	4.5	4.9	6.0	7.1	8.5	9.9	12.0	13.6	12.9	13.9
Spirits (%)	58.2	58.4	55.0	51.4	48.0	44.6	39.7	35.6	36.1	34.4	34.9	37.1
Beer (%)	16.4	18.7	20.4	23.8	27.0	31.5	36.5	41.9	45.2	48.8	50.1	49.9
Other liquors (%)	25.4	22.9	24.6	24.8	24.9	23.9	23.9	22.5	18.7	16.7	15.1	13.0
Ethyl alcohol (MT)	0.4	0.5	0.5	0.6	0.7	0.7	0.8	0.9	1.0	1.1	–	–

Note:
'Other liquors' include wine, champagne and other fruit liquors.
Source: Garnaut and Ma (1992a).

The most remarkable change has been the rising importance of feed grain in China's overall grain demand.

Grain demand projections

The projection of grain demand to the year 2000 is based on the following assumptions and methodology.

It is assumed that in the year 2000 the Chinese population will be 1.3 billion, implying an average 1.3 per cent per annum population growth rate in the 1990s.

It is assumed that a reasonably high average rate of economic growth will continue through the 1990s. By implication, this assumes that there are no major social and economic fractures. The implications of two possible growth scenarios are examined: the normal-growth scenario and the high-growth scenario. The normal-growth scenario assumes a 6 per cent growth rate of per capita real GDP – the official objective through the 1980s. The high-growth scenario assumes a per capita GDP growth rate of 7.2 per cent – the average rate during 1978–90. The high-growth scenario thus assumes per capita output expansion a bit below the rate in Taiwan in the 1960s, and well below the (unsustainable) levels of 1992–4.

Underlying consumer demand

Overall grain demand is estimated from different sources of direct and indirect underlying consumer demand for food items which are constrained only by budget (income) growth and prevailing market prices. Implicitly, a more or less free trade regime is assumed for China in the year 2000, with international grain relative to other prices not varying much from the levels of the early 1990s. It is recognised that consumption of grain would be affected substantially if China were to follow Japan, Korea and Taiwan into high agricultural protectionism as incomes grow. It would also be affected if China opted for free trade in grain and world prices rose. These possibilities are discussed separately, as departures from the assumptions of the basic projections.

Consumer demand growth

In most cases average income elasticities estimated in existing studies on China's consumer demand are applied to the two assumed GDP growth rates in projecting the annual growth rates of consumer food demand. For the normal-growth scenario, the lower estimates of these income elasticities are used, while their averages are taken for the high-growth scenario.[2]

Confidence in these elasticities is increased by their similarity to those of Taiwan at comparable per capita income levels.

Derived grain demand

Adjusted estimates of food grain consumption and a modified balance-sheet approach have been shown to be consistent with both the demand-side and supply-side estimates. The demand-side approach is used to predict demand for feed grain on the basis of projected consumption of meat, eggs and dairy products, and the minimum grain–feed conversion ratios that are generally used by analysts in China. Grain demand derived from liquor consumption is treated similarly. In addition, possible grain-saving technological changes which would result in a 10 per cent reduction in the grain–meat ratios by the year 2000 are allowed for. (This may underestimate the extent of technological improvement in the production of non-staple foods, and correspondingly overestimate indirect demand for grain.)

Price

A scenario is assumed in which there are no major changes in relative prices from those ruling in 1992, the base point from which projections are made. Domestic grain prices, following increases in 1991–2 and late 1993, are now quite close to international prices. The relatively low prices in the base period may have led to some overestimation of domestic consumption and underestimation of domestic production in the following projections. International prices are projected by international organisations to decline slightly in real terms during the 1990s from current levels, so 'free trade' could see some fall in Chinese prices through the remainder of the 1990s. This is not certain, and another view is that strong grain market internationalisation in East Asia, and the implementation of the Uruguay Round settlement more generally, will lead to a small increment in world grain prices. Future world prices in reality depend on trade policy and grain consumption and supply in many countries, notably China and the former Soviet Union.

Any overestimation of Chinese grain demand resulting from the relatively low domestic prices in the base year (1992) is unlikely to be large, because the effective price at the margin to consumers in earlier years, taking into account the availability of ration coupons, was far higher than the controlled price, and may have been the full market price. Nevertheless, any exacerbation of the price increases of late 1993 may result in significant shortfalls of demand from the projected levels.

Table 4.11 *Projections of grain demand in the year 2000*

	1992	2000 Normal-growth scenario	2000 High-growth scenario
Aggregate (million tonnes)			
Food grain	261.1	289.5	295.5
Feed grain	122.0	161.8	195.6
Other uses	59.5	73.4	80.5
Total	442.6	524.7	571.6
Per capita (kg)	377.6	403.6	439.7
Composition (%)			
Food grain	59.0	55.2	51.7
Feed grain	27.6	30.8	34.2
Other uses	13.4	14.0	14.1
Total	100.0	100.0	100.0
Annual growth of			
aggregate demand (%)	–	2.1	3.2

Note:
Unmilled grain.
Sources: Garnaut and Ma (1992a); SSB, ZTN (1993).

On the other side of the scale, there are a number of issues that may have led to some underestimation of future demand. It was thought best to make these assumptions clear, and to allow the reader to follow them through to their logical conclusion. None of these possible sources of underestimation or overestimation would be as powerful as the major divergence between assumed and actual rates of growth in the Chinese economy as a whole.

To emphasise again, projected grain demand is based on underlying consumer demand unconstrained by major government interventions.

Projections of grain demand in the year 2000

The projections of consumer demand for various food items and the projected total grain demand in the year 2000 under both scenarios are summarised (table 4.11). Comparisons of projections under the two scenarios with the consumption patterns of Taiwan in 1971–3 suggest that the results presented here are plausible and reasonable.

The normal-growth scenario projects an aggregate grain demand of 525 million tonnes in the year 2000. In the high-growth scenario it is 572 million tonnes. These results represent increases of 82 million tonnes (or 18.5 per cent) and 129 million tonnes (or 29 per cent), respectively, from the actual level of 1992.

The normal-growth scenario reflects an economy experiencing slower structural changes in the 1990s than in the 1980s. The high-growth scenario reflects a dynamic economy with substantial liberalisation in prices, trade and relatively unrestrained choice by consumers within their budgets.

Under both scenarios, it is projected that feed grain will be the most important source of increased grain demand, accounting for 50 to 57 per cent of the increase in total grain demand between 1992 and the year 2000. As a result, the food grain share in total projected grain demand falls in both scenarios, from 59 per cent in 1992 to 55 per cent in the normal-growth scenario, and to 52 per cent in the high-growth scenario, in the year 2000. The share of feed grain rises from 27 per cent in 1992 to 31 per cent and 34 per cent, respectively. In both scenarios, the share of other grain uses remains roughly at the 1992 level of 13–14 per cent.

How would these projections be affected by major variations in relative prices? The experiences of China in the 1980s and Taiwan in the 1960s suggest that increases in relative prices for food would need to be very large to diminish substantially the projected demand growth. This is underlined by the fact that some increase in relative prices is embodied in the China and Taiwan experience from which estimates of demand growth are drawn.

These projections leave China's per capita direct and indirect demand for grain (404 kilograms and 440 kilograms) somewhat higher than Taiwan's in 1971–3 (400 kilograms) when grain embodied in imported final products is taken into account. The projection for the mainland may at first sight look too high from this perspective, but not so clearly when the consumption-constraining effects of protection and high food prices in Taiwan, and the 'Taiwan fish factor' are taken into account.

The average Taiwan consumer absorbed about 36 kilograms of fish annually in 1971–3, about three to four times the projected mainland China average in the year 2000. The bulk of Taiwan's fish supply is from ocean catches, while about half of mainland supply is from fish farming. If half of Taiwan's fish consumption during 1971–3 were substituted in mainland Chinese consumption by 6 kilograms each of farmed fish, pork and poultry, that would raise per capita mainland Chinese food grain demand relative to Taiwan's by 42 kilograms per annum on this account alone. If 42 kilograms per annum were added to Taiwan's total grain demand to allow for the 'Taiwan fish factor', Taiwan's overall grain demand would rise to 442 kilograms per annum for 1971–3. This would exceed our estimate of China's grain demand in the year 2000.

Meeting Chinese food demand

The major change in Chinese food consumption since the early 1980s, has been the strong growth in high-value food in sharp contrast to stagnation and decline in staple food. This change is very similar to that which took place in China's neighbouring East Asian economies during the 1960s and 1970s.

A wide spectrum of important factors have affected and will continue to influence Chinese food and grain consumption in the 1990s. They include economic growth, price trends, institutional changes and the trade regime. These factors are themselves closely related. Income growth is likely to be the dominant factor, though changes in relative prices of grain are also expected to play an important role.

Assuming something like a regime of free trade and liberalised domestic markets, China's aggregate grain demand is projected to be between 550 and 590 million tonnes in the year 2000, depending on the growth scenario used, and in per capita terms, between 420 and 450 kilograms. Important qualifications apply to this projection due to the unreliability of income and price elasticities, the recent grain price reforms and the actual course of China's evolving trade regimes. Nevertheless, this projection represents a benchmark case under relatively free trade.

Garnaut and Ma (1992a) argue that without trade protectionism, China is unlikely to exceed the peak grain output achieved in 1984 (400 kilograms level of grain output per person) by the year 2000. This is somewhat lower than suggested earlier by Garnaut and Ma (1992a), because the base year for the current projections, 1992, embodies the grain consumption-damp-ening effects of the structural reforms in 1991 and 1992. The base case (normal growth scenario) projection presented here thus suggests a net grain import of 30 to 70 million tonnes for China in a relatively free trade environment around the year 2000. Any increase in net imports of grain to these levels would not imply the failure of Chinese agriculture. On the con-trary, if it emerged naturally from open trade and market forces, it would allow China to achieve a more efficient allocation of resources and faster economic growth in the years ahead.

This expansion of foreign trade is not an inevitable outcome. It is open to China to choose what has become the characteristic pattern of north-east Asian economies when they reach high incomes: restriction of imports so that domestic food prices rise, choking off consumption growth and, probably more powerfully, artificially encouraging domestic production. Trade restrictions in other north-east Asian economies have been supported by high subsidies to production. Responses along these lines would complicate China's foreign economic relations and contribute to domestic problems of economic instability and, associated with rising food prices, perhaps political unrest.

It is also known, from analysis and the experiences of other countries, that agricultural protection is not a cost-effective means of raising incomes of poor farmers. But in practice, the choice between East Asian-style farm protectionism and open trade will be as contentious in China as in other countries. It will be affected by Chinese perceptions of the reliability of foreign markets to absorb increasing quantities of its exports, and to supply reliably increasing quantities of grain at reasonable prices. The fateful choice between free trade and protection in grain is likely to be forced by developments in the mid-1990s.

Notes

1 These issues are discussed elsewhere (Garnaut and Ma 1992a).
2 For other, less important assumptions, see Garnaut and Ma (1992a).

5   Rural poverty in post-reform China

Carl Riskin

The beginning of the reform period coincided with the rediscovery of poverty in China. It was claimed at this time that 100–200 million people were unable to feed, clothe and house themselves adequately. The Party Central Committee and the State Council turned their attention to the problem in September 1984 and called for 'speeding up transformation of poor areas'. In 1986 the National People's Congress included anti-poverty projects in the Seventh Five Year Plan (1986–90). In the same year the State Council set up the Leading Group on Economic Development in Poor Areas to co-ordinate national and local anti-poverty efforts.

Chinese poverty has been treated primarily in recent years as a regional problem, and with some justification. Vast areas of the country, particularly in the northwest and southwest, suffer from climatic conditions that make farming difficult or impossible. Much of this area is mountainous or hilly, with poor soil and inadequate rainfall. Deforestation and erosion are advanced. The rural people who live in these regions, though a small fraction of the country's population, still comprise a large group, and experience low levels of well-being in comparison with the average for China. The prohibition against migration, in effect through much of the history of the People's Republic, tied the inhabitants of these regions tightly to their impoverished circumstances.

Thus the Chinese government anti-poverty effort is focused on some 18 regions of the country designated as poor. These contain 664 poor counties, or 30 per cent of the total. Although 23 provinces contain one or more of these counties, more than three-quarters of them are located in the western and central part of the country (Office of the Leading Group 1989: 39–41; Stone *et al.* 1991: 32).

To focus on geographic and climatic causes of poverty is to imply that social institutions and government policies play a lesser role in its genesis. Areas that are perenially dry and stripped of natural vegetation over the generations are necessarily going to be poor areas, at least until some of their inhabitants are able to migrate and/or non-agricultural employment becomes available. Moreover, such a focus also implies that poverty is not significantly present among the bulk of the population living outside the designated poverty regions. Indeed, poverty in ordinary, non-poor localities is routinely treated as a problem of special circumstances – illness, injury, old age or natural disaster – rather than as a generic problem afflicting ordinary people in normal circumstances.

Of course, the admission in the late 1970s that millions of Chinese were living in circumstances of want because of government policies which deprived them of the means or the motivation to improve their living conditions, made clear that geographic disadvantage was not the only cause of poverty. When those policies were changed, a massive upsurge in rural incomes occurred, including those of the poor, with the result that the incidence of official poverty declined sharply.

Reforms leading to the disbanding of agricultural collectives and the leasing of land to households largely on a per capita basis meant that household income distribution was no longer collectively controlled. Such control in the commune era had kept intra-village inequalities in household income very low while permitting substantial differences to grow up among villages and regions. If one was poor under these conditions, it was because one belonged to a poor village. With collective control of income distribution greatly weakened, income began to accrue to individual households in accordance with their relevant characteristics, including education and skill, but also financial capital and political connections, to say nothing of plain luck. It became possible for individual households and persons to become rich or poor within non-rich or non-poor villages.

The data set, definition, measurement and incidence of absolute poverty

There is very little published information about poverty outside of the poor regions of western China. One objective of this study is to produce an independent estimate of the incidence of poverty in rural China, and an independent estimate of its disposition, as regards the poor and non-poor regions of the country.

The basis for such an estimate is an independent survey of household income in 1988, the China Household Income Project (CHIP), carried out in spring 1989 by a Sino-US team of social scientists. This study surveyed some 20,000 rural and urban households. As the rural sample used in the CHIP study is a sub-sample of the State Statistical Bureau's rural panel, this study inherits some of the problems of the parent sample, such as possible downward bias due to underrepresentation of the poor. Nonetheless, the CHIP survey provides a basis for investigating poverty more fully than was previously possible.

Although Chinese specialists have worked out a more refined version of a rural absolute poverty line, the Chinese government has used a simple line of 200 yuan in 1985 prices.[1] This has been taken to be based on a rough estimate of the money cost of the basic necessities needed to maintain a minimum standard of living, but in fact it seems to have been chosen as corresponding to 50 per cent of the mean rural per capita income in 1985 (Yang 1990a). On the basis of this line, corrected for price changes, some 27 per cent of the rural population was poor in 1979, or more than 200 million people, and this number declined to 12.3 per cent, or 102 million people, in 1985 (Ahmad and Wang 1991: 234; see also Office of the Leading Group 1989), and further to 11.3 per cent or 70 million people in 1986 (*Far Eastern Economic Review*, 10 September 1987: 84). Such a decline would mean that the absolute number of rural poor fell by more than 100 million people in seven years, a remarkable accomplishment.

Starting about 1985, however, the decline in the incidence of poverty slowed and may have been reversed. One set of estimates for example, based on State Statistical Bureau data, finds the percentage of the population below the poverty line reached a trough of 12.3 per cent in 1985, then rose to 14.8 per cent in 1988 (Ahmad and Wang 1991: 238). Per capita food grain production in designated poor counties fell by 5 per cent between 1983 and 1987 and the proportion of these counties producing less than 200 kilograms per capita of grain – the food-based poverty line used by the Chinese government – increased from 8 per cent in 1984 to 15.3 per cent in 1987 (Stone *et al.* 1991: table 4).

It is probably true that absolute poverty declined substantially in the boom years of the early reform period, and rose again thereafter. Rural reforms spread fastest at first in the poorer localities, some of which had been very adversely affected by Maoist policies towards agriculture, especially the grain-first policy. Moreover, the biggest improvements in agriculture's terms of trade with industry came early in the reform period. By the mid-1980s farm input costs were probably rising faster than output prices. But the precise scale of the problem and of its change over time is far from clear. For instance, some delegates to the National People's Congress in March 1985 (when relatively independent expression was permitted) criticised the government's depiction of rural conditions as overly rosy (Lee 1989), and several students of poverty and income distribution in China have concluded that the State Statistical Bureau household income survey samples underrepresent the absolute poor, in which case recent counts would be underestimates. Some of the poorest households are illiterate and innumerate and thus unable to keep the accounts required for inclusion in the State Statistical Bureau sample.

Moreover, another official source reveals a quite different picture of fluctuating numbers of abolute poor, with no clear trend through the 1980s. The State Statistical Bureau (State Statistical Bureau 1989b) gives figures implying that the number of poor varied between 65.3 million in 1978 and 102.3 million in 1986 (Ahmad and Wang 1991: 234), falling to 97.5 million and 88.5 million in 1987 and 1988, respectively (State Statistical Bureau 1989b: 326). However, no definition of poverty is given in this source.

For China the problem of defining poverty is compounded by a lack of correspondence between measured income and basic welfare outcomes found in many other countries. By the mid-to-late 1970s China had achieved a life expectancy at birth of more than 68 years, according to official sources, or 63–4 years according to Western demographic estimates (Banister 1987: 86). These are very high levels given China's low level of measured income and have been achieved through the spread of basic preventive health care, hygiene, literacy and rudimentary systems of relief from climatic or personal disaster. Yet some observers think that one-third or more of the rural population lived in absolute poverty at that time (Stone *et al.* 1991: 23). Indeed, the Chinese government's own poverty line, extrapolated backwards to 1978, surpasses the estimated income of 65 per cent of the rural population in that year (Ahmad and Wang 1991: 238).

Income and other measures of well-being, such as life expectancy, morbidity or literacy, can and do move in opposite directions (Dreze and Sen 1989, 1990), and there is some indication that they did so in China in the early reform period as the reforms weakened the existing social welfare system. Thus, when the income coefficients of important welfare outcomes such as longevity are small, as in China, income measures of poverty need to be supplemented with explicit consideration of these outcomes. This chapter concentrates on income for a number of reasons: the Chinese discussion of poverty itself focuses on income (as well as on food grain consumption); other national poverty lines generally take the form of income thresholds; income, properly measured, in fact tells us a great deal about well-being; and, finally, the data used here are for income and its components.

An income measure of poverty

An income or consumption-based poverty line consists of two parts: the cost of minimum nutritional intake and other basic necessities, and an additional value reflecting 'the cost of participating in the everyday life of society' (World Bank 1990b: 26). Whereas both components have a measure of variability, the second inherently reflects social judgements as to what constitutes a necessary minimum standard.

This is recognised by Chinese experts from the Rural Investigation Team of the State Statistical Bureau who devised such a standard (Small Group 1989). Their poverty line, defined in terms of net per capita income, is meant to encompass a minimum basket of goods and services needed to maintain 'simple reproduction' (the ability to live and work): food, clothing, housing, health care, tools, education and so on.

The food component is based on a relatively high average daily requirement of 2,400 calories, 11 per cent higher than the World Bank standard. The Small Group explains this choice by reference to the poor and unvaried structure of China's average diet and the typically high energy expenditure required in manual work. The food component is costed at 168.1 renminbi.

The minimum basket includes 7 square metres per person of living space, plus 2 square metres of auxiliary space (for storage of grain, fuel and the like), together valued at 18.6 renminbi. Clothing and other necessities are estimated at 42.7 renminbi, and everything else (including travel, fuel, medical care, education, work materials and so on) is costed at 30.3 renminbi. The minimum basket adds to 259.7 renminbi.

The CHIP survey found that about 13 per cent of rural households (or 13.8 per cent of individuals) fell below this poverty line when income was defined according to the State Statistical Bureau. The survey, however, employed a more comprehensive income definition which comes to 763 renminbi per capita, 40 per cent higher than the official State Statistical Bureau estimate of 545 yuan.

Should the poverty line be redefined in accordance with the broader definition of income? The answer depends upon whether the original poverty line of 260 renminbi is regarded as a complete representation of the cost of a minimum acceptable subsistence bundle of goods and services.

One of the three major components of the difference between the two estimates of income is wages and receipts from non-household enterprises; 42 renminbi per person more in the CHIP than in the State Statistical Bureau survey. This appears to be a genuine addition to income not counted by the State Statistical Bureau.

A second contributor to the difference in incomes is imputed rental value of self-owned housing, included by the CHIP study as equal to 8 per cent of the equity value (total current value minus amount of outstanding housing debt). This averaged 65.6 renminbi per person. The State Statistical Bureau excludes this item from income, although it includes in the poverty threshold an estimate of minimum necessary housing expenses equal to 18.6 renminbi. This estimate is replaced with the average rental value of housing for low-income households of 31.6 renminbi per capita. This raises the threshold by 13 renminbi to 273 renminbi.

The largest component of the difference between the two estimates is income from household grain production. Almost all of this difference is due to the method of valuing self-consumed output. The State Statistical Bureau in 1988 used official contract (quota) prices well below market prices, whereas the CHIP study used market prices. Market prices are a better representation of the opportunity cost of consuming self-produced grain, as well as of the marginal cost of obtaining grain. Moreover, the State Statistical Bureau team used actual prices for grain sales substantially below those reported in the CHIP survey or in other published sources.

The food grain component of the poverty line is revalued using market prices to value production for self-consumption, then by calculating an expenditure-weighted average price received for grain,[2] and finally by using that price to value the minimum food grain component (194.4 kilograms) used by the State Statistical Bureau in its poverty line. The result is to raise the share of food grain in the total basket from only 29.5 per cent – a very low share for staple food in the poverty-level income of a low-income country – to 42.8 per cent in the revised line. The share of all food rises from 65 to 71 per cent. For rural China as a whole in 1988, when self-consumed grain is valued at state prices, about 24 per cent of net per capita income was spent on grain and 47 per cent on all food. The revaluation of food grains adds 60 renminbi to the poverty threshold, bringing it to 333 renminbi. This value is used in the following analysis.

In addition to these steps designed to make the poverty line consistent with the CHIP definition of income, the threshold is also adjusted for economies of scale in household size and for provincial differences in the cost of living.

Economies of scale in use of income are available to larger households, and individuals of different ages have different income needs. To reflect these factors, the State Statistical Bureau Small Group uses an equivalence scale, on the basis of the average propensity to consume of households of different sizes. Taking a household of five as the norm (100), the effect of household size on average per capita consumption expenses is estimated to range from 106.8 for a single individual to 96.8 for a household of seven or more members. This scale implies a much smaller impact of household size on income efficiency than others used internationally, such as the OECD scale, which assigns the values 1.0, 0.7 and 0.5 for the first adult, subsequent adults and children (Ringen 1991). Nevertheless, it is used on the assumption that it reflects Chinese rural conditions better than the known alternatives.

In the absence of a publicly available index of regional variations in the rural cost of living, an index by province of rural market prices expressed as a ratio of state commercial prices is adopted. As state prices tend to be relatively uniform nationally, this index suggests the differences in provincial market price levels. The provincial deviations of market from state prices, expressed as a ratio of the national average deviation, are multiplied by the estimated provincial agricultural commercialisation rate (derived from CHIP survey data). This method probably understates provincial average price differentials substantially, but it enables some allowance for such differences to be made. The resulting index is used to adjust the poverty line.

The poverty headcount in 1988

The revised poverty line of 333 renminbi, adjusted for household size and provincial cost of living, yields an incidence of poverty of 12.1 per cent of households. As poorer households are on average larger than richer ones (averaging 5.29 members as against 4.95), they contain 12.7 per cent of the rural population. This is slightly below the poverty share produced by the State Statistical Bureau definition of income and the unadjusted State Statistical Bureau poverty line. The difference is chiefly due to the treatment of housing. In the approach adopted here the addition to measured income is greater than that to the poverty line, so fewer people fall below the poverty line. The effects of the family-size scale and provincial price adjustment are minimal.

The headcount of rural poverty corresponding to a rate of 12.7 per cent depends on the definition of 'rural' accepted (table 5.1). The definition based on the 1984 standard for town formation departs greatly from the usual conception of an urban place, permitting areas of which 90 per cent of residents are farmers to be designated as towns. Both the alternative definitions are better representations of the urban–rural distinction. Using the State Statistical Bureau definition in *Zhongguo tongji zhaiyao* [Statistical Abstract of China] (State Statistical Bureau 1991a), according to which 74.2 per cent of China's 1988 population was rural, some 105 million persons fell below the poverty line in that year.

Despite the apparent precision of the steps taken to obtain a measure of rural poverty, estimates must be regarded as rough. Uncertainties surround the level of the poverty line, prices used in its calculation, adjustments for provincial price levels and household size, and the significance of the differences between CHIP and State Statistical Bureau concepts of income. Perhaps, most important, current income in a single year is an inaccurate guide to living standards.

Table 5.1 *Alternative estimates of China's rural population in 1988, and corresponding poverty counts*

Basis of definition	Rural population (million)	Total population (%)	Poverty count (million)
Rural *hukou*[a]	867.25	78.1	110.1
1984 standard for urban place[b]	552.45	50.4	70.2
State Statistical Bureau definition[c]	823.65	74.2	104.6

Notes and sources:
[a] Permanent population with household registration in the countryside. Based on the 1964 standard for town designation. *Source:* SSB (1989b: 34).
[b] In 1984 the standard for town designation was considerably relaxed and a change also took place in governing procedures that permitted cities and towns to incorporate large numbers of surrounding farm households within their administrative boundaries. The result was a rapid nominal growth in urbanisation, resulting in half the population being urban by this standard in 1988. For a discussion of changing concepts of urbanisation, see Lee (1989). *Source:* SSB (1989b: 87).
[c] This is the rural population figure given and explained in SSB (1991: 14). It is a residual left after a detailed delineation of the urban population, consisting of the following components: district populations of cities comprised of districts; neighbourhood populations of cities not comprised of districts; residential committee populations of towns under the jurisdiction of cities not comprised of districts; and residential committee populations of county towns. Underlying data are from the Fourth National Population Census.

Characteristics of the poor

The income of poor households, on average, would have to be raised 39 per cent to reach the poverty line. It is only 27 per cent of that of the non-poor group (table 5.2). The poor on average get only about three-quarters of the per capita grain supply of the non-poor.

Houses of poor households averaged only 46 per cent of the current market value of houses of the non-poor. Only 29 per cent of poor households reported financial assets, compared with 53 per cent of non-poverty households, and the former's asset value averaged only 44 per cent of the latter's. Twenty-seven per cent of poor households were in debt and the poor had a smaller average debt than did the non-poor, suggesting greater difficulty in accessing credit. There have indeed been complaints that as banks and farm credit institutions became profit

Table 5.2 *Characteristics of poverty and non-poverty rural households* (*poverty line=333 renminbi*)

	Non-poverty households			Poverty households		
	Number	Mean	%	Number	Mean	%
Number of households	8,907		100.0	1,221		100.0
Average size of HH (persons)	4.95			5.29		
Number of individuals	44,090			6,459		
HH mean per capita adjusted income		893			240	
Number HHs getting						
<188 kg food grain	1,321	295	14.8	419	275	34.3
Productive capital	(7,845)	1,220	88.1	(1,005)	1,212	82.3
Cultivated land (*mu*)	(8,559)	11.3	96.1	(1,153)	16.5	94.4
Irrigated land (*mu*)	(5,667)	6.3	63.6	(433)	5.4	35.5
House value	(8,074)	4,997	90.6	(974)	2.274	79.8
Financial assets	(4,733)	932	53.1	(356)	413	29.2
Debts	(1,977)	967	22.2	(329)	637	26.9
Resident of 'poverty region'	1,564	n.a.	17.6	433	n.a.	35.5
'Five guarantee HH'	12	n.a.	0.1	5	n.a.	0.4
Get welfare fund income	190	239	2.1	7	186	0.6
Get relief grain	32	273	0.4	10	194	0.8
Borrow grain	314	468	3.5	64	631	5.2
Grain per capita	8,780	631	98.6	1,173	490	96.1

Notes:
Household per capita income here includes imputed rental value of self-owned housing.
Numbers in parentheses are numbers of non-zero observations.
Households with negative incomes have been excluded from both categories of households in this table.
Source: China Household Income Project.

conscious they concentrated their lending on rural industries at the expense of poorer farmers.

Despite the regional concentration of poverty, available evidence suggests that the majority of rural poor are located in more normal income areas, or in poor areas that have not been so designated by the government (table 5.3). Almost two-thirds of poor households are located outside of officially designated poverty areas. Regionally focused anti-poverty policies may miss much of their target.

How extensively did individual household-aimed welfare policies reach poor households? Only 17 households of the over 10,000 in the 1988 survey sample reported being 'five guarantee' households. Of these, five were poor – only 0.4 per cent of poor households. A lower percentage of poor households (0.6 per cent) got income from the local welfare fund than did non-poor (2.1 per cent). The most likely explanation for this observation is that the size and disposition of local welfare funds depends on local economic conditions. Wealthier areas can afford to collect and redistribute a larger amount of support, and to observe a less-demanding poverty line, than poorer areas. Similarly, only 42 households reported receiving relief grain. Of these, only 10 were poor. It would seem from these results that the welfare measures examined here do not reach the overwhelming majority of the poor.

Non-poor households do significantly better in housing and financial assets. Unexpectedly, they have only slightly more productive capital than poor households, while also possessing less land. This is perhaps the biggest anomaly. That poor households actually cultivate more land is the result of the relative concentration of the poor in arid and hilly areas of the west and northwest, where farms tend to be larger in acreage but of low productivity. Thus, 64 per cent of the better-off group, but only 36 per cent of the poor sub-group, had irrigated land. Moreover, the former irrigated 55 per cent of their land, on average, while the latter irrigated only 33 per cent. But why do poor households have virtually as much productive capital as non-poor households?

Productive capital as specified in the CHIP survey includes livestock, tools and machinery for farming and non-farming activities, structures used for production or storage, and other productive fixed assets. An examination of these components indicates that poor households reported a larger value of livestock, non-farm tools and agricultural machinery than did non-poor households, and a smaller value of farm tools, industrial and transport machinery, and production structures. While reflecting to some degree the greater diversification of production structures among the better-off rural population, this division requires further investigation.

Causes of poverty

The following model investigates the relationship between various household characteristics and the distribution of household income. Included variables are defined as follows:

RYP = household income per capita
WORKMEM = ratio of working to total members of household
EDU = average years of education per working household member
WAGE = ratio of wage-earning to working members
IND = ratio of gross non-agricultural income to total gross household income
AGE = average age of household members
CAP = current market value of household's productive assets
IRRIG = irrigated proportion of household's cultivated land
COMMZN = ratio of agricultural output sold to total agricultural output
ENTREP = number of owner-managers of private or individual enterprises
CHEM = quantity of chemical fertiliser used
ASSETS = net value of 'non-productive assets', including house value and financial assets minus debts
WEST = location dummy: takes value of 1 if household is in Sichuan, Guizhou, Yunnan, Shaanxi, Gansu, Qinghai or Ningxia provinces
CP = party membership dummy: takes value of 1 if one or more household members are members of the Communist Party

The most important explanatory variables are IND, WAGE and COMMZN (table 5.3). Per capita income rises by 5.4 renminbi for each percentage point increase in the ratio of wage earners to total working members. For example, in a household with three working members, one additional wage-earning job among them will generate an expected increase in household per capita income of 180 renminbi – an amount equal to one-third of the overall mean per capita income.

Similarly, per capita income rises by almost 6 renminbi for each percentage point increase in WAGE, the share of gross non-agricultural income in total household gross income. COMMZN, the measure of the percentage of farm output sold, encompasses economic locational characteristics. For households located near a major urban market, for instance, COMMZN will tend to have a high value, whereas in the underdeveloped hinterland

Table 5.3 *Factors affecting per capita income: results of Model 1*

Variable	Parameter estimate	Standard error	t for Ho: parameter=0
INTERCEP	−104.32**	28.37	−3.63
WORKMEM	320.33**	27.41	11.69
EDU	4.22**	1.97	2.13
WAGE	537.33**	29.72	18.08
IND	567.51**	29.81	19.04
AGE	3.86**	0.62	6.25
CAP	0.00	0.00	0.27
IRRIG	175.65**	12.83	13.69
COMMZN	386.39**	25.76	15.00
ENTREP	22.10	16.69	1.33
CHEM	0.01**	0.01	1.99
ASSETS	0.03**	0.00	34.33
CP	53.78**	14.15	3.80
WEST	8.06	13.43	0.60

Note:
** indicates significance at the one per cent level. Adjusted R^2 is 0.33.

its value will be low. On average, a 10 point increase raises per capita income by 39 yuan.

WORKMEM, the inverse of the dependency rate, also has a large and significant coefficient. One additional 'labour power' (full working member) in a family of five would bring an expected increase of 320 yuan in total household income.

Increases in the proportion of irrigated acreage have a large, positive effect on income. Average age and education of household members are both significant: per capita income advances by almost 4 yuan for each year in average family age, and by over 4 yuan for each year in average amount of schooling per working member. Surprisingly, productive capital has no significant effect on income. This is in part because the impact of productive capital is limited to income from household production, whereas the dependent variable includes other components of household per capita income as well.

'Non-productive' assets are highly significant. Household income advances by about 17 yuan for each 100 yuan in assets. As for chemical fertiliser, each 100 kilograms used produces on average an increase of only 12 yuan in household income, perhaps a reflection of the increasing costs of farm inputs.

Of the two dummy variables, only Party membership is significant. Per capita income rises by 54 yuan if the household includes a Party member. Location in one of the western provinces, *ceteris paribus*, has no significant effect on income. This model however, does not indicate whether the impact of the dummies is autonomous or works through other variables. To examine this question, coefficients of interactive variables consisting of the products of the dummies and the continuous variables are estimated.

Model 2 contains 35 variables on the right side, consisting of the 13 variables in the first model plus 11*2 = 22 interactive variables (table 5.4).

All of the continuous variables significant in Model 1 remain so except productive capital, and the order of magnitude of their values stays roughly the same. ENTREP, not significant before, becomes so now: each private business owner in a family adds 293 yuan to household net income. The sign of the coefficient of CP changes from positive to negative and this variable loses its significance. CP members do not appear to be better earners *per se*; rather, having a Party member in the household enhances the income-earning potential of other household characteristics. The main such characteristic is the degree of commercialisation. The coefficient of COMMZN is much higher for households with a CP member than for those without. It is not clear how and why CP membership enhances the value of commercialisation. Party members could be more energetic and/or ambitious, on average, or they could get better prices from the state or from the market. Perhaps they take advantage of Party networks to avoid assignment to low-value crops. These questions still need to be investigated.

CP membership also interacts positively with average household age and negatively with private ownership. CP membership actually *reverses* the efficacy of private ownership of a business. This effect is highly significant statistically. Indeed, the negative effects of Party membership (as well as of western location) upon private ownership would seem to explain its lack of statistical significance in the first model. Why households with Party members should benefit less from private entrepreneurship is not clear.

The coefficient of WEST becomes significant in Model 2. Taking into account the disadvantages of western location for other income-earning activities, it curiously turns out to have a substantial positive residual effect on income! The size of the positive coefficient (186) however, is dwarfed by the sum of the significant negative interactive coefficients (731). The chief negative impact of western location is on household off-farm employment and family sideline activity (WESTIND). Western location has a similarly negative (but smaller) effect on the advantage of raising the commercialisation rate. Selling more of household output to

Table 5.4 *Effects of location and Party membership on per capita income: results of Model 2*

Variable	Parameter estimate	Standard error	t for Ho: parameter=0
INTERCEP	−124.45**	35.08	−3.55
WORKMEM	320.60**	33.02	9.71
CPWORK	7.72	74.37	0.10
WESTWORK	−21.57	67.95	−0.32
EDU	5.41**	2.44	2.21
CPEDU	−7.35	5.62	−1.31
WESTEDU	3.72	4.51	0.83
WAGE	522.26**	35.49	14.72
CPWAGE	−52.61	70.63	−0.75
WESTWAGE	−9.86	108.59	−0.09
IND	637.59**	35.57	17.92
CPIND	124.95	80.46	1.43
WESTIND	−513.70**	79.29	−6.48
AGE	3.26**	0.73	4.48
CPAGE	4.70**	1.77	2.65
WESTAGE	−0.62	1.59	−0.39
CAP	−0.00	0.00	−0.51
CPCAP	−0.00	0.01	−1.08
WESTCAP	0.02**	0.01	3.05
COMMZN	403.61**	30.88	13.07
CPCOMMZN	191.45**	70.84	2.70
WESTCOMMZN	−217.95**	65.42	−3.33
IRRIG	181.92**	15.07	12.08
CPIRRIG	4.27	33.74	0.13
WESTIRRIG	−32.83	35.89	−0.92
ENTREP	58.79**	20.10	2.93
CPENTREP	−110.46**	40.30	−2.74
WESTENTREP	−62.71	50.52	−1.24
CHEM	0.02**	0.01	2.45
CPCHEM	−0.01	0.01	−0.37
WESTCHEM	−0.01	0.02	−0.31
ASSETS	0.03**	0.00	29.15
CPASSETS	−0.00	0.00	−0.40
WESTASSETS	−0.00	0.00	−0.97
CP	−124.60	79.26	−1.57
WEST	186.41**	62.75	2.97

Note:
** indicates significance at the 1 per cent level. Adjusted R^2 is 0.34.

the state or market brings a smaller reward in the west than elsewhere in China. Both of these effects can probably be satisfactorily explained by the poorer and less-developed state of the western provincial economies, which limits the market for high-value crops and sidelines. Finally, the returns to private ownership are negated in the west. This is possibly due to more restricted market opportunities, but also to greater political conservatism in the inland western regions, and the consequent presence of various bureaucratic barriers to, and infringements upon, private economic activity.

On the other hand, of interest also are the dogs that do not bark – for example, the rewards that party membership apparently does not bring. There is no indication, for instance, that CP members get preferential treatment in the wage-earning sector; the coefficient of CPWAGE is actually negative, though not significant. Similarly, western location might be expected to enhance the efficacy of irrigation in raising income because arid conditions are probably a greater barrier to farm productivity in the western provinces on average than in the east. However, the relevant coefficient is the wrong sign although insignificant.

Combating poverty in China

Poverty affected some 13 per cent of the rural population in 1988, or 105–10 million people. Two-thirds of the rural poor live outside officially designated poverty areas. A strong implication of this finding is that anti-poverty policies confining themselves to such areas will miss the majority of the poor. This implication is supported by the finding that anti-poverty measures tracked in this study benefited only a small minority of poor households.

The scale of rural poverty as defined here is small relative to total income and to the incomes of the non-poor population. An average tax rate of only 1.6 per cent on the rural non-poor or 2.4 per cent on the substantially richer urban population, net of the costs of administering the tax and resulting expenditure program, would be sufficient to eliminate defined poverty. This burden is seemingly modest, especially when viewed against the fact that government fiscal intervention (net taxes/subsidies) in 1988 had a net effect of taking away from the rural population some 4 per cent of its income and giving to the urban population some 40 per cent of its income (Khan et al. 1992). The highly regressive urban bias characterising Chinese distribution policy needs careful re-examination.

The coefficients of the model suggest broad policy directions that might make big inroads on rural poverty. Policies of rural industrialisation (especially if jobs were earmarked for the poor) and diversification of production structures would seem to offer much promise for reducing poverty. Because income from marketed output has a disequalising effect on the distribution of rural income in China (Khan *et al.* 1993), in the sense that relatively less of it accrues to poorer households, policies adopted should specifically channel to the latter the resources needed to increase market access.

The conclusion that China's rural poverty problem is of modest dimensions needs to be treated with caution. It could be that the poverty threshold adopted is too low, or that the bias towards better-off households in the sample is greater than suspected. Caution should also be exercised over the conclusion that remaining poverty could be removed relatively simply: 'throwing money at the problem' is not always an adequate solution, even if the required amount is small. Poor households practising subsistence farming in remote villages without roads or electricity or access to modern inputs most need the infrastructure and other resources that they are individually incapable of providing.

It is possible, however, that the apparently modest dimensions derived for rural poverty in China are more or less accurate. The low mortality rates and high life expectancy in China are not consistent with large-scale grinding poverty. The 'basic needs' strategy followed during the early years of the PRC of providing sanitation and preventive health care systems, increasing rural literacy and constructing rudimentary relief programmes, may indeed have paid off as intended in less poverty and more welfare.

Government anti-poverty efforts are regionally defined. If the findings presented are accurate, most rural poor reside outside officially designated poor regions and anti-poverty measures do not reach most of them. A continuation of China's admirable record in containing the scope and intensity of rural poverty would thus seem to require a re-thinking of the nature of the government's approach to the new institutional and economic conditions of the reform era.

Notes

I am grateful to Ma Guonan, Andrew Watson and Jon Unger for valuable comments and criticisms of an earlier draft.
1 'Zhongguode pinkun zhuyao shi nongcun pinkun' [Poverty in China is Mainly Rural Poverty] in Small Group (1989: 1)
2 This refers to processed grain. For self-produced grain, we use extraction rates of 0.85 for wheat and miscellaneous grains and 0.63 for rice.

Marketing and price reform

6 Price reform for agricultural products

Li Bingkun

Agricultural product price reform has been crucial within rural economic reform, and represents a fundamental test of whether a socialist market economy can be established successfully in China's rural areas. Changes to the system of pricing agricultural output have also played an important role in economic reform and development throughout the Chinese economy. Successful price reform is necessary to motivate wider systemic reform during the process of establishing a market economy in rural areas.

Three stages in the reform of agricultural product prices

China's agricultural product price reform has been proceeding gradually since rural reform was initiated at the end of 1978. The scope of reform widened over time, and its objectives became more explicit. Reform of agricultural product prices has now reached a critical stage.

The evolution of China's system of pricing agricultural output can be divided into three distinct but closely related stages. The first was dominated by adjustment of state prices. The second included both adjustments to government-set prices, and partial price liberalisation. The third has involved deliberate transformation of the price setting mechanism towards reliance on markets.

The first stage occurred between 1979 and 1984. The main thrust of reform was to raise the prices of agricultural products against those of industrial output, and to adjust relative prices within the farm sector, with the aim of stimulating agricultural development.

Before 1979, China's agricultural prices were controlled centrally and had been frozen for almost three decades. Prices did not accurately reflect the value of economic activity. Agriculture became the weakest sector and this in turn seriously hindered the development of the whole economy.

Following the decision to initiate reform the State Council, in 1979, raised the state procurement prices of 18 important agricultural products, including grains, edible oil, cotton and pork, by an average of 24.8 per cent. Several similar upward price adjustments were implemented in the following years. The cumulative effect was a gradual rationalisation of relative prices. Agricultural product prices rose faster than industrial product prices and agricultural output increased rapidly.

Over this period, negotiated procurement and sales prices and free transactions in country fairs were reintroduced for some agricultural products. A 'two-tier' price system for agricultural products began to form, and market forces were introduced into price determination for agricultural products. Nevertheless, price reform of agricultural products occurred within the general framework of the traditional planned economy.

During the second stage of price reform, 1985 to 1991, problems created during the first stage of reform started to emerge. The most obvious was the difficulty experienced by the state in making correct and timely responses to changes in the economy. More and more people began to accept that central control of the prices of some agricultural products had to be removed and prices instead had to be determined by market supply and demand.

Prices of agricultural products regarded as important to people's livelihood and the whole economy, such as grains and cotton, were still for the most part managed by the state through the mandatory plan. Price adjustment for these products was directly controlled by the state, but part of their exchange was left to the markets. The state released guideline prices for some products from time to time. Market forces played a major role in determining prices for other farm products, mainly non-staple foods such as vegetables, meat, milk and eggs. The co-existence of guideline and market-determined prices constituted the 'two-tier' price system.

Production and supply of agricultural products not subject to price control generally increased faster, and their prices tended to stabilise after initially rising to some extent. Production and supply of the agricultural products under 'two-tier' prices, however, were far from satisfactory.

After 1991, reform of agricultural product prices entered a third stage. The theory of the socialist market economy requires markets to provide the basis of price formation for agricultural products.

As economic reform deepened, it became more generally recognised that emphasis had to be placed on changing the mechanism for price formation, making full use of market forces, and establishing and strengthening the corresponding macro-regulation system based on market rules. Price reform of agricultural products since 1992, although similar in many aspects to changes during the second stage of reform, has been deeper and more extensive. During the second stage, prices were freed as an expedient measure. There were still doubts about the role of the market in price determination, and the most important farm products were not free of price controls.

During the third stage doubts about the market mechanism have been replaced by conscious efforts to enhance and improve the market system. The new reform programme began to build the framework of regulation that was necessary if prices were to be freed. The most important agricultural products were freed from price control. In a remarkable decision, the State Council announced in September 1992 that local governments could remove state control over the procurement and sale prices of quota grains supplied to urban residents. Grain prices were to be determined by markets from that time.

Price control for other important agricultural products such as cotton was also gradually reduced. By May 1993, the complete removal of government control over grain procurement and sale prices had been effected in both rural and urban areas including such big cities as Beijing, Shanghai and Tianjin. The 40-year system of urban grain quotas and coupons has now all but been abolished. It is expected that reform of agricultural product prices will continue and result in complete removal of controls.

Significant achievements of agricultural price reform

In the 15 years since reforms were initiated, the speed of China's reform of agricultural product prices has surpassed the expectations of many people and played an important role in encouraging the rapid, stable and co-ordinated development of agriculture and the national economy. This is reflected in the following three ways.

First, unreasonable price relativities between rural and industrial products have been substantially removed. From 1978 to 1991 the overall farm procurement price index rose by 174 per cent, considerably higher than the 77 per cent for industrial products. Although there is some incomparability in the statistical series, there is no doubt about the direction of change.

From 1979 to 1984 in particular, China's agricultural production grew rapidly and laid a solid foundation for the development of the whole economy. This was attributable in part to the important role played by price adjustments.

Second, a new pattern of price determination by markets has been established, at least in a preliminary way. At the beginning of the 1980s there were 113 kinds of agricultural products under state price control; by 1986 there were only 17 directly under state price control, and 11 under state price guidance. By 1991 the state directly controlled the prices of only nine kinds of agricultural products, and released guideline prices for another 19. In 1992 the State Council decided to implement several important measures to liberalise the procurement and retail sales prices of grains. These measures further expanded the range of agricultural products under market rules. By 1993 markets determined the prices of about 90 per cent of agricultural products entering commercial exchange, compared with about 10 per cent in the early 1980s.

Third, attempts have commenced to establish a new regulatory system for agricultural markets. China, as it entered the era of price reform, lacked practical experience as well as effective management methods and instruments for regulating agricultural product markets. Since the mid-1980s some regions have made efforts to establish appropriate regulatory systems. These efforts have been extended since 1990 to the whole country under central government guidelines. To maintain price stability for agricultural products and to protect the interests of producers, operators and consumers, the state has established a system of reserve stocks for grains and is making efforts to provide sufficient funds to reduce price risk in grain markets. The establishment of new wholesale markets for agricultural products is also seen as being helpful to price stability. Funds to reduce price rises for non-staple foods such as vegetables have begun to be established in some large and medium-sized cities.

The necessity of further reforming agricultural product markets

China is only part way towards establishing a nationwide market economy. There are still many problems to be resolved and dilemmas to be understood.

First, there are still serious price imbalances between industrial and agricultural products. In 1993 some agricultural prices remained well below world prices. This affected farmers' incentives to engage in agricultural production. It was one reason that investment in agriculture fell in the first half of 1993. When the national economy is growing at a low rate the resulting outflow of funds from agriculture is relatively small. Once the national economy shifts into high-speed growth, funds are in great shortage. As result, funds flow on a large scale away from agriculture and into manufacturing and tertiary industries that have comparatively higher returns, leading to a large difference between the growth in agriculture and the rest of the economy.

From 1984 to 1988 the Chinese economy grew rapidly. Agriculture lagged behind. During the period of rectification and adjustment (1989–91), the relative growth of agricultural output was higher. In 1992 the Chinese national economy entered another period of high growth when agriculture again lagged.

Part of the relative decline in agricultural output at times of high national growth is a normal and rational reflection of economic forces.

But the tendency has been exaggerated by the unreasonable price relativities between industrial and agricultural products.

Second, the market mechanism of price determination is immature. Although 90 per cent of farm prices were determined by the market by 1993, this is no more than a start. The market lacks the essential rules that are required if it is to reflect value reliably.

The debate about market reform takes place around two polar extremes: let the market decide prices without any control; or let the state determine all the prices. Neither extreme makes sense. The former brings exaggerated price fluctuation, while the latter depends entirely on the (unlikely) correct government response to changing supply and demand in the market. Decades of unproductive dispute over non-interference or monopoly of agricultural product prices continues and is still far from resolved.

The correct path lies between these extremes: prices need to be left to the market; but the market requires rules to ensure that the balance of supply and demand is reliably reflected in prices, and that prices are no more unstable than is necessary to reflect underlying economic realities. Certainly, China needs further agricultural price reform. Future reforms will be influenced by the policy of greater opening to the outside world. The highest priority is to accelerate the process of China's re-entry to the World Trade Organization (WTO). To meet this goal, China's systems of market exchange and regulation need to be made consistent with internationally accepted principles. The agricultural price system should meet not only the requirements of establishing a nationwide market economy but also those of WTO principles.

As a WTO member, China will find that many of its farm products face competition from the international market. For some agricultural products, domestic prices for poorer quality goods are higher than world prices. Comparing the 1990 domestic and international market prices at the official exchange rate, domestic prices for wheat, corn, beans, vegetable oils and sugar were higher than their international counterparts by proportions ranging from 20 per cent to 100 per cent. Domestic relative prices were substantially lower at secondary exchange rates (Garnaut, Fang and Huang, chapter 14). China must establish a more competitive price system based on liberalised domestic markets open to international exchange. This will cause it to make the best use of comparative advantage in some agricultural products and at the same time increase imports of agricultural products that cannot be competitively produced domestically.

China will participate more fully in international agricultural trade. It is urgent and important to establish a price system which suits the needs of international market competition.

Suggestions for future reform of agricultural product prices

The time from now to the end of the century is critical for the development of China's economy as well as for its economic reform. This is the period during which China will establish a preliminary framework for a socialist market economy. At the core of the Chinese rural economic reform is agricultural price reform.

The first requirement is the total liberalisation of producer and consumer prices for agricultural products, step by step. Although nationwide grain price liberalisation has started, it will experience some problems. Efforts should be made to liberalise the prices of cotton and silkworm cocoon by 1995 or 1996.

The liberalisation of grain prices could start with procurement (producer) prices and be followed by sales (consumer) prices. Following liberalisation, the price of state grain purchases could be set in the market. Grain production efficiency would be improved if, in most areas, government procurement was based on fixed quantities, rather than the fixed prices which have prevailed. Under this system government grain departments would guarantee to purchase a specified quota of grain, and farmers would undertake to sell to the government the same amount. The procurement price would fluctuate according to market supply and demand. Farmers could sell their remaining grain output through other channels. Price liberalisation would also allow measures to be taken to improve efficiency in supply. One major step could involve replacing the practice of supplying production inputs (fertiliser, diesel oil and so on) in proportion to the grain sold to the state, with cash payments that compensate for the removal of price differences between state and market prices for these inputs.

The second requirement is to maintain rational and reasonably stable relationships between prices for agricultural products and inputs. Price changes for agricultural inputs, such as fertiliser, pesticide, plastic film, machinery and diesel oil, have important effects on the price trend of agricultural products (Zhang and Zuo, chapter 8). While prices should be set in markets, care should be taken to avoid instability and distortions due to bottlenecks and artificial scarcity of inputs or outputs.

In the early 1990s the prices of agricultural production inputs increased by a large amount. The fast growth of the economy increased the demand for energy, raw and other processed materials, driving up the prices of agricultural production inputs made from petroleum, steel and other raw materials. The market prices of grains and most agricultural products dropped substantially at the same time due to excessive stocks of low-quality grain. In 1992 the prices of farm production inputs were 6.7 per cent above 1990 levels, but agricultural product procurement prices had only increased by 1.3 per cent. More efficient production and marketing arrangements for farm inputs would have reduced this erosion of farm profitability. Competition is essential to allow market forces to reflect the scarcity of farm inputs.

Steps can be taken to increase the efficient supply of agricultural products. The government should provide farmers with education in productive responses to market demand. This would lead to a reduction in the production of unsaleable and overstocked agricultural products, and to increased supply of products which are of high quality and in great demand. Prices and farmers' incomes will rise if products fit market demand.

The main way to increase farmers' income is to speed up the transfer of surplus labour from agriculture to other spheres of activity and gradually to achieve the optimal scale of agricultural production.

Third, China should develop more efficient and effective market rules. Price liberalisation and regulation are two inseparable aspects of a market economy – the former to increase the vitality of the economy, and the latter to guarantee order in economic affairs. Government regulation has a large role to play in the development of an honest, efficient market, with clear rules properly enforced and supported by adequate infrastructure and information.

Now that rural China has entered the third revolution, with market determination of prices for agricultural products, it is important that the Chinese government establishes a framework of law that institutionalises an appropriate role for both economic forces and administrative processes.

In a market economy, there is a valid role for the state in influencing agricultural prices through the establishment of price stabilisation funds and a commodity reserve stock system, especially for grain and cotton which are important in the national economy and people's livelihood. One of the sources of funds for grain price stabilisation is the fiscal subsidy that was previously applied to grain consumption. The funds could be used to purchase grain for buffer stocks when prices fell to unusually low levels, and sold when prices were unreasonably high. The reasonable limits of prices should be set by reference to average international levels and the operation of the buffer stock system would help to reduce price fluctuations. The experience of other countries suggests that buffer stock transactions accounting for 5 to 10 per cent of total grain purchases and sales can be effective in stabilising prices. The quantity of grains necessary for effective price stabilisation in China must be discovered and tested by experience.

Alongside price stabilisation, attention must be paid to the establishment of wholesale markets for agricultural products (Xu, chapter 9). The state, when purchasing and selling, can only trade in the volumes required for price stabilisation in wholesale markets. The wholesale markets in turn affect retail markets. The whole system depends on the effective functioning of markets at all levels. The effective functioning of markets requires efforts to ensure fair and honest competition, adequate physical and legal infrastructure, and other measures to make the markets attractive and to achieve high transaction volumes.

7 Grain marketing: from plan to market

Tang Renjian

The grain marketing system in the People's Republic of China has gone through four distinct periods

the free market system of the early 1950s

the state marketing system established in 1953

the dual system of market and plan which replaced the monopoly system in 1985–90

the post-1990 period created by the liberalisation of procurement and urban retail prices and grain marketing generally that is currently spreading across China.

This chapter describes and analyses reform of the grain marketing system in the fourth period.

Reform of China's grain marketing system is still incomplete, though the immediate targets of the fourth stage have largely been achieved. The goals and measures associated with the current reform process are quite clear. Review of progress so far promotes understanding of the directions in which the system will evolve in the future.

Background of the reform

In 1979 the government made a number of adjustments to grain marketing and price systems. One of these led to increases in state procurement prices. Another saw state mandatory procurement quotas gradually lowered, and prices for additional procurements increased by 50 per cent. These measures substantially improved incentives to increase production.

Urban retail prices were kept at the level established in 1965, resulting in a gap between producer and urban consumer prices. This gap was subsidised from the government budget. With rapid increases in grain production and state sales, the cost of this subsidy rose sharply, accounting for 13.5 per cent of state expenditure in 1984.

The reforms introduced in 1979 helped to bring about the abolition of the state monopoly over purchase of agricultural products, through changes in the procurement system, while maintaining low urban retail prices. This created new problems. Contract procurement became more monopolised than ever in the period 1985–8, alongside stagnating grain production. The government was obliged to raise prices again so as to increase incentives to production. This meant more government subsidies, however, and created a cycle of increased prices leading to budgetary problems and lower prices to reduce the subsidy leading to falls in production and pressures for price increases.

The cost of changing the purchase system without changing the retailing system was high from several viewpoints. First, for producers, the small change in contract procurement prices from 1985 was insignificant compared with the large increase in the prices of agricultural inputs and manufactured goods. The opportunity cost of producing grain rose swiftly. While many factors contributed to the stagnation in grain production in 1985–9, the reduced profitability of grain production relative to other crops was particularly important. Second, the grain subsidy was a huge fiscal burden. Government subsidies for grain and oil accounted for one-sixth of total government expenditure in 1985–9. Finally, from the viewpoint of consumers, grain was particularly cheap and thus greatly stimulated consumption, some of it wasteful.

Some consumers were dissatisfied with the low quality of the grain, despite the low prices, and impatient with the coupon system of fixed quantity, fixed place and fixed time. The author in 1990 conducted a survey of nine cities in five provinces. There were 1,597 participating households. Nearly 40 per cent did not know that their grain was subsidised by the state.

The five years of stagnation in grain production associated with contract procurement from 1985 affected the whole economy. During 1985–8 the state retail price index rose by 8.8 per cent, 6 per cent, 7.3 per cent and 18.5 per cent annually instead of the 1 or 2 per cent that was usual before 1984. It has been calculated that 40 per cent of the increase in the price index was due to increases in grain and edible oil prices. In turn, high inflation also affected grain production. Before 1984 the annual increase in the retail price index for rural manufactured goods did not exceed 1.5 per cent. In the four years between 1985 and 1988, however, it rose by 3.2 per cent, 3.2 per cent, 4.8 per cent and 15.2 per cent respectively.

And so the partial reforms implemented up to the mid-1980s left the grain problem in China even more complicated. Although the government spent a huge amount on grain subsidies, it failed to satisfy consumers, producers or traders. The contract procurement system had reached a dead end.

Sales system reform: breakthrough in experimental regions

The heart of the problem in reform to the mid-1980s was that it failed to face up to the issue of urban consumer benefits, and the monopolised grain marketing system that had been built to protect those benefits. This was recognised widely, but the necessary changes were easier to identify than to undertake.

The central government had hoped that local governments would take the first step. In 1988 the State Council gave approval to Xingxiang city in Henan province and Yulin city in Guangxi province to undertake an experiment in reform. Local governments had plenty of incentive for reform, as they carried much of the fiscal burden of buying at a high price and selling at a low price. They were responsible for most of the grain subsidy; 75 per cent of price increases was subsidised locally.

Shanxi province, a less developed inland province with poor grain production conditions and a large grain deficit (1 million tonnes in 1988), was the first to carry out the urban grain reform. The provincial government decreed that from 1 April 1988 the non-rural population, college students and army personnel would only be permitted a quota of 14 kilograms of grain per month at subsidised prices. The rest would be sold at negotiated or market prices. The amount of subsidised grain sold in Shanxi decreased by half a million tonnes in that year, and by another 0.6 million tonnes in 1989. Workers were given a monthly subsidy to compensate for the gap between the subsidised and negotiated prices, which were announced quarterly. This subsidy was included in enterprise management costs or in operational and administrative expenditure. The state procurement quota was cut in order to transfer the benefit to farmers. In 1988 Shanxi province reduced 'taxed' grain procurement from 215 thousand tonnes to 150 thousand tonnes. Two million tonnes of contract grain was purchased at negotiated prices.

A number of careful preparations were made before this reform was implemented. Before 1 April 1988 the local grain departments acquired an additional 50 thousand tonnes of wheat flour, and 235 thousand tonnes of grain were set aside as the provincial reserve stock. To protect consumers from the real income effects of price increases for grain-related products, each worker was given a subsidy of 3 yuan per month. Also, it was announced that grain coupons would remain valid. Controls were implemented over the gross profit margin of the processed food industry in the range 3–5 per cent. And finally, a price ceiling was established in case of a serious grain shortage.

Reform of the system in Shanxi province was carried out smoothly, achieved its intended results, and enhanced confidence in the reforms.

Grain production was stimulated, and because of the reduction in state procurement quotas, farmers' income increased by 44 million yuan in 1988 and 260 million yuan in 1989. The areas sown to grain remained steady in these two years, while the grain yield per hectare increased by 25 kilograms and 8 kilograms respectively. As a result, total grain production increased by 1.06 million tonnes in 1988 and by 0.61 million tonnes in 1989. The growth of grain consumption was constrained. Finally, the rate of increase in the subsidy on grain and edible oil was reduced: in 1988 and 1989 the subsidy for grain and edible oil increased by 8 per cent and 42 per cent, respectively, in China as a whole, but in Shanxi province the rise was only 5 per cent and 12 per cent in these two years.

Liaoning province decided to reduce the subsidised sale of grain from 1 November 1989 by 735 thousand tonnes. A number of other provinces quickly followed suit. Some provinces and regions took the lead in reducing subsidised grain sales for city dwellers. For example, Jiangxi province cut the monthly quota by 1.5 kilograms per person without compensation. Hainan, Guangxi and Hunan provinces also implemented these measures.

The reform measures taken by most provinces and regions took the form of reducing the quantity purchased and sold by the state. Another approach implemented in economically developed coastal areas such as Guangdong and Fujian that needed large amounts of imported grain involved raising prices set by the state.

In 1989 Guangdong government paid as subsidies to agricultural inputs 12 yuan for each 100 kilograms of quota grain procurement. This was equivalent to raising its procurement price from 38 yuan to 50 yuan per 100 kilograms. Urban retail grain prices were raised to 60 yuan per 100 kilograms. A lump-sum monthly subsidy of 6.95 yuan was provided to each city dweller, financed jointly by the government budget and enterprises, with individuals accepting incomplete subsidisation. This raised both procurement and urban retail prices and had a far-reaching effect on grain marketing reform in other regions.

With the rising price of production inputs, and the increasing opportunity cost of grain production as alternative economic activities became more profitable, the Guangdong provincial government again raised grain procurement prices in 1991, this time from 60 yuan to 124 yuan per 100 kilograms. In addition, the subsidised supply of fertilisers increased from 30 to 84 kilograms for every 100 kilograms of state-procured grain. Thus the effective procurement prices paid by the Guangdong provincial government rose significantly.

Another variation of grain marketing reform was to adjust both the price and quota of grain procurement. Reform in Yulin city, Guangxi province consisted of three steps. The first, undertaken in April 1989, sought to adjust the purchasing price and improve the effectiveness of subsidy delivery, while leaving the procurement quota unchanged. The second step, which took place in 1990, saw the abolition of the grain procurement quota and the relaxation of price controls so as to produce a genuine contract purchase system. The third step involved the elimination of the consumer subsidy by removing the grain subsidy and paying compensation in the form of higher salaries, in the case of enterprises absorbed as increased production costs. At this point, reform of the grain marketing system in Yulin city was largely complete.

Reform in Xinxiang city, Henan province was implemented in two steps. The first involved reforming the grain procurement system away from contract purchase to state mandatory procurement, increasing agricultural tax in the form of grain, and raising the state price of diesel oil and fertilisers. Procurement prices for grain and edible oil were then increased using the fiscal revenue from the increases in agricultural tax and the prices of agricultural production inputs. The second step involved reform of the sales system in order to reduce the subsidised grain supply. Reform in Xinxiang city can be characterised as 'reform at its own expense'; in other words, increases in procurement prices were funded by more agricultural tax and higher prices for agricultural production inputs. However, it was still within the old tradition of 'increasing procurement prices without increasing urban retail prices', and this doomed it to failure. Fortunately, the second step of the reform led to a reduction of grain supply at the official low price.

A third variation was to remove price controls. Before 1991 this policy was only implemented in Zhouzi county in the Inner Mongolia Autonomous Region, a pastoral area with a sparse population and severe grain shortage. At that time, removal of price controls was regarded as a breakthrough in reform of the grain marketing system, but it was generally not thought practical to employ it throughout the entire country at that time.

Equalising procurement and sales prices

The success of grain marketing reform in these local experiments encouraged the central government to put nationwide reform on its agenda. In fact, conditions were favourable for reforming the grain marketing system around 1990.

First, grain production in 1989 reached the record level of 1984, and in 1990 increased again by 9.5 per cent. It was estimated that grain output in 1989 was 4.8 million tonnes more than total demand. This 'surplus' increased to 31.1 million tonnes in 1990 and was still 11.8 million tonnes in 1991. Farmers' grain stocks exceeded the level necessary for food security.

Second, since the implementation of the rectification programme in 1989, the macro-economic climate had improved and inflation was under control. Retail prices in the country increased by only 2.1 per cent while the index of agricultural procurement prices dropped by 19.6 per cent in 1990.

In addition, reform of the grain marketing system was regarded as an urgent task to ease the government's budget burden. Government expenditure on grain and edible oil subsidy reached an alarming 40 billion yuan in 1990.

On 1 May 1991 the central government made an historical decision to adjust the urban retail prices of grain and edible oil. The average price of three main kinds of grain (flour, husked rice and corn) increased by 0.2 yuan per kilograms, and the average prices of six main kinds of edible oil increased by 2.7 yuan. Meanwhile, the monthly food and edible oil subsidy for urban residents was increased by 6 yuan.

The majority of people accepted the price increases with minimal complaint. The market prices of grain and edible oil were stable, the effect of policy on market demand was limited and the adjustment of grain and edible oil prices had generally achieved its goals. These were certainly encouraging results for the policy-makers, even though the urban retail price was 0.22 yuan per kilogram below the state procurement price following this first round of adjustments.

In April 1992, in order to consolidate its achievements from the first-round price adjustment, the central government again adjusted the sales prices of grain and edible oil upward to match urban retail prices with procurement prices. As a result, the average price of grain increased by 0.22 yuan per kilograms and the food subsidy for urban residents increased by 5 yuan monthly. This time there was little consumer reaction.

Removing price control: the end of the 'two-tier' price system

Equalising the state sales and purchase prices after the above two adjustments of the urban retail prices provided the basis for setting prices through the interaction of supply and demand. Substantial progress was made in changing from a grain planning system to a market one.

In the event, equalisation of sales and purchase prices was achieved under the traditional planning system. Equalisation was important in helping to reduce the government's expenditure on food subsidies, but it did little to solve some of the fundamental problems rooted in the old planning system. Further steps were required to liberalise grain price control and to allow grain to enter the market as a commodity.

Prior to 1991 grain price control had been relaxed in some provinces, prefectures and counties. The measures implemented in Guangdong were to have a far-reaching significance for the relaxation of grain price control throughout the whole country.

Guangdong liberalised grain prices in three major steps. First, a guidance plan was adopted for grain procurement. Grain management departments at the grass-roots level signed purchase contracts with farmers according to the guidance plan and guidance prices. If the price was not stipulated in the purchase contracts, the purchase was to be made at market prices. If no purchase contract were signed, free exchange was permitted between producers and consumers. Second, the grain sales price in urban areas was decided by grain traders themselves based on market demand and supply, and had to be reported to the price administrative departments. No subsidy was added for urban residents due to the small difference between actual market prices and official prices under the urban supply plan. Third, for the purpose of strengthening the government's macro-regulation of the grain market, grain reserve systems were established at provincial, prefectural and county levels.

Based on Guangdong's experience, one year after the historical readjustment of sales prices for grain and edible oil, liberalisation of grain prices was rapidly extended across China in 1992 and 1993. By October 1993 purchase and sales prices had been liberalised in 95 per cent of China's counties; the policy of 'stabilising purchase prices and liberalising sales prices' had been adopted in two provinces; and the policy of 'reducing procurement quota and liberalising sales prices' had been introduced in two other provinces. Generally speaking, grain price liberalisation in these provinces took a similar form to that in Guangdong. There were some differences. One approach involved state guarantee of the procurement volume without price control (that is, the state purchase quota remained in place), while the price was decided by the market. Another approach was to retain some subsidy for consumers.

The liberalisation of grain price control has achieved a number of desirable outcomes. First, farmers have been granted the right to decide what they produce. Second, urban residents have benefited from a wider choice. Free market prices of grain did not rise very much, and even dropped in some regions. High quality grain is now readily available at a reasonable price in the market. Third, the government has gradually reduced the subsidy for state-run grain enterprises and limited the increase in the consumption subsidy for urban residents. Fourth, the relaxation of grain price control has facilitated increased market orientation and produced a strengthening of management in state grain enterprises.

By mid-1993 all but 25 of China's 2,100 counties had adopted a market-determined pricing system for both sales and purchases of grains.

System restraints after grain price liberalisation

Liberalisation of grain purchase and sales prices was an important step forward, but not sufficient in itself to establish an effective grain marketing system. Prices reflect supply and demand in the market. Agricultural producers are often in an unfavourable position due to the special features of agricultural production, including market price instability due to low elasticity of supply and demand. The removal of control over grain purchase and sale prices signals the end of the state policy on mandatory procurement of grain rather than the establishment of the perfect grain marketing system.

A number of problems were perceived by government and farmers after the price reform. First, grain market prices were at a low level, and felt by farmers to be too low. After the relaxation of grain price control, the grain marketing organisations reduced their purchase of grain due to relatively large grain stocks. In many regions, particularly in main grain producing areas, the grain price dropped somewhat, though this trend was suddenly reversed in late 1993. Second, the grain purchasing price was not yet genuinely determined in markets. The grain marketing departments signed purchase contracts with farmers at the basic price set down by the state in 1993. According to estimates, this ('protective') price is lower than unit production costs. At the same time, production costs rose, because some preferential policies related to the contract purchase of grain, such as the supply of fertiliser and diesel oil at subsidised prices, were cancelled. Third, the share of purchases by state-run enterprises in the market shrank. It became apparent that it is very difficult to guarantee the volume of grain purchase at actual market prices.

Further analysis indicates that there are several fundamental difficulties in establishing a new grain marketing system in China. First, it is difficult for individual grain farmers to enter the market, due to small production scales and self-consumption. Some progress was made in reforming and revitalising agricultural marketing co-operatives, although they were not always seen by farmers as being helpful: they are just separate economic entities, responsible for their own profits and losses, and not farmers' organisations with democratic management. Seventy per cent of collective economic organisations run by the community provide little marketing service, and only 40 per cent of those service entities established by farmers themselves, are engaged in marketing.

Second, it is difficult to establish a unified grain market. The local governments retain some responsibility for organising grain supply. Therefore, they are prone to interfere in the grain market, including in relation to grain shortage. One reason that wholesale markets at both central and local levels are not booming at present is the existence of different regional interests, and the different relations between local government and grain enterprises across regions (Xu, chapter 9). Free trade between producers and consumers in different parts of the country is a distant goal.

Third, it is difficult to define clearly the relation between the government and state-run grain enterprises in a way that separates the regulatory role of government from ownership.

Fourth, there is anxiety in China about whether grain production will fall precipitously without government protection after the grain price is set in the market.

Finally, it is difficult for urban industrial enterprises to bear the risk of grain price instability when the price is set by markets. There is therefore a danger that enterprises and government will use government and market power to influence the grain market when these interests are threatened by free market outcomes. The solution lies in further market reforms, and particularly in the development of future markets in grain to allow the sale of price risk to enterprises or people who are in the best position to carry it.

Suggestions for establishing a new grain marketing system

The above problems came to the fore in late 1993 when there were sharp rises in grain prices. Between November and December grain prices rose by more than 50 per cent. This resulted from regional demand–supply gaps, general inflation and the institutional problems of the grain departments and enterprises. The government responded by imposing a price ceiling, selling off grain reserves, and allocating more transport capacity for the inter-regional transfer of grains.

In order to establish a new grain marketing system, attention should be paid not only to short-term policy adjustments but also to long-term institution building.

To solve problems affecting the implementation of a grain pricing policy, a number of steps were being considered early in 1994. The first was advance payments to farmers. The second was compensation for the difference between official and negotiable prices for fertiliser and diesel oil by arms of government that do not have responsibility for grain. But it should be clear that this shifts the fiscal burden of subsidising farm inputs from higher levels of governments to local government, which in turn could hurt the development of other sectors.

A third step being considered was basing government purchase of grain on the principle of guaranteeing the purchase volume of grain at the actual market price. The grain purchased by the government would then be used as a buffer stock, to stabilise market prices. The government could sign a purchase contract with farmers before harvests. There is an expectation that, because the grain purchased by the government is used for stabilising the market, losses should be covered by state finance. There is a potential conflict between the requirements of public finance and the desire to stabilise grain prices.

To avoid this conflict, commercial transactions should be subject to the rules of free trade. Commercial organisations involved in the purchase of grain should aim to make profits, and commercial transactions should be voluntary. No commercial organisations should have the power to force farmers to sell grain. One of the ways in which commercial organisations can play a role in stabilising the grain market is for them to sign a commercial purchasing contract before harvests. In order to protect the interests of both buyers and sellers and to ensure execution of the contract, it is necessary to find a way of distributing market risks between sellers and buyers, rather than the government accepting all of the risk through the budget.

It is important to establish effective mechanisms for market stabilisation. The development of grain wholesale markets is a key to establishing a new grain marketing system in China. Priority should be given to strengthening the functions of existing wholesale markets. To achieve this, the following measures should be taken. First, a range of economic and regulatory measures should be taken to ensure that the wholesale market encompasses trade between provinces. Second, purchases for and sales from the government's special grain reserves should be transacted through wholesale markets. Third, grain imports and exports should be integrated with domestic grain trade through wholesale markets. Fourth, regulatory reforms must ensure fair competition and increase the number of traders on wholesale markets and strictly forbid market administrators from participating in trade activities. Fifth, wholesale markets need to be made more attractive by ensuring that transportation is available to support trade on wholesale markets and by improving the processes through which contracts are organised.

Farmers' marketing co-operative organisations have a role in an efficient grain marketing system. Three types of co-operative organisations have been proven to be effective

  various marketing co-operative organisations, including: marketing co-operatives set up by farmers themselves; marketing co-operatives collectively run by the community; and some of the traditional supply and marketing co-operatives that have been taken over by organisations set up by farmers since the reform

  various farmers' specialised associations which are not economic entities but support production and marketing through the provision of technical, research, training and advisory services

organisations which provide integrated services covering production, supply and marketing. Due to their importance, it is suggested that the government take steps to promote farmers' marketing co-operative organisations.

'Protective' or minimum prices for farm products are applied in many market economies. China can learn from the experience of other countries, for there can be large costs to the government budget and consumers associated with these policies, and China will need to take care in implementing them. There is less cost associated with, and therefore a stronger case for, policies that seek to stabilise prices around an average level that is close to international prices. When the market price was lower than the 'stabilised price', the Chinese government would purchase grain on the market, adding some strength to market prices. It is not easy, however, to anticipate the stable domestic prices that will end up corresponding to average international prices. There is a danger that pressure from farmers will in practice lead to prices well above world prices, and to large unnecessary costs for society.

Any consumer subsidies that remain should be carefully targeted at low income groups. This could be implemented through official grain shops, which could provide channels for subsidies for low-quality grain, so as to ensure the subsidies go to low-income groups at low operational cost.

The grain buffer reserve is the appropriate instrument for government to stabilise grain prices. Priority should now be given to the following three measures. First, it is necessary to place the financing of grain reserves on a sound long-term basis, ending the situation where the grain reserve depends on special financial allocations. Second, it is necessary to decide what level of reserve is reasonable. The experience of other countries and Chinese conditions suggest that the grain buffer reserve should make up 5 per cent of the annual output of grain. Third, it is important to speed up the construction of storage facilities.

Finally, the government needs to improve the regulatory environment for the grain trade. Priority measures should cover anti-monopoly provisions, measures to monitor qualifications for traders to enter the market, and measures to protect producers' interests against fraud and unfair practices.

8 Fertiliser price

Zhang Wen Bao and Zuo Chang Sheng

Between one-third and one-half of the increase in world grain production is attributed to the increased use of fertiliser in recent decades. In China, as elsewhere, agricultural development is closely related to the increase in the application of fertiliser. China's large population and limited arable land causes increases in the supply of agricultural products to depend on increasing yields, and gives fertiliser an important role in expanding supply. The price of fertiliser is a key variable affecting fertilisation use and agricultural yields, also having an important influence on farmers' incomes.

China's fertiliser price system

Before economic reform, China's chemical fertiliser prices were determined in the planned economy. Central government plans for agriculture were passed down to local governments. All agricultural products, except those that were retained as inputs into agricultural production or for peasants' consumption, were purchased by the government at fixed prices. At the same time, most materials needed in agricultural production, such as fertiliser, pesticides, diesel and high quality seeds and stock, were provided to peasants by the government at fixed prices through designated commercial networks.

In the 1950s the state transferred most of the surplus value created in agriculture, to industry, to provide capital for industrialisation. This was effected through the state purchasing agricultural products at lower prices than would have been available in a free market, and selling industrial products to the peasants at artificially high prices. This represented a hidden income redistribution.

To maintain low prices of agricultural products, the state subsidised fertiliser to keep prices low. Thus a system of 'subsidy, low-priced fertiliser, and low-priced agricultural products' was established.

In 1985 the Chinese government replaced the system of planned state purchase of agricultural products by state contract purchase for grain, cotton, edible oil and other principal agricultural products. Production above contract requirements could be sold in free markets. The fertiliser management system was also transformed: more marketing organisations were allowed to enter the fertiliser business, and market prices were introduced for the exchange of fertiliser in excess of quantities specified in the plan.

Under the new system, there were three means by which fertiliser prices were set. The first was the government fixed price, or the planned price. The state sold part of the available fertilisers to the peasants in proportion to the amount of agricultural products sold to the state. These fertilisers were provided to the peasants by state-owned farm material companies and commercial co-operatives at the planned prices. State regulations determined that the government would provide a peasant with 30 kilograms of fertiliser at planned prices with the purchase of 100 kilograms of soybean, 20 kilograms for 100 kilograms of corn or wheat, and 70 kilograms for 100 kilograms of cotton. Fertiliser sales at the planned low prices were also available for disaster relief and other special purposes.

The second type was the negotiated price. The farm material departments and the commercial co-operatives could buy fertiliser directly from factories and other firms at a negotiated price, and then sell to the peasants at a price that fluctuated with the market. These price fluctuations could be larger within the price ceiling imposed by the government.

The third type was the free market. Other marketing organisations could participate at prices determined freely on the market.

After the fertiliser market had been opened up and its price set free, demand that had been suppressed in the planned system was released. There was some chaos in the market and prices rose sharply. Many fake and inferior quality products appeared on the market and brought great loss to the peasants.

In response, the government restored the special fertiliser management system in 1989. Most fertiliser distribution gradually came to be managed only by state-owned farm material companies and commercial co-operatives. Only a small proportion of fertiliser for technological extension was sold to the peasants by the grass-roots agricultural extension departments. There were effectively two different administrations over fertiliser price: the planned and the unplanned, with planned and negotiated prices. Although the fertiliser markets were closed, other ways of dealing remained, so there was still a market price of fertiliser. The importance of the market price was heightened by the fact that each district, each farm material company and each commercial co-operative had its own independent economic interests in a high or low fertiliser price, and in practice sought as high or as low a price as the market would bear.

Characteristics of fertiliser prices in China

The relationship between grain and fertiliser prices

It has been pointed out that a very important part of China's fertiliser price policy is the provision by government of subsidies to support lower prices of fertiliser supplies for agricultural production. The purpose of this arrangement is to allow the prices of agricultural products to be kept low. As both inputs and outputs of agricultural production come under the low price policy, the profitability of fertiliser application is determined by the relative prices of inputs and outputs.

The relative price of fertiliser to grain was low in China relative to international levels, and therefore favourable to grain production. This is consistent with the following policy goals: the extension of fertiliser use to increase agricultural production, especially of grain; and the return of part of the surplus value created in agriculture to the peasants to ensure a steady growth of peasants' income.

From 1978 the Chinese government raised the prices of agricultural products considerably, but the fertiliser price remained stable till 1985. This caused a substantial increase in the price ratio of grain to fertiliser. For example, the official price ratio of nitrogen fertiliser to rice dropped from 4.0–5.0:1.0 in 1978 to 2.8–4.2:1.0 in 1984. Over the same period, the official price ratio of fertiliser to wheat dropped 2.7–3.6:1.0 to 2.1–3.1:1.0. This raised fertiliser usage and the standard of living for peasants considerably. Fertiliser application rose from 8.8 million tonnes to 17.3 million tonnes, almost doubling in six years. The average annual net cash income of peasants rose from 134 yuan to 355 yuan in the same period.

Both negotiated, and market prices which better reflect economic scarcity, have risen a great deal since 1985. This has increased the fertiliser to grain price ratio. The ratio in 1988 was 1:1.04, compared with 1:1.14 in 1978, and 1:1.50 in 1979–83. The ratio returned to 1:1.40 in 1990. The high price of fertiliser relative to grain may be the cause of stagnation in grain production during 1985–9.

The relationship between different types of fertiliser prices

It has been noted that the same fertiliser has different prices at the same time and at the same place. With the planned price, both the purchasing price and the subsidy are set by the government. Price does not reflect market conditions, and often remains unchanged for several years. When it is changed by the government, the change is often quite small. On the

Table 8.1 *Changes in different types of fertiliser prices in Xinxiang city, 1982–8 (yuan/tonne)*

	Purchasing price	Planned price	Negotiated price
1982	411	450	–
1983	411	458	–
1984	494	520	622–650
1985	494	520	520–670
1986	461	520	540–700
1987	461	520	700–1,000
1988	461	520	700–1,000

Source: Ministry of Agriculture (1991).

other hand, the negotiated prices of fertiliser often fluctuate with supply and demand, and the fluctuations are frequently large. Changes in the two different types of fertiliser prices in Xinxiang city in Henan province illustrate these points (table 8.1).

Excess demand at planned prices caused sharp increases in market prices when these were allowed after 1984. At the national level, the negotiated prices of some fertilisers were twice the planned prices. As could be expected, such price distortions led to 'rent-seeking', and to consequences that conflicted with the objectives of policy. State-owned business enterprises often sold low-priced fertilisers at higher negotiated prices, so peasants did not receive the government subsidies.

Regional fertiliser price differences

There is no regional variation in planned prices. But non-planned prices vary widely with location, market conditions and management costs. For instance, the non-planned price of urea is only about 800 yuan per tonne in some provinces that have their own large and medium-sized fertiliser factories, and range as high as 1,200–1,400 yuan per tonne in others. Large regional differences in non-planned fertiliser prices are evident (table 8.2).

The large regional price differences are caused by many factors. The most obvious is transport costs from centres of fertiliser production. A second is the underdevelopment of the market for chemical fertilisers, which cannot circulate freely all over the country. The regional imbalance of supply and demand is also exacerbated by local protectionism in China.

Table 8.2 *State ceiling retail price of urea in different provinces*

Province	Ceiling for retail price (yuan/tonne)
Hainan	1,400
Helongjiang	1,350
Shandong	870
Guangdong	860

Source: Ministry of Agriculture (1991).

Relative prices of different fertilisers

The relationships between prices of chemical fertilisers containing different nutrients, and between prices of different fertilisers containing the same nutrient, both need to be analysed.

First, we examine the relative prices of fertilisers containing different nutrients. Taking planned prices of different fertilisers in 1988, the price of nitrogen was a little higher than phosphorus, and they were both higher than potassium. This was the reverse order to world market prices. While in the world market the price of potassium is generally higher than the price of nitrogen, in China the price of nitrogen is 50 per cent higher than the price of potassium.

Relative prices in China developed within a closed economy, and had two causes. First, the marginal yield increase from a given increase in the application of nitrogen is greater than that of phosphorus, and the latter is greater than that of potassium. This was revealed in the second national chemical fertiliser experiment started in 1957. The later third national chemical fertiliser experiment of 1980 confirmed this finding. It remains valid today. For the main grain products, on average, we can get a range of output responses from the application of an additional kilogram of various chemical fertilisers: 9–13 kilograms of grain for nitrogen, 5–10 kilograms for phosphorus, and 2–5 kilograms for potassium.

The second cause of the price differentials had its origin in the policy objective of generating what the government considered to be a correct balance between usage of the three fertilisers.

Let us now turn to the differences between prices of fertilisers containing the same nutrient (based on nutrient content). The differences across planned prices are quite different from those under the market system.

Table 8.3 *Price of nitrogen content of various fertilisers, 1988*

Fertiliser	Planned retail price of nitrogen (yuan/tonne)
Urea	1,130
Ammonium nitrate	1,160
Ammonium carbonate	1,156
Ammonium sulphate	1,286

Source: Ministry of Agriculture (1991).

One would expect that a fertiliser with a larger, favourable effect on output and a lower application cost would have a higher price. But planned prices of fertiliser in China have the opposite characteristic (table 8.3). Among the four listed fertilisers, urea had the lowest price, but the greatest quality. The purpose of such a price policy was to raise the profits of fertiliser factories, especially from small and medium-sized factories, to what the government considered to be satisfactory levels. This sometimes meant setting higher prices than for equivalent imported fertilisers. While this increased domestic supply of the chemical fertiliser, it also brought distortion and confusion to the fertiliser market.

Factors affecting fertiliser prices in China

Microeconomic factors

In the past, fertiliser prices were set by the government, so the effects of market conditions on prices were not obvious. After the government adopted a dual-track system, the proportion of market-determined fertiliser supply increased steadily, and the importance of the market in determining price levels became greater. The price of fertiliser began to fluctuate with changing market conditions.

Two main factors affect the supply of fertiliser in a market environment within a closed economy. The first is the production cost of fertiliser. The prices of raw materials, capital and labour have increased greatly in China in recent years, and this has increased the production cost of fertiliser considerably. This is the main cause of the rise in prices of fertilisers made in China. It is not necessarily a cause of increased relative price of fertilisers, since all industries are affected by factor price increases. The improvements of technology in the fertiliser industry have contributed to the fall in the production cost of fertilisers, but not enough to offset the effects of the increase in the prices of production factors. Management of fertiliser enterprises has in general become more efficient, and lowered costs. There have been periods, however, when management costs have risen. One was after the reform of the fertiliser management system in 1985, leading to a period of market chaos with high costs.

The second factor affecting the supply of fertiliser is the industry's production capacity. Over the short and medium term, the supply of fertiliser will increase with the capacity of the industry, and this can cause prices to fall. It is open to China to dampen the rise in fertiliser prices by increasing its investment in the fertiliser industry. Of course, beyond some point this would cease to be a cost-effective use of China's scarce capital.

Further effects also come from management costs and the import of fertiliser. Normal management costs have the same effects on the price of fertiliser as the cost of other inputs into production. After the reform of the fertiliser management system in 1985, the market entered a period of chaos, and management costs increased greatly. The management policy adopted in 1989, which entrenched monopolies, has done nothing to ease the chaos. Increased competition is necessary to force down management costs.

In an open economy, such as China is becoming, the price of fertiliser in world markets becomes the main influence on price. As the price of fertiliser in the world market (in 1993) is lower than the domestic market price, China can reduce and stabilise its fertiliser price by importing more fertiliser. This, of course, is an indication that at least a substantial part of the fertiliser subsidy does not help farmers or encourage agricultural production, but simply offsets the effects of various internationally traded input prices being higher in China than in world markets. It underlines the dangers and costs, to agriculture especially, of protecting an uncompetitive fertiliser industry.

There are two main factors influencing the demand for fertiliser. The first is the input–output ratio of fertiliser application. The application is optimal when the marginal cost equals the marginal return measured at undistorted market prices, and is therefore linked to world prices. The demand for fertiliser would continue to increase as long as the marginal return is higher than the marginal cost. A bigger gap would lead to increased demand, and stronger demand would also lead to a higher price. By this test, current fertiliser application in China is far below optimal levels and the input–output ratio is rather low. The gradual correction of this weakness will tend to increase demand for fertiliser, and therefore the price.

The second influence on demand is the purchasing power of the peasants. The effective demand for fertiliser would stagnate if peasants could not afford to buy it, even if their experience had proved that it would be profitable to use more fertiliser in agricultural production. Because of the poor state of development of rural credit markets, it is difficult for peasants to obtain loans from banks or financial co-operatives. So their purchasing power for agricultural production inputs is mainly determined by their own income.

Of course, among the factors that affect the price of fertiliser, some are specific to particular types of fertiliser.

Pricing principles in the planned price system

Before the economic reform of 1985, all fertiliser prices were controlled by the government. The reform in 1985 allowed some to be sold on a free market. But a large part still remained under the planned price system. Although there have been some changes in the planned prices, they have been almost totally unrelated to market conditions. The planned prices of fertiliser are set by the government according to such principles as the following

to maintain a uniform planned price of fertilisers all over the country, no matter how large the distribution management and other costs

to keep the planned prices of fertiliser stable (so that prices often remain unchanged for many years)

to keep planned prices low, so as to promote production and to safeguard peasants' incomes.

Consideration is also given to factors such as production cost, management cost, the grain to fertiliser price ratio, and relative prices of different fertilisers.

Fertiliser subsidies

The planned price system of fertiliser is supported by government subsidies. The total amount of price subsidies on imported and domestic fertiliser provided to the peasants at planned prices was about 3.4 billion yuan in 1990.

The government subsidises fertiliser in three ways. The first is through subsidies to fertiliser enterprises to make up for losses incurred when the factory-gate price is set by the government below costs of production. Enterprises are usually separately subsidised by the central government and local governments according to the form of enterprise, location and products. Large and medium-size enterprises are normally subsidised by the central and provincial governments, and small enterprises by the county governments.

The second way in which the government provides subsidies is through the departments of state responsible for fertiliser distribution. Under the planned price policy, current in late 1993, the distribution department would suffer a loss of about 27 yuan for distributing one tonne of fertiliser. If annual distribution was 20 million tonnes, the total loss would be as high as 0.54 billion yuan. This is so large a burden that the government has to subsidise the distribution departments.

The third form of subsidy is on the import of fertiliser. There are price differences between the world market and the domestic planned low prices, which are covered by government subsidy. Since the beginning of the 1980s the subsidies for price differences of the imported fertiliser have been maintained at a high level: 2.3 billion yuan in 1988 and 3.2 billion yuan in 1989.

Before the reform of the chemical fertiliser price and management systems, all fertilisers were covered by the plan. Subsidies had helped to keep fertiliser prices below the international and domestic market-clearing levels. After the dual-track price system was introduced, fertilisers sold by negotiation and market exchange assumed a dominant position. The subsidy for fertiliser is now of little importance to its retail price. The proportion that actually benefits peasants is decreasing. The subsidy is mainly used to make up losses in the fertiliser industry and the management departments. Subsidies applied to fertiliser in the present way are not a cost-effective way to promote the development of agriculture in China.

Effects of fertiliser prices on agricultural production

The effects of fertiliser price on agricultural production may be divided into two groups: the effects of the general price level of fertilisers, and the effects of price differentials among fertilisers.

Let us first review the effects of the general price level of fertilisers. A higher fertiliser price would lower the input level of the fertilisers and lower the profitability of agricultural production. The marginal return of fertiliser application is very high in agriculture, so a decline in fertiliser input would cause agricultural production to fall. The price indicators of fertiliser were rather low before 1985 (except in 1984) when the price system of fertilisers was reformed, and grain production continued to rise rapidly in the same period (table 8.4). The price of fertiliser rose greatly in 1984, only slowly mid-decade, and strongly again in the boom conditions of 1988 and 1989.

In an economically efficient (that is, undistorted) market, a high marginal return is associated with a high price for fertiliser. If the high price is

Table 8.4 *Retail price index of fertiliser and grain production, 1978–90*

	Annual retail price index of fertiliser (%)	Grain production (million tonnes)
1978	0.0	305
1979	−0.3	332
1980	0.1	321
1981	0.0	325
1982	0.8	354
1983	2.8	387
1984	11.9	407
1985	3.8	379
1986	−0.7	391
1987	8.3	403
1988	18.6	394
1989	17.3	407
1990	3.5	435

Source: SSB, ZTN (various issues).

an equilibrium market price, reflecting costs of production and marginal productivity in use inside China, and international prices externally, the discouraging effects of high price may be economically appropriate. A high price can be the mechanism through which marginal revenue from the use of fertiliser comes to equal price, through which the marginal cost of production of fertiliser comes to equal price, and through which the Chinese price comes to equal the international price.

Grain production dropped in 1985 following the fertiliser price increase. It stagnated until 1989, when the government restored elements of the old controlled system for fertiliser and other agricultural inputs. The strong rising trend of fertiliser prices was brought under control in 1990 and growth in grain production was restored. The close association of changes in fertiliser price with changes in grain production is suggestive.

Let us now examine the effects of price differentials among fertilisers. It has been noted that the price of nitrogen is higher than the price of phosphorus, and the latter is higher than the price of potassium. Although at the national level the marginal return from the use of nitrogen is larger than that of phosphorus and potassium, the fact is that two-thirds of the arable land is short of phosphorus and a considerable part of the arable land is short of potassium. Balanced fertiliser application would have a more important effect on these lands than the sole application of nitrogen. Balanced fertiliser application would also raise the marginal return from nitrogen itself. The way to bring about the economically efficient use of different kinds of fertiliser is to allow the market to set prices in China, and to allow open trade between the Chinese domestic market and the international market. Such an approach would lead to large changes in the relative prices of fertiliser within China. Over time, it would allow the increased agricultural production value from the use of an increment of each type of fertiliser to equal the price of that fertiliser; the cost of production to equal the price for each type of fertiliser; and the domestic price to equal the international price for each type of fertiliser.

Effects of the planned prices of fertiliser on agricultural production

Planned prices have both positive and negative effects on the volume of agricultural production. It has been noted that low planned prices of fertilisers have stimulated farm output and profitability. This section analyses the negative effects of the planned prices of fertiliser.

The government distributes fertiliser at the planned price to peasants according to the amount of contracted agricultural products. Peasants who sell more products to the government receive more chemical fertiliser from the government. The marginal product of fertiliser has begun to diminish in the high-yield regions as their application of fertiliser is already high. But the marginal return of fertiliser is much larger in the low-yield regions. According to economic principles, distribution and application of fertiliser can be optimal only when marginal returns are equal in all regions. Taking the overall supply of chemical fertiliser as given, it would thus help to raise national agricultural production if fertiliser supply to the high-yield areas were reduced and to the low-yield areas increased. But such an adjustment is seriously restricted by the present price and distribution systems.

This situation can be contrasted with that where distribution is through efficient markets. Expanded fertiliser use in areas where marginal product is high would raise prices, leading to lower usage in regions where marginal product was low. Falling use causes marginal product to rise in the high-usage areas where it had been low, and rising use causes marginal product to fall in the low-usage areas in which it had been high. The end point of the adjustment is the equalisation of marginal product in the various areas.

Other negative effects of low planned prices include fiscal burdens and inflationary effects, which are damaging to agriculture as well as to other sectors.

Basic trend in fertiliser demand, supply and price

The production and application of fertiliser has increased greatly since 1949. Production in the five years from 1951 to 1955, measured by its nutrient components, was only 0.3 million tonnes, and application was only 0.7 million tonnes. Annual production rose in 1990 to 18.8 million tonnes, and application to 25.9 million tonnes. The establishment of many large-scale fertiliser factories in the late 1970s led to large increases in supply in China. Domestic production has increased rapidly since the early 1980s, but fertiliser application increased more rapidly. The gap between domestic production and application of fertiliser increased from 0.4 million tonnes in 1980 to 7.1 million tonnes in 1990.

In the long run, the Chinese government's strategic objective of 400 kilograms of grain production per person in the year 2000 will be difficult to attain. Its achievement will mainly depend on the increase in yields which in turn will depend on the quantity and quality of fertiliser. Fertiliser use would need to rise to 150 million tonnes (in terms of gross weight) at the end of the century if the strategic objective were to be met. It seems that China's production capacity of fertiliser will be able to rise to only 120 million tonnes, even if the industry is on the state investment priority list. The gap between demand and domestic supply would be about 30 million tonnes. The difference may be made up from imports, but this will not be without anxiety about the availability of foreign exchange and the effects of such large imports on world prices.

The level of fertiliser use and domestic production will, of course, depend on the institutional arrangements and the prices that emerge under those arrangements. Higher prices under a market system linked to international prices would lead to a slower increase in fertiliser use and tend to stimulate domestic production.

Under the old planned price system, there were few and small changes in the price of fertiliser. After the adoption of a dual-track price system, the annual increase of fertiliser price was large (except for 1986) until the government restored the planned management system in 1989 and successfully controlled the increase in price.

In the long run, in the expectation of movement towards a market economy, two factors will influence the general trend in fertiliser price. One is the general trend in demand–supply conditions; the other is the probable reform in the fertiliser price and distribution system, including the import regime.

The abolition of the planned management of fertiliser would soon lead to large fluctuations, even if the planned price system remained unchanged. On the other hand, as the amount of fertiliser administered under the planned price is still very large, and the difference between the planned price and the market price is also large, a price reform towards a free market would raise the retail price. The longer the subsidy continues, the greater the eventual adjustment problem.

Policy implications

The rate of agricultural development depends heavily on the efficient supply and price of fertiliser. But what amount of supply and what price are optimal in the context of the Chinese economy as a whole?

The Chinese government has been spending a large amount of foreign currency on importing agricultural products such as grain, sugar and vegetable oil. It may be more profitable to spend this foreign currency on importing fertiliser. The test of whether this is so is whether it is profitable to produce more fertiliser or more grain when barriers to trade are removed. It may be that the removal of import barriers to grain as well as fertiliser would lead to less import of agricultural products and more fertiliser; if so, such a pattern would promote more efficient agricultural development.

It would be productive to again relax government controls over fertiliser. The reform in 1985 was well conceived. The problems after the reform were mainly caused by the under-development of the fertiliser market and inappropriate government administration. The restoration of the old planned management system is not an effective response to these problems. In order to develop an efficient market economy, the Chinese government has to relax its control on the management of fertiliser. To avoid the problems which emerged in 1985–8, the government must improve the administration and regulation of fertiliser markets.

It is important to abolish the planned price subsidy for fertiliser step by step. The main purpose of the planned price subsidy for chemical fertiliser is to promote the development of agriculture. As the subsidy is not given to the peasants directly, a considerable part of it has been absorbed by the industrial and commercial enterprises, often to cover deficits caused by simple mismanagement. The price subsidy therefore does not have the desired effect of encouraging domestic production, which it was intended to have. It would be better to use this expenditure for public purposes, including in agriculture, that can be justified by the social returns that they generate, or to reduce the budget deficit. The government ought gradually to abolish the planned price subsidy for fertiliser and free the price of chemical fertiliser from government control.

9   Agricultural wholesale markets

Xu Boyuan

In what is a new development in Chinese agricultural marketing, many wholesale markets have sprung up since the mid-1980s. The first were for vegetables. In Shangdong, the Shoiguang Vegetable Wholesale Market was set up in a major vegetable producing area in 1984. The first grain wholesale market was opened in Guangzhou in October 1990; the first central meat wholesale market in Chengdu in October 1991; and the first sugar wholesale market in the north of China was established in Tianjin in January 1992.

These markets take two forms. One type formed spontaneously and are administered by the Industrial and Commercial Bureaus. The second type has been established by state commercial organisations. Industrial and Commercial Bureaus were administering nine times as many agricultural wholesale markets in 1992 as in 1983.

The role of wholesale markets

Wholesale markets are an important vehicle for deepening agricultural marketing reform. They provide markets for many commodities that lack them. They coordinate dispersed production with concentrated urban requirements, and seasonal patterns of production with continuous consumption.

The wholesale markets have increased efficiency. In the Taiyuan Hexi Agricultural Wholesale Market, the efficiency of labour is high and costs are low. More than 80 products are traded. The market provides two-thirds of the vegetable requirements of nearby urban residents and transacts throughout 24 provinces. The collection of management fees has risen steadily and the market has only 16 administrative employees.

Market mechanisms equilibrate supply and demand, and the wide regional reach of the wholesale markets allows this process to occur with less price instability than would otherwise be present. Wholesale markets

113

also ensure lower prices than would otherwise be the case. According to a survey conducted in Beijing's Dazhongshi Agricultural Wholesale Market from June 1988 to June 1991, among 12 vegetable varieties, the prices of eight decreased or were stable, and four rose.[1] Consumers felt that the prices of vegetables from the south, such as tomatoes and cucumbers, were lower than before. Total costs, including wholesale distribution, were lower than local greenhouse production costs.

Wholesale markets also facilitate dispersion of market information. For example, the two largest meat wholesale markets, the Chengdu Wholesale Meat Market and the Shanghai Wholesale Meat Market use computerised long-distance communication. This has strengthened their roles in providing market information and forming prices.

The wholesale market system encourages peasants to enter market exchange and to transfer agricultural labour to non-farm sectors. In the process, it helps peasants move land and labour into their most productive uses.

Wholesale marketing is itself a major industry, employing many people. A survey in the Chengdu Hehuaci Agricultural Wholesale Market revealed more than 10 thousand self-employed peddlers.

Wholesale markets and state enterprises

The new system has put pressure on state wholesale organisations. Following the establishment of agricultural wholesale markets and the reform of state agricultural purchase monopolies, state enterprises have begun to participate in the creation and operation of wholesale markets. State enterprise reform has taken two forms. The first reform is of the management structure. In Chongqing, the state-operated commercial organisations decided to make their own decisions on hiring labour, setting prices and entering into new business. Some organisations sought to adapt to market conditions by integrating the management of agriculture and marketing, rebuilding wholesale channels, taking part in market competition, using labour more economically and enhancing internal management.

The second is state enterprise participation in wholesale markets. Reformed state enterprises play important roles as traders in wholesale markets – in the process increasing market efficiency. It is estimated that in the ten largest wholesale markets, with transaction volumes in 1991 exceeding 100 million yuan and paying more than 10 million yuan in taxes, more than 2,000 state businesses and enterprises were actively participating in trading.

In addition, more and more state businesses play a role in the construction of agricultural wholesale markets. There have been great changes in the infrastructure of the markets and increases in the scale of investment:

in 1991 the total volume of investment in construction was 3.8 billion yuan, an increase of 95 per cent over 1990.

There are a number of differences between markets administered by Industrial and Commercial Bureaus (spontaneous) and those run by state commercial organisations (official). The spontaneous markets cover fresh as well as dried products, while the official markets are mainly limited to grain, oil, meat and sugar. Spontaneous markets mainly use spot transactions, while official markets rely primarily on traditional methods of state trading. Market forces determine prices in the first type of market while official intervention (and related market failure) occurs in the second. In the first type of market, anybody can enter for trading; but in the second only members can trade. Members are almost exclusively state business corporations formed under the traditional marketing system. The first type of market has a solid basis but is short on rules, while the second has good standards but lacks vitality.

It is important to combine the advantages of these two types of wholesale markets.

Officially supported wholesale markets have several problems. First, they are often subject to close government administrative intervention. Sometimes market managers receive administrative orders to manipulate supply and demand, and this often results in heavy losses that administrations cannot afford to compensate.

Second, these markets are often fragmented. Governments introduce administrative measures to ensure that local products dominate local markets. For example, after the building of the North China Wholesale Sugar Market in Tianjin, both departmental and regional trade barriers remained. Light industry and agriculture business systems had to sell outside the market. So much sugar was sold outside the wholesale market that the price fell to a damaging extent.

Third, some markets lack the necessary operating funds and staff. Fourth, tax policy appears to have affected market development in some of these wholesale markets.

In sum, the officially sanctioned wholesale markets rely on administrative monopoly to underwrite market shares and on subsidies to keep running. The market administration is extremely bureaucratic and inefficient.

Three obvious steps could be taken to make state-sponsored wholesale markets more active and efficient. Administrative and proprietary rights should be separated, so that wholesale market management can be carried out according to market rules. Official intervention in price formation should be withdrawn, so that supply and demand freely determine prices. Emphasis should be placed on improving management and the quality of administrative staff.

The wholesale markets formed spontaneously need improvements of different kinds. These markets draw their strength from the many parties that participate in transactions. Many dealers are individual peasants who are not well organised. Marketing co-operatives may be good vehicles for organising peasants entering into trade, but to be effective they must first change the bureaucratic working style. The physical and legal infrastructure, including for contract enforcement, also needs to be improved.

Extending and consolidating the system

How much should the system be extended, and in what locations? Are all parts of the system worth consolidating?

Some of the growth in wholesale markets seems to have no economic justification. For example, in one case, there are three agricultural wholesale markets within one kilometre. Market establishment needs to proceed gradually to avoid wasteful investment.

China should regard the establishment of wholesale markets as an important part of agricultural marketing reform. Governments have a role in co-ordinating market development. As a general rule, an agricultural wholesale market may be justified to service each major, distinct catchment area and range of services, although the practice of locating markets according to regional administrative divisions should be avoided.

A number of conditions need to be met if an agricultural wholesale market is to be justified:

Production in a market's neighbourhood should provide abundant merchandise.

A wholesale market should be close to cities with good transportation infrastructure

The neighbourhood of a wholesale market should be relatively liberalised and well developed.

There should be a large group of wholesalers and retailers, including individual peddlers and specialised mongers in the locations, or the potential for these to emerge quickly.

The location should have good service facilities.

The superior experience with spontaneous markets suggests that agricultural wholesale markets should be established after a period of natural convergence of traders.

The role of government: Zhenzhou and Dazhongshi compared

There is a public policy case for government assistance in the founding of agricultural wholesale markets. Public investment will often be needed to support construction of wholesale markets, alongside other sources of investment including private equity. It will often be appropriate to use the land of state-owned commercial or other economic organisations, or if new land is necessary, for the regulatory authorities to provide approvals.

Wholesale markets should offer paid service to customers and cover running costs from income. Departments of commerce, tax, price, public security and others should make common efforts to administer and supervise the markets, but not participate in trade, directly or indirectly. Steps must be taken to ensure that prices can function as signals for resource allocation.

The Zhenzhou Wholesale Grain Market illustrates the issues and problems associated with government involvement in the official type of market. It has two price setting systems: auction and negotiation. Both are used in the exchange hall, within price ranges determined by the government. Contractual formalities are completed at the moment the exchange is made.

The auction system serves the ends of open and fair competition better than the negotiation system, but the majority of the traders have not adjusted to it. Because of this and other factors the auction system is not often practised. Though not as competitive as the auction system, negotiation is closer to the trading tradition of China. Price negotiation may be influenced by such information as the most recent selling price and quotation in other places. As traders adjust to modern market operations, the auction system should become dominant.

The Zhenzhou market has also made great progress in forward price transactions. If at a relevant time the forward contract price is within 6 per cent of the current spot price, the buyer and seller alone share the price risks. If it varies by 6 to 10 per cent, the government may partially compensate the party against whom the market has moved. Under these arrangements, mid-term and long-term contracts (longer than three months) have accounted for one-third of contracts signed.

Zhenzhou market prices have begun to exert an influence on grain trades across the country and many enterprises use them as an important indicator in managing their production activity. Even farmers are beginning to use the Zhenzhou market price to inform their sales decisions.

The Zhenzhou price is not entirely unbiased. There are gaps in the market's formal laws and rules. Only a small proportion of grain trading takes place in the Zhenzhou market. The fact that most grain trading takes place on other markets, where regulation is poor, information blocked and transparency low, casts doubt on the Zhenzhou market prices. Administrative interference in the forms of price and subsidy affect trading outcomes.

The role of government and associated problems are very different in the spontaneous type of market, exemplified by Beijing's Dazhongshi Agricultural Wholesale Market. Prices in this market were monitored from June 1988 to June 1991 and were found to be fairly stable. Five characteristics of the Dazhongshi market explain this outcome.

First, demand and supply are concentrated. The volume of vegetables traded accounted for one-third to one-quarter of total vegetable trading in Beijing.

Second, competition is considerable. The market's network includes 26 provinces and cities and nearly 600 counties. In the vegetable season (from May to August), produce from outside Beijing accounts for 80 per cent of market trading, and in the slack season (from September to April), 95 per cent. Sellers include farmer mongers, producers selling their own products and individual long-distance peddlers. On the purchase side, peddlers account for more than 70 per cent, collective units for about 20 per cent and individual customers for 5 to 6 per cent. Buyers and sellers agree on prices through negotiation.

Third, there are no subsidies or other administrative interventions in the Dazhongshi market, beyond normal taxes and management fees.

Fourth, the transparency of the market is high and information flows easily. Each day the market records detailed price information. These data are analysed each month by the market management. As a result the market has become one of the vegetable price formation centres in Beijing.

Fifth, Dazhongshi is regulated efficiently. The departments of tax, security, industry and commerce, and others, are invited into the market to enforce market order. Due to this regulation there is confidence that contracts will be implemented as agreed.

Lessons and open questions

Despite achievements in the establishment of wholesale markets in recent years, there is an urgent need to formulate appropriate regulations. Problems that need to be addressed include unco-ordinated overlapping administration by several different authorities, and arbitrary interference in management by government departments.

Some important issues remain the subject of debate. For example, should the regulatory agencies (the Industrial and Commercial Bureaus) be allowed to establish markets? As the wholesale market is a public facility, should the government, rather than the rural collectives, assume the responsibility of construction? Both the Chengdu Bebuaci Agricultural Wholesale Market, established by the Industrial and Commercial Bureau, and the Beijing Dazhongshi Agricultural Wholesale Market, set up by rural collective units, have been booming.

It is very useful to learn from the successful and not so successful experiences of specialised wholesale markets – the Zhenzhou Wholesale Grain Market, the Chengdu and Shanghai wholesale meat markets, Beijing's Dazhongshi and Shandong's Shouguang wholesale vegetable markets, and the Chongqing Wholesale Fruit Market – in drafting provisional regulations for wholesale markets.

Regulations include those made by the market management bodies themselves and those made by the government. While the former may be shaped according to the distinguishing features of each product, it would be the best for the latter to be formulated in an integrated way by the agricultural and commercial ministries, the Industrial and Commercial Bureau and the Development Research Centre of the State Council, with leadership from the State System Reform Committee.

Notes

1 Survey conducted by author.

10 The 'wool war' and the 'cotton chaos': fibre marketing

Zhang Xiaohe, Lu Weiguo, Sun Keliang,
Christopher Findlay and Andrew Watson

Textile fibres are at once a major source of farm output and income (ranking after grain), and a major input into industrial production (ranking after coal and oil). The textile industries have contributed the largest component of the increase in industrial production in both urban and rural areas since the commencement of reform. Production, trade and utilisation of natural textiles is thus an important part of the story of the Chinese rural economy in the reform period, interacting with agriculture, rural industry, trade between rural and urban areas, and economic exchange between the farms and township and village enterprises.

A study of the production, trade and absorption of natural textile fibres illustrates many of the problems and contradictions of China's partially reformed economic system. Nowhere were the contradictions more costly, or revealed more dramatically, than in the struggle that emerged in the late 1980s for possession of the rents generated by controlled and distorted markets for natural fibres. These came to be known in China as the 'wool war' and the 'cotton chaos'.

A highly competitive and internationally oriented processing industry co-existed alongside problems in the supply of raw material. Constraints on local production of raw materials were not the problem, as natural fibres are internationally tradable, and the textiles and clothing sector has been a net importer of raw materials. Access to the world market permits a separation between the fibre production stage and the processing stage. A simple model here is based on these characteristics of the industry – a model of a two-stage production process is utilised here in an attempt to identify the origins of the fibre wars and shortages.

The UNIDO Secretariat has examined the changing patterns of world trade in textiles and clothing, describing a four-phase development path. The UNIDO model indicates that the developing economies were *traditionally* net importers of textiles and clothing products but with economic development and change they have become net exporters (UNIDO

120

Secretariat 1989). Anderson and Park (1988) and Park and Anderson (1988) suggest a hill-shaped export pattern of textiles and clothing products with respect to the growth of per capita income. As many textiles and clothing activities tend to be labour intensive, they will be among the items initially exported by a newly industrialising, less densely populated economy. As demand for raw textile materials increase, the country's net exports of natural fibre diminish or net imports of natural fibre increase. The greater the density of its population, the longer textiles and clothing dominate an economy's exports.

According to Zhang's (1990) classification, China's textiles and clothing sector can be treated as a typical set of labour-intensive activities, with the clothing industry ranked first and the textile industry ranked fourteenth out of 40 industries in terms of labour-to-capital ratios.

This analysis suggests that China, with a high population density, can be expected to specialise strongly in the production and export of textiles and clothing. Furthermore, it suggests the international market provides a mechanism for separating processing activity from the procurement of raw material supplies. That is, the capacity to produce finished products need not be restricted by the domestic capacity of the fibre industry.

The data on China's trade indicate the importance of the textiles and clothing sector. In 1993 textiles and clothing exports were valued at US$27.1 billion and accounted for about 30 per cent of China's exports. China overtook South Korea and Taiwan in the early 1980s to become the second largest textiles and clothing exporter among developing countries. Hong Kong, which is nominally the largest exporter, now mainly re-exports mainland manufactures. According to UN trade data, China's share of world textile trade rose from 4.9 per cent in 1980 to 7.4 per cent in 1992. Its share of world clothing trade also rose from 4.1 per cent to 12.8 per cent during the same period. Overall, about one-third of textile output is exported and about 20 per cent of raw material requirements are imported. These ratios vary between regions of China – for example, they are much higher in Shanghai.

There is some debate in China about the appropriate size of the textile industry, but we ignore that issue here. While a country of China's size cannot expect to limitlessly increase its exports without affecting price, these effects do not yet or forseeably suggest the end of Chinese export expansion. (For purposes of analysis, the following section adopts the simplifying assumption that world prices do not fall as China increases its exports.)

China's textiles and clothing trade over the decade of the 1980s show that the distinguishing characteristics of China's textiles and clothing trade is in its intra-industry pattern (table 10.1). China imports fibre and

Table 10.1 *China's textile and clothing (TC) production and trade, 1970–93*

	Total TC Exports		Of which			Share of China's total exports %	China's share of world exports %	Total TC imports		Of which		
	Value (million US$)	Average annual growth %	Fibre (million US$)	Textile (million US$)	Clothing (million US$)			Value (million US$)	Average annual growth %	Fibre (million US$)	Textile (million US$)	Clothing (million US$)
1970	596		100	340	155	26.37	2.6	156		110	45	1
1975	1,631		245	1,033	353	22.48	3.0	484		395	89	
1978	2,832		401	1,723	708	29.06	3.5	1,060		857	202	1
1980	4,953	22.25	544	2,756	1,653	27.11	4.6	2,896		2,040	835	21
1981	4,998	0.91	454	2,680	1,864	22.71	4.7	4,042	39.57	2,644	1,383	15
1982	5,034	0.72	589	2,496	1,949	22.55	4.9	2,355	-41.74	1,486	852	7
1983	5,638	12.00	672	2,906	2,060	25.37	5.4	1,399	-40.59	832	564	3
1984	7,275	29.04	930	3,692	2,653	27.83	6.3	1,653	18.16	693	954	6
1985	6,438	-11.51	1,145	3,243	2,050	23.54	5.2	2,740	65.76	1,118	1,607	15
1986	8,283	28.66	1,148	4,220	2,915	26.77	5.5	2,689	-1.86	1,055	620	14
1987	11,044	33.33	1,508	5,790	3,749	28.08	5.8	2,996	11.42	1,131	1,848	17
1988	13,002	17.73	1,672	6,458	3,872	27.35	6.2	4,362	45.59	1,946	2,388	28
1989	14,670	12.82	1,546	6,994	6,130	27.95	6.7	5,169	18.50	2,286	2,845	38
1990	14,940	0.18	1,094	6,998	6,848	23.66	6.2	4,637	-10.29	1,841	2,748	48
1991	17,858	19.53	1,125	7,735	8,998	23.30	7.9	5,995	28.42	2,205	3,688	61
1992	26,004	45.62	669	8,587	16,748	29.80	10.2	10,138	70.24	3,042	6,695	400
1993	27,790	6.87	658	8,704	18,428	n.a.	n.a.	9,670	-4.62	2,373	6,787	510

Source: Zhongguo fangzhi gongye nianjin (1994: 14, 114, 116 and 127).

Table 10.2 *Gross output value of China's textile and clothing industries, 1970–92 (1980 constant prices)*

	·1970		1980		1990		1992	
	(billion yuan)	(%)	(billion yuan)	(%)	(billion yuan)	(%)	(billion yuan	(%)
Total textiles	29.32		66.66		136.16		151.60	
Chemical fibres	0.84	2.86	4.98	7.47	17.44	12.81	23.27	15.34
Cotton textiles	26.63	70.36	43.89	65.84	69.61	51.12	75.22	49.62
Knit fabrics	2.15	7.33	6.39	9.59	11.11	8.16	11.35	7.48
Wool textiles	1.37	4.67	3.47	5.20	9.41	6.91	11.60	7.65
Bast fibre	0.42	1.43	1.00	1.50	2.64	1.94	2.90	1.91
Silk and spun silk	2.45	8.35	4.58	6.87	10.10	7.42	11.30	7.45
Textile machinery	n.a.	n.a.	1.26	1.84	2.75	2.02	3.41	2.25
Textile accessories	n.a.	n.a.	0.35	0.53	0.73	0.54	0.85	0.56
Apparel	n.a.	n.a.	n.a.	n.a.	10.23	7.51	11.70	7.72

Notes:
The data in this table refer to the enterprises under Ministry of Textile control only.
Cotton textile includes all cotton spinning, weaving, dyeing and printing processes.
Bast fibre includes bast fibre spinning and weaving.
Data before 1987 do not include apparel industry.
Source: Zhongguo fangzhi gongye nianjin (1990: 13).

textiles and exports mainly textiles and clothing. China is a net importer of fibre but a net exporter of textiles and clothing. This position was disturbed by good harvests in 1984 but returned to the long-run trend after 1987. The pattern was reinforced in the period up to 1993. Net exports of clothing have increased dramatically, most likely as a result of China's outward-oriented trade policy and the development of rural industries.[1]

The Chinese textiles and clothing sector is dominated by the natural fibre industries with the cotton sector accounting for more than 66 per cent of total textiles and clothing production in 1980 and that its share declined to less than 50 per cent in 1992 (table 10.2). According to Findlay and Li (1991), cotton textile production is the most labour-intensive sector, ranking above the wool textile sector, which in turn is more labour intensive than the chemical fibre sector. The factor intensity ranking of China's seven main sub-branches of the textiles and clothing sector in 1985, are consistent with their results (table 10.3). Measured in terms of indicators of capital intensity, such as fixed capital per worker, the

Table 10.3 *Factor intensities in China's textile industry*

	NVFA total (million yuan)	Total employees (thousand)	NVFAW (yuan)	Skill ratio (%)	Net output value (million yuan)	NOVW (yuan)	Wage bill (million yuan)	Wage bill/ NOV (%)	Ranking by capital intensity
Total textiles	30,346	6,830	4,443	1.40	25,050	3,668	6,590	26.31	
Chemical fibres	7,125	259	27,510	4.97	2,695	10,405	321	11.91	1
Cotton textiles	17,028	3,685	4,621	1.58	13,794	3,743	3,662	26.55	4
Knit fabric	3,867	1,060	3,648	1.10	3,278	3,092	949	28.95	5
Wool textiles	3,858	605	6,377	1.83	3,492	5,772	632	18.10	2
Bast fibre	1,196	247	4,872	1.09	772	3,126	224	29.02	3
Silk and spun silk	3,186	906	3,517	1.14	2,662	2,938	838	31.48	6
Apparel	3,060	1,998	1,532	0.47	4,900	2,452	1,707	34.84	7

Notes:
Cotton textiles include all cotton spinning, weaving, dyeing and printing processes.
Wool textiles include all wool spinning, weaving, dyeing and printing processes.
Bast fibre includes bast fibre spinning and weaving.
Apparel and chemical fibres are not included in total textile data.
The data include all enterprises above the township level.
NVFA: net value of fixed assets.
NVFAW: net value of fixed assets per worker.
NOV: net output value.
NOVW: net output value per worker.
Skill ratio is denied as the share of technicians to total employees.
Capital intensity is ranked ascendingly for NVFA, NOV, and skill ratio and descendingly for wage bill/NOV.
Source: China's Industrial Survey Data 1988, vol. 3:172–81, vol. 8: 18–51, reported in Zhang (1991).

importance of skilled workers in the labour force, value-added per worker and the share of the wage bill in value-added, the cotton textile industry ranks fourth, the wool textile industry second and the chemical fibre industry first (the most capital intensive). These rankings are also consistent with those of Anderson (1989) and Park and Anderson (1988) for South Korea and Japan.

China is clearly a highly internationally competitive supplier of textiles and clothing products, especially natural fibre products. Despite this international competitiveness, however, there appear to be serious shortages of raw material supplies to the textile industry. It has been estimated that the degree of overall capacity utilisation in the industry fell over the second half of the 1980s. The decline in capacity utilisation over this period reflects both the slowdown in domestic demand[2] and the problem of obtaining raw materials.[3]

In addition to falling capacity utilisation, the marketing of fibre within China has been fragmented by barriers to inter-regional trade. These include export embargoes and taxes. Regional governments have attempted to inhibit the movement of wool and cotton out of their jurisdiction, sometimes in contradiction of the objectives of the central government.

Model of a two-stage production process[4]

Figure 10.1 shows a partial equilibrium model of a two-stage production process. There are two products in this model, the finished good (clothing, for instance), and the raw material input (for example, fibre). Both goods are traded on world markets and their world market prices are P_c and P_f respectively. It is assumed that units are specified so that each unit of the final good requires one unit of fibre; this permits comparison of prices on the same diagram. For simplicity, it is assumed that the good is produced only for the world market and therefore the diversion of output on to the domestic market is ignored. In free trade, the price for fibre in the domestic market would be P_f. The fibre producers' supply curve is shown by S_f so at price P_f they would produce Q_f. The clothing producers can buy as much fibre as they want at the world price, from domestic producers and from the world market. Their supply curve is shown by S_c, with a rising margin on the cost of fibre.[5] At a world price of P_c their output of clothing is shown by Q_c, they earn a surplus shown by area A, and fibre imports are equal to $Q_f Q_c$. In the case depicted, the economy is an exporter of finished products but an importer of fibre.

Suppose then that the government regulates the fibre market and holds the price at P_g below the world market price.[6] If producers had the choice

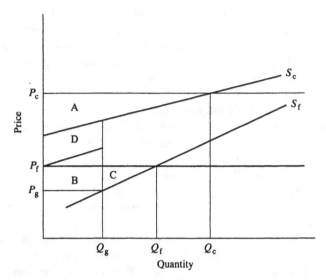

Figure 10.1   Model of a two-stage production process
Source: Zhang Xiaohe 1991.

they would cut output to Q_g. Part, but not all, of their surplus would be transferred to the clothing makers (area B equal to area D); and the deadweight loss of this policy is area C. In these circumstances, imports of fibre increase to $Q_g Q_c$.

Under a centrally planned system, however, P_g might only be an accounting price. Other mechanisms could be used to obtain a higher level of output than Q_g such as Q_f. In that situation, the planner behaves like a monopsonist who makes the growers an 'all-or-nothing offer' in order to extract their surplus. The deadweight cost of the regulation could be less. Instead it involves a greater transfer component but not necessarily a distortion of output. This may be relevant up to the late 1970s. However, in the period after 1978 producers were given more autonomy over output levels. In terms of figure 10.1, this means that they were more likely to be responding to marginal prices for their output. They would be operating according to their supply curve, rather than being forced off it by the planning system.

The policy of keeping down prices paid for industrial raw materials has other implications. There will be a variety of attempts to evade the price distortion. The export price becomes higher than the domestic price as a result. Producers of fibre can earn higher returns on the export market so they have incentives to evade the distortion by exporting. The policy could therefore induce simultaneous import and export of fibre.

A domestic secondary market in fibre could develop. Its price would settle at P_f. In that case, P_g would be supplied through the planning system and $Q_g Q_f$ through the market. Imports would return to their original level. The planners might initially sanction the secondary market, on the expectation that they could still procure the supply they wanted at price Pg. But the presence of a secondary market creates the incentive to switch supplies out of the planned system on to the free market. It makes it more difficult for the planners to fulfil their expectations.

An option for trying to recapture some of the rents created by the distortion (namely area B) is for the fibre makers to integrate forward into processing. It is easier to capture these rents if the processing capacity they build becomes part of the planned system. Otherwise they have incentives to withhold supplies of fibre from the planned system in order to process it locally.

The struggle over supplies in China took the form of interventions in the distribution system by different levels of government to procure supplies, leading to the 'fibre wars'. The pursuit of rents in the processing activity, as predicted by our model, could involve a disruption in the planned system. In addition, regional governments might prefer to see rents created by the price distortion captured by local processing enterprises in their jurisdiction, rather than see them recaptured by fibre producers receiving higher prices in secondary markets. Another element of the fibre wars is therefore likely to be intervention by regional governments in fibre producing regions to divert products from secondary markets into local processing (that is, some form of export tax or export quota).

Commentators have also suggested that there were 'shortages' of fibre, the evidence being the low level of utilisation of existing capacity.[7] In the model as specified so far there will be no 'shortages' of supplies, since the secondary market will continue to clear and imports will make up any remaining shortfall in fibre-poor regions. Shortages could appear if the secondary market worked imperfectly and if there were quantity controls on imports as well.

In summary, a planning system which tries to lower the fibre price relative to the finished product price will lead to

increased imports of fibres

switching of fibre supplies on to the export market and simultaneous export and import of fibres

development of a secondary market and diversion of supplies to that market

integration by fibre producers into clothing production and diversion of fibres destined for the planning system into local processing capacity

efforts by regional governments to divert local supplies into local processing rather than be sold on secondary markets

'shortages' of fibre and low levels of capacity utilisation, in the event
that secondary markets work imperfectly or when there are import
restrictions.

The cotton chaos[8]

Supply side

China's cotton production and net exports reached their peak in 1984 and
1986 respectively, but after 1988 cotton imports increased rapidly. Self-sufficiency fell to a low point of 72 per cent in 1989 (table 10.4).

Zhang (1991) identifies a number of forces affecting the distribution of
cotton over the second half of the 1980s. The first was the change in the
marketing arrangements for cotton, shifting the relative returns away from
cotton towards other crops. Prior to 1985 the state was the only purchaser
of cotton. Producers had to meet a basic quota with higher prices offered
for over-quota output. There were also other subsidies for inputs and
access to cheap grain in proportion to cotton output. The state procurement system for cotton was replaced by contract purchases in 1985 but the
continuing low contract prices, and the decline in the extent of other subsidies, saw producers switch out of cotton.

From the producers' point of view, the main substitute on the supply
side was grain. After 1978 the price of grain relative to cotton fell but then
rose again from 1983 onwards (table 10.5). Cotton production peaked in
1984 and then, responding to its falling relative price, fell in 1985 and
again in 1986.[9]

The supply of coupons for low-price foods, and the provision of chemical fertilisers and insecticides, for example, are all relevant to agricultural
decision-making. Several investigations into the impact of these non-price
factors on cotton supply indicated that their impact was significant, especially the elimination after 1985 of access to subsidised foods and to dis-
counted industrial inputs (table 10.6).[10]

This drop in output, in the face of steady increases in demand, led to
severe competition for supplies, forcing up the price of raw cotton. Market
prices for cotton exceeded the plan price by at least 50 per cent in 1988 and
1989. The quality of raw cotton also declined (with, for instance, adulteration and shorter fibre lengths). Cotton-producing regions also refused to
supply raw cotton at the state price without receiving other rewards (for
example foreign exchange, low-cost debt funds, or other goods such as fertiliser).[11] Regional governments attempted to raise their bargaining power

Table 10.4 *China's cotton production, industrial consumption and trade, 1980–92*

	Production (1,000 mt)	Purchases (1,000 mt)	Consumption (1,000 mt)	Exports (1,000 mt)	Exports (million US$)	Imports (1,000 mt)	Imports (million US$)	Self-sufficiency (%)	Trade balance (million US$)
1980	2,707	2,681	3,176	–	–	898	–	82	–
1981	2,968	2,910	3,424	10	2	801	1,534	84	–1,532
1982	3,598	3,497	3,569	4	6	473	714	96	–708
1983	4,637	4,481	3,555	58	74	230	331	129	–257
1984	6,258	6,001	3,502	189	276	40	80	149	196
1985	4,147	3,550	4,080	347	433	–	–	106	433
1986	3,540	3,794	4,570	527	745	–	–	83	745
1987	4,245	4,071	4,390	761	500	9	15	93	485
1988	4,149	3,778	4,310	468	719	35	59	88	660
1989	3,783	3,306	4,600	273	431	519	709	72	–278
1990	4,508	4,091	4,700	167	300	417	711	87	–411
1991	5,675	5,290	5,461	200	361	371	631	97	–270
1992	4,508	4,358	4,346	145	211	133	430	100	–219

Notes:

Self-sufficiency is defined as the ratio of domestic purchases to domestic consumption.

Trade balance is defined as exports minus imports in value terms.

The export and import values after 1985 in terms of US dollars are derived from the exchange rates in each year. Consumption data in 1991 and 1992 are estimated from domestic purchases minus exports plus imports.

Sources: SSB, ZTN (1994: 641, 644); *Zhongguo fangzhi gongye nianjin* (1994: 37).

Table 10.5 *Comparison of cotton and grain production and price changes, 1978–92*

	Cotton production				Grain production				Index of grain to cotton price (1978=100)
	Output (1,000 mt)	Unit output (KG/MU)	Sown area (million mu)	Price index (1978=100)	Output (1,000 mt)	Unit output (KG/MU)	Sown area (million mu)	Price index (1978=100)	
1978	2,160	30	74	100	304,770	169	1,809	100	100
1979	2,200	33	68	117	332,120	189	1,789	121	103
1980	2,700	37	74	129	320,560	183	1,759	121	94
1981	2,960	38	78	129	325,020	189	1,724	126	98
1982	3,590	41	87	129	354,500	209	1,710	126	98
1983	4,630	51	91	158	387,280	227	1,702	177	112
1984	6,250	61	104	159	407,310	241	1,693	198	125
1985	4,140	54	77	156	379,110	232	1,633	201	129
1986	3,540	55	65	155	391,510	235	1,664	222	143
1987	4,240	58	73	162	402,980	241	1,669	239	148
1988	4,140	50	83	176	394,080	239	1,652	274	156
1989	3,780	49	78	224	407,550	242	1,683	348	156
1990	4,500	54	84	291	435,000	242	1,799	325	112
1991	5,670	58	98	297	435,293	258	1,685	305	103
1992	4,500	44	103	282	442,658	267	1,658	321	114

Notes:
KG/MU: kilogram per mu (7.6 hectares).
Sources: SSB, ZTN (1993: 265, 358–9, 363–6).

Table 10.6 *Changes in non-price incentives for China's cotton production, 1978–90*

Incentives	1978–85	After 1985
Purchasing regime	monopsony	contract purchases until 1987
Food reward proportion	1 kg cotton to 2 kg grain rewards	1 kg cotton to 1 kg grain or none rewards
Over-quota rewards	basic quota, 30% premium	proportional price margin, 6:4 in south, 2:8 in north
Fertiliser rewards, etc.	provided and subsidised	reduced or none
Capital input supply	provided and subsidised	not sufficiently, price increased dramatically
Payment	cash	'white receipt' (IOU) used frequently

Source: Zhang (1991).

by asserting their administrative control over the cotton produced in their region. These responses by regional governments are consistent with predictions from the previous section.

The State Council in 1989 attempted to close the secondary market and to limit the power of regional governments by requiring that all raw cotton be sold to the state only (*Zhongguo fangzhi gongye nianjian* 1990: 119). This reinstated the system which had previously been abolished in 1985. Also in 1989 and 1990 the price of cotton in the planned system was increased (table 10.5) so that by 1990 the relative gain to the cotton price fell by nearly 30 per cent. Cotton output initially responded positively to these price changes. By 1991 it was at its highest level since 1984. Subsequently, however, a rise in production costs, a drop in purchase prices and serious pest problems led to a sharp decline in output (Li Zhigiang 1994). By 1993 sown area had dropped to 74.8 million acres and output to only 3,739 million tonnes. (SSB 1994: 62–4). Inevitably, this major decline prompted a further round of government concern. State purchase prices for 1994 were increased by some 21 per cent (SWB, FE/1934/G/1, 1 March 1994), state intervention in the cotton market was reaffirmed (Zhu Rongji, September 1994), and there was a reported increase of 7 million acres in sown area (SWB, FE/2094/G/8, 7 September 1994).

Nevertheless, these changes took place at a time when most agricultural product markets were being deregulated and grain prices were also rising. The prospects for major improvement in cotton output in 1994 thus remained doubtful. Mid-year reports referred to a decline in cotton quality and problems of adulteration (SWB, FE/2064/G/5, 3 August 1994), and the likelihood of further short supplies led to warnings about the potential for renewed 'cotton wars' as processors competed for supplies (Zhu Rongji, September 1994 and *Renmin Ribao*, 2 September 1994: 1). Towards the end of the year, growers were being exhorted not to hold on to stocks in the hope that subsequent panic purchasing would force up prices, and there were references to illegal trading in cotton and direct purchasing by local cotton mills (SWB, FE/2144/SI/5–6, 4 November 1994).

As predicted by our model, the efforts by the government to regulate production and prices and to intervene in the market was again leading to the development of a secondary market and to competition for supplies. The planning system is thus still having difficulty meeting expectations. For example, it was reported in 1990 that only 40 per cent of the cotton requirements of state-owned enterprises were being met by the state and that many cotton mills were operating at 50 per cent capacity utilisation (*Textile Asia*, April 1990: 96). An explanation of this phenomenon requires more attention to the boom in processing capacity in the second half of the 1980s.

Demand side

While cotton production was discouraged by its low price, the textile industry experienced increased profits. As predicted in the preceding section a large number of enterprises were created, especially in rural areas where cotton was produced. Table 10.7 shows that spindle numbers in the cotton textile industry increased from 16 million in 1978 to over 41 million in 1992. The growth of capacity in rural China was especially rapid. Over this period, the gross value of output in rural enterprises increased by about 830 per cent, while in the state-owned enterprises it increased by only 38 per cent (table 10.8). Furthermore the ratio of rural to urban output rose from 7 per cent to 39 per cent. Thus the growth of rural enterprises made it more difficult for the state-owned sector to obtain fibre supplies, mainly because regional governments were doing their best to divert supplies of raw cotton to local processors.

The consequence was competition for supplies, rising prices for raw materials, administrative intervention to control the physical movement of cotton, and illegal efforts to divert supplies. During 1993 the industrial use cotton price rose from Rmb 8000 per tonne to Rmb 12,000, and by March 1994 was as high as Rmb 16,000 in some areas (Dong Ying and Cheng Jianhua 1994: 34).

One possible response to the increased demand for cotton would have

Table 10.7 *China's cotton textile production capacity, 1978–92*

	Cotton spindles (1,000)	Cotton looms (1,000)	
		Total	Shuttleless
1978	15,619	496.5	..
1979	16,632	514.9	..
1980	17,797	539.1	5.0
1981	18,935	570.6	5.5
1982	20,190	595.0	5.4
1983	21,406	624.7	4.9
1984	22,197	633.5	4.0
1985	23,238	667.7	5.2
1986	24,026	700.1	8.3
1987	26,026	746.0	10.1
1988	31,545	798.2	12.3
1989	35,656	838.2	15.5
1990	38,821	860.4	16.9
1991	41,920	904.5	19.2
1992	41,896	886.7	23.6

Sources: Zhongguo fangzhi gongye nianjin (1994: 13).

been to increase imports, a possibility suggested by the analysis of the model in the preceding section. But in the period in which the cotton chaos was at its height, export volumes also reached their peak. It was not until late 1989 and 1990 that exports fell and imports increased (table 10.4). Furthermore, the brief surge in output in 1991 was again associated with a rise in exports. The high level of exports in the face of the steady growth of demand for cotton within China is an indication of the presence of price distortion.[12]

Another option would have been to use more chemical fibres. Unlike the wool textile industry, the cotton industry has not made a significant switch into chemical fibres (table 10.9).

Summary

The cotton sector experience illustrates the effects of the combination of a rapidly growing and internationally-oriented processing industry relying on supplies of raw materials from a distorted domestic marketing system. There has been evidence of

 attempts by local governments to protect their own processing industries by restricting 'exports' to other provinces of raw cotton

Table 10.8 *Growth of the cotton textile industry, urban and rural, 1984–92*

	Urban industry			Rural enterprises			Ratio of rural to urban enterprises		
	Gross output value (million yuan) (1980 constant prices)	Employees (1,000)	No. of enterprises	Gross output value (million yuan)	Employees (1,000)	No. of enterprises	Gross output value (%)	Employees (%)	No. of enterprises (%)
1984	54,453	2,892	2,917	3,583	489	5,114	7	17	175
1985	59,031	3,069	3,007	5,850	622	5,792	10	20	193
1986	62,105	3,252	3,065	8,496	789	6,867	14	24	224
1987	65,060	3,428	3,192	11,678	953	8,488	18	30	766
1988	68,690	3,644	3,368	17,715	1,172	9,837	26	32	192
1989	69,520	3,724	3,569	20,786	1,229	10,223	30	33	286
1990	69,610	3,720	n.a.	19,103	1,273	10,458	27	34	n.a.
1991	69,476	3,890	n.a.	22,454	1,306	10,122	32	34	n.a.
1992	75,222	3,800	n.a.	29,705	1,179	9,784	39	31	n.a.

Notes:
Urban industry denotes enterprises under the control of the Ministry of Textile only. Rural enterprises include township and village-run enterprises only.

Sources: Zhongguo fangzhi gongye nianjian 1989: 423, 424, 502. 1990: 317–18, 355–6; 1993: 209–10, 1994: 12, 13; China's Rural Industrial Statistical Data, 1989: 35, reported by Zhang (1991).

Table 10.9 *Consumption of chemical fibres in the cotton and wool sectors (per cent) 1978–91*

Year	Cotton sector	Wool sector
1978	12.60	25.40
1979	15.60	39.80
1980	18.90	40.30
1981	21.80	43.60
1982	17.18	41.70
1983	22.10	44.10
1984	25.70	39.10
1985	25.10	43.03
1986	21.11	50.67
1987	19.20	47.70
1988	16.50	55.10
1989	19.26	59.08
1990	23.50	64.10
1991	22.65	58.68

Source: Zhongguo fangzhi gongye nianjian (various issues).

(especially over 1985 to 1989) followed by reinstatement of central government control in order to stop the 'chaos'

the development of local processing capacity in rural industry in an attempt to capture some of the rents created by the distorted prices (especially in 1988 and 1989)

the diversion of raw cotton on to the export market (from 1985 onwards) and simultaneous export and import of raw cotton

imperfectly working secondary markets and restrictions on imports by producers not having access to domestic raw cotton, leading to 'shortages' and low levels of capacity utilisation.

The 'wool war'

In the first half of the 1980s raw wool production in China remained at about 180–200 mkg. This output was higher than in 1978 and 1979, but up to 1986 there was little sustained growth in output (table 10.10). Wool purchases by the state marketing system rose from 138 mkg in 1978 to about 220 mkg in 1986. But by 1985 purchases were greater than production and stocks accumulated in previous years were being run down. Also imports of raw wool had been growing and by 1985 were over 100 mkg. At this

136   Zhang Xiaohe *et al.*

Table 10.10 *Raw wool production and consumption, China, 1978–93*

Year	Raw wool production (mkg)	Total purchases (mkg)	Wool imports (mkg)	Raw wool availability (mkg)	Domestic purchases as a % of availability
1978	137.8	138.2	10.3	148.5	93
1979	153.2	149.1	16.9	166.0	90
1980	176.0	161.0	37.4	198.4	81
1981	189.0	170.1	59.1	229.2	74
1982	202.0	179.9	87.0	266.9	67
1983	194.0	177.7	88.4	266.1	67
1984	183.0	154.8	55.8	210.6	74
1985	178.0	219.0	113.4	332.4	66
1986	185.0	218.0	152.2	370.2	59
1987	209.0	212.0	151.3	363.3	58
1988	222.0	200.0	187.4	387.4	52
1989	237.0	156.0	104.4	260.4	60
1990	239.0	200.0	56.1	256.1	78
1991	240.0	178.0	157.5	335.5	53
1992	238.0	155.0	209.0	364.0	43
1993	240.0	n.a.	237.5	n.a.	n.a.

Notes:
Wool import is a mixture of greasy, clean and tops.
Sources: Findlay and Watson (1991), updated from SSB, ZTN (1991 and 1993);
SSB (1994: 108).

stage, however, the industry was still about 70 per cent self-sufficient (down from 90 per cent in 1978).

The picture changes post-1985. Production grew much faster after 1986. Except for 1989, purchases of raw wool remained at about 200 million kilograms. But imports boomed then busted, reaching a peak of 187 million kilograms in 1988 and slumping to 56 mkg in 1990. The level of self-sufficiency was 52 per cent in 1988 but back up to 78 per cent by 1990. These shifts reflect events on both the supply and demand sides of the market.

Supply side

Even after the reforms of 1978 there was no over-quota price or negotiated price for raw wool. All raw wool was marketed through the state system. Purchase prices changed very little in the first half of the 1980s

Table 10.11 *Wool, meat and grain prices, China, 1952–92* (1978=100)

	Wool purchase price (yuan/kg)	Sheep meat price (yuan/head)	Grain price (yuan/tonne)
1952	61	60	53
1972	88	91	97
1975	90	95	97
1978	100	100	100
1979	100	120	126
1980	101	148	137
1981	102	174	145
1982	105	170	149
1983	108	189	149
1984	110	197	150
1985	148	266	158
1986	177	280	177
1987	185	298	193
1988	317	377	214
1989	267	361	285
1990	195	329.2	272
1991	178	338.7	257.3
1992	206	414.1	268.2

Sources: SSB, ZTN (various issues); SSB, *Statistics on China's Domestic and Foreign Trade,* (various issues); SSB, *Statistical Yearbook of China's Domestic Market* (various issues).

(table 10.11). By 1984 the raw wool purchase price was only 10 per cent higher than in 1978. But by 1984 the meat price was double the 1978 level (the grain price was also 50 per cent higher). In 1984 the market for meat was completely deregulated and the meat price rose even faster. By 1992 it was four times its level of 1978.

While the relative prices for wool had changed little, the responsibility for the management of its production had changed. In the first half of the 1980s the ownership of sheep was passed back to households. As a result, sheep-owners became more sensitive to the opportunity costs of different activities. Furthermore, it was not only wool and meat prices which mattered but also the returns to time and effort in other activities, including off-farm work. As a result, relative price changes encouraged the use of sheep for meat production, so slaughter rates were higher, the age structure of the flock tended to be lower, and wool production was reduced. Sheep numbers reached a peak in 1981 of 110 million but then fell to 94 million in 1985.

Another disincentive for wool production arose from the logistical difficulties in the state marketing system. Although the demand for wool was
growing rapidly, the state was having difficulty storing the wool which it
purchased. The drop in purchases in 1984 and the drop in imports that
year are attributed to these problems.

About this time (1983–4) there emerged the first signs of the development of a secondary market in wool. Findlay and Watson (1991) report
instances of textile enterprises forming direct links with producers and of
small-scale traders shifting wool across provincial boundaries. At this time
these trades were strictly illegal.

There was a major change in the marketing arrangements for raw wool
in 1985 when the centralised marketing system was replaced by purchase
through contract or through the market. It was intended that state contracts be filled first and that excess wool then be sold on the free market.
The incentives instead encouraged the movement of as much wool as possible to the market. The number of private dealers increased and a wider
range of prices emerged. The state found it difficult to obtain the wool it
wanted and the state purchase price rose (table 10.11).

This was the peak of the 'wool war'. Demand for raw wool had
increased in the wool producing provinces. Those provinces were pursuing
a policy of 'own production, own use and own sales', and grew reluctant
to supply outsiders. Findlay and Watson (1991) document the forms of
barriers to 'exports' that were imposed, including taxes on exports and
road blocks.

The wool war lasted through to the start of 1989. Wool prices in
1988 were 70 per cent higher than in 1987 (table 10.11). Import volumes
were also high over the period of the wool war (table 10.10). The system
of trade in wool is discussed in detail by Martin (1991), who stresses
the impact of the foreign exchange retention system. In the case of
wool imports, it was the secondary market in foreign exchange in
conjunction with the world price of wool that set the domestic price
of imports, and which in turn would have affected the prices for domestic wool. These relatively liberal arrangements however were cut
back in 1988 when a system of import quotas and permits was introduced to control the volume of imports. Importing provinces had to
apply to the State Planning Commission for a quota and to the Ministry
of Foreign Economic Relations and Trade for a permit before signing
contracts.

The high prices for wool also led to a rapid rise in sheep numbers, which
reached a record level in 1989 (table 10.12). The raw wool yield had
changed little over the 1980s (remaining at about 2 kilograms per head)
with reported instances of falls in quality (Findlay and Watson 1991). For

Table 10.12 *Sheep numbers, China, 1978–93*

	Sheep numbers year-end (million)	Raw wool yield (kg/head)
1978	96.40	1.43
1979	102.57	1.49
1980	106.63	1.65
1981	109.47	1.73
1982	106.47	1.90
1983	98.92	1.96
1984	95.19	1.92
1985	94.21	1.89
1986	99.01	1.87
1987	102.65	2.04
1988	110.57	2.01
1989	113.51	2.09
1990	112.82	2.12
1991	110.86	2.17
1992	109.72	2.17
1993	111.62	n.a.

Source: SSB, ZTN (various issues); SSB (1994: 66).

example, the clean weight yield of scoured wool had dropped to about 30 per cent or even 20 per cent by 1987. This was due in part to the lack of quality premia in the pricing system and the incentives created to adulterate the wool (for example, there are cases of 'wool processing centres' set up to help the peasants blend their wool with dirt, oil, sugar, water and sand).

Demand side

The increase in the demand for raw wool was driven by the increase in the processing capacity in China. This number of wool spindles in China increased five times over a decade (table 10.13). By 1993 the number of spindles continued to rise to 3.4 million. According to data reported by Findlay and Li (1991), even by 1987 about 40 per cent of these spindles were in rural industry, twice the share of two years before. The rents created by the suppressed prices of raw wool artificially encouraged investment in processing in wool growing provinces.

The rise in prices of raw wool had a couple of effects. The profitability of the textile industry was squeezed. There were incentives to switch into

Table 10.13 *China's wool textile production capacity, 1978–93 ('000 spindles)*

	Total	Knitting wool	Worsted	Woollen
1978	478.1	95.8	268.5	94.8
1979	532.9	111.3	292.9	107.5
1980	600.5	176.1	295.1	103.3
1981	744.4	228.6	328.0	139.5
1982	888.8	375.4	300.7	166.4
1983	1,005.3	308.5	445.1	209.5
1984	1,205.2	325.1	497.6	283.7
1985	1,394.9	368.6	606.6	379.5
1986	1,685.3	525.3	731.9	392.8
1987	1,992,0	638.6	821.0	489.3
1988	2,266.7	756.1	898.5	562.2
1989	2,522.7	881.5	969.2	598.1
1990	2,658.7	1,110.7	1,010.2	638.0
1991	3,030.2	1,110.7	1,145.8	709.8
1992	3,292.5	1,292.3	1,187.9	736.2
1993	3,390.0	n.a.	n.a.	n.a.

Sources: Zhongguo fangzhi gongye nianjin (1994: 79).

chemical fibres by the early 1990s their share increasing to about 60 per cent, compared with less than 40 per cent at the start of the 1980s (table 10.9).[13]

The end of the wool war

By the end of the 1980s there were some reforms underway to try to solve the problems of the quality of the raw wool delivered to the textile industry. Findlay and Watson (1991) report efforts to introduce auctions, to base prices on clean yields, and to encourage direct links between wool producers and textile mills. But the regional conflict over supplies persisted. The intensity of this struggle was reduced by the credit squeeze and the deflationary policies adopted in 1989. Domestic demand slumped and stocks of finished products in the wool textile sector rose rapidly. These products, designed for the local market, could not be cleared on to world markets.

The slowdown in sales of finished products also reduced the demand for raw wool. Import volumes crashed in 1989 and 1990. But sluggish domestic production combined with continued growth in processing capacity inevitably led to a rebound in imports, which rose to new high levels in 1992 and 1993.

At the end of 1989 the stockpile of raw wool was estimated to be 140 million kilograms and by the end of 1990 this had risen to 230 million kilograms (about one-year's production). The extent of the stockpile reflected not only the slowdown in domestic demand but also the low quality of Chinese wool and the lack of interest in that wool by the mills (Lin Xiangjin 1991). Thus, even when stocks were increasing in 1989 and 1990, China continued to import wool (wool growing areas such as Xinjiang and Inner Mongolia were also importing wool at this time). Furthermore, as the economy recovered from the austerity period, dependency on imports increased.

The relative stability in the domestic market after 1988 and the fact that domestic output had clearly reached a plateau of around 240 mkg per year provided the opportunity for further reform of the market. In 1992 control over marketing was relaxed in many areas. In Xinjiang, the major fine wool production province, both prices and marketing channels were deregulated (*Zhongguo Fangzhi Bao* [China Textile Paper] 2 June 1992: 1). Since that time the market situation has remained stable and the growth of imports has made up for the imbalance between domestic supply and demand. Provided government intervention in the domestic market and imports remains limited, the potential for a renewal of the 'wool war' is lessened.

Summary

Reform of the domestic wool marketing system lagged behind reform in other sectors. The slower pace of reform meant the price of wool was distorted relative to the price of finished products, implying
- rapid growth in processing capacity in rural industry in China, as wool growing regions integrated forward into the production of finished goods in an attempt to grab the rents available
- intervention in the marketing system by regional governments to inhibit 'exports' of raw wool to other regions
- the development of a secondary market in raw wool, followed by reforms of the marketing system that sanctioned trades in wool outside the state system (and unlike the cotton sector, the state monopoly over wool purchasing was not reinstated)
- an increase in imports of raw wool at the height of the wool war, although subsequently the level of imports was subject to quantitative controls.

Conclusion

The fibre wars have their origins in the segmentation of the marketing system in China. The barriers to inter-regional trade, in turn, have their origins in the protectionist motives of regional governments. These governments had, after reforms to the fiscal system, a higher degree of autonomy to invest in industrial activity. They sought to capture rents present in the marketing system created by the distorted price of fibre relative to finished products. These distortions may have originally been motivated by a desire by the central government to protect urban processing industries but they became the target of regional governments. These governments then set up barriers to exports of local fibres, in the forms of taxes and export controls. These were the weapons employed in the fibre wars.

The presence of inter-regional wars over fibre supplies, does not explain fibre shortages in China. Shortages were reflected in the very low levels of capacity utilisation in the textile industry. Secondary markets could have been expected to develop in the face of supply restrictions from fibre producing regions, thus raising prices, encouraging more production or even encouraging producers faced with export controls to evade those regulations. Secondary markets, in particular the market for foreign exchange, could also have facilitated the diversion of demand for fibre on to world markets, which would have been an attractive option for the coastal, urban and internationally oriented part of the industry. The suppression of secondary markets for cotton within China, the lack of institutional development in wool markets, the inability of these markets to generate quality margins, and the quotas on fibre imports inhibited this aspect of the response to the fibre wars.

Consequently, the textile industry has been plagued in China by both war and shortages. The intensity of hostilities fell in 1990 and 1991 because of the slowdown in the economy. In the second half of 1991 growth returned to double digits, and accelerated subsequently. The conditions are thus again present for another series of fibre wars as the economy recovered, pending either further and far-reaching steps to allow markets to operate freely, or the exercise of greater power over the fibre marketing systems by the central government. In the case of wool, the decline of government intervention and the absence of rents to be obtained by trading between plan and market distribution has meant that this has not occurred. In the case of cotton, all of the dangers indicated by our model remained very real at the end of 1994.

Notes

Part of the work reported in this chapter was supported by a grant from the Australian Wool Research and Promotion Organisation.

1 China's rural textiles and clothing exports reached 12.963 million yuan in 1989, a 50 per cent increase over 1988. Rural industry textile exports increased by 43 per cent and clothing exports increased by 62 per cent. Rural textiles and clothing industries now account for 29 per cent of total textiles and clothing exports (*Zhongguo fangzhi gongye nianjian* 1990: 31,44). Rural enterprises accounted for 70 per cent of total clothing output alone in 1990, and their exports represented two-thirds of the national total (*Textile Asia* 1991: 701).

2 Domestic sales of textile products were 11.5 per cent yuan lower in 1989 than in 1988 and a further 9 per cent lower in 1990. Between 1989 and 1990 domestic sales of cotton and wool products fell even faster; namely by 20 per cent.

3 There may be also other factors contributing to low rates of capacity utilisation, such as shortages of electric power or working capital.

4 The model reported in this section is a simplified version of those developed and reported by Zhang (1991).

5 S_c is drawn relative to P_f and not to the domestic supply of fibre.

6 Yang (1991) reports that the planned prices of cotton and wool were 36 per cent and 6 per cent lower than world prices in 1988. We discuss the motivation for these sorts of distortions in more detail below.

7 To some extent this drop in capacity utilisation reflects a drop in domestic demand for finished products and the inability to divert that capacity to production for the world market. In terms of the model in this section, we have abstracted from this possibility by assuming that export goods and domestic goods are identical.

8 This section and the next on the wool war also use material reported in Lu (1991) and Sun (1991).

9 A number of authors have argued that the falling relative price of cotton was the main reason for the drop in output after 1985. See, for example, Li (1989), Song (1990) and Liu (1990).

10 See references in note 3. Over the period 1987 to 1988 the peasants said that 'the price of agricultural inputs is flying, the price of manufactured goods is running and the price of agricultural goods is just crawling'.

11 Details of these sorts of deals are reported in various issues of *Textile Asia*, for example, May, June, August and December 1989, and September 1991.

12 There were also barriers to imports; described in more detail in discussion of the wool war.

13 The degree of fibre substitutability and the response to relative price changes in the wool and cotton sectors is a topic for further work.

11 Conflict over cabbages: the reform of wholesale marketing

Andrew Watson

Rapid economic growth brings about significant changes in opportunity costs, generating a need for a new balance between economic sectors. Rebalancing in turn entails a cascading sequence of change in a whole range of social relations, institutions and technology. The interplay between economic growth and further economic reform is thus crucial to the next phase of China's development. The evidence suggests that the economic forces at work cannot be halted or reversed. A study of the 'struggle' to deliver the humble Chinese cabbage to the dinner tables of China's urban residents provides insights into the nature of China's reform process, the forces driving the reform agenda, and how China's economy is changing.

The reform period since 1978 has seen changes in the pattern of demand and in the organisation and location of production, the growth of new regional linkages, reform of the marketing system, a general trend towards higher prices, and problems caused by inflationary effects and burgeoning government subsidies. These changes have had important consequences for economic and political organisation and for the technical aspects of production, infrastructure and marketing. Producers need new inputs, more services and more information. Institutional systems originally geared towards local self-sufficiency now have to play a role in regional interdependency. The institutional boundaries between production, transport, wholesale and retail which form obstacles to an integrated marketing network have to be swept aside. New mechanisms need to be found to handle the competing interests of producers, consumers, different urban administrations and different ministerial systems. Transport and other types of infrastructure have to be developed if the demands of the consumers and the aims of the producers are to be realised. The distortions and waste caused by subsidies have to be addressed. All of these issues also relate to such things as the nature of ownership of land and assets and the bearing that has on market organisation and infrastructure.

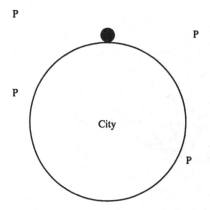

Figure 11.1   Free market model

The underlying argument here is that the forces at work are, in essence, economic. Although many of the tensions generated require political, social and institutional solutions, the reform program is being shaped by these economic pressures.

Two marketing models

Two models of wholesale marketing – one for industrial market economies (figure 11.1) and the other for China's planned economy before the reforms began – are background to the discussion of these changes (figure 11.2). These models are simplified. They do not take into account the possibilities for different types of specialisation, or for the combination of wholesale and retail functions.

A wholesale market in industrial economies can typically serve the needs of a large city with a population of around one million. Such a market handles about half a million tonnes of fruit and vegetables a year, and its design and technical specifications are shaped to minimise waste, to maximise ease and speed of handling and to facilitate commercial exchange. Such a market has a large geographical reach and the producers serving them may be hundreds or thousands of kilometres away, or even in another country, allowing the market to balance seasonal variations in output and fluctuations in regional production. The role of transport is thus fundamental to the way the market functions. The markets require highly standardised systems of packaging and handling. Direct human handling tends to be minimised since this is a major source of damage to produce. Most of the washing, sorting, packing and storage of produce is carried out by the producer rather than the market. The market depends

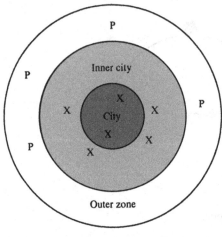

X = Purchasing station   P = Producer

Figure 11.2   China's pre-1978 model

on a range of support services: middleman activities, banking and credit facilities, market information networks, standards and regulations, and contractual laws.

By contrast, China's pre-1978 vegetable marketing system was based on the idea of urban self-sufficiency. As far as possible, cities aimed to rely on vegetables produced according to plan in zones around the urban core. Producers delivered their output quotas to state purchasing stations around the city in return for plan prices and, particularly in later years, subsidised inputs. The state stations then redistributed the vegetables to shops or urban units. This system aimed to promote urban self-sufficiency and to guarantee urban supplies at low prices. It aimed to reduce transport costs by keeping inter-regional flows to a minimum. It was controlled and operated by urban governments, with the costs involved forming part of the urban budget. It was associated with large subsidies to producers, to commercial units and to consumers. There was little variety of produce, entailing local monotony of diet. Sorting, packaging and storing were carried out by state agencies, meaning that any benefits from value-added accrued to the state unit but that the produce itself was handled several times, with slow movement through the system and resulting deterioration and loss of quality. It lacked any in-built incentives to promote quality and reduce waste.

The contrast between these two models is very clear. They reflect quite different sets of priorities and methods of economic management. China is in the process of moving from the latter model to the former, a process initiated by economic reforms and accelerated by the rapid economic growth which ensued.

Pre-reform production, marketing and prices

Vegetable production in China is a major function of the agricultural system. The World Bank estimate for total annual consumption in 1985–7 was 163.9 million tonnes (World Bank 1991b: 154). In 1989 urban per capita vegetable purchases were reported to be around 144 kilograms (SSB, ZTN 1990: 306). In the same year, peasant per capita consumption was estimated at 133 kilograms (SSB 1990a: 209). A very approximate calculation suggests that total consumption in that year therefore had to be at least 120 million tonnes.

These total figures are not very reliable in detail. The figures for rural consumption, in particular, must be open to question since so much is self-produced and self-consumed.

Before the reforms, urban governments aimed to meet as much of their vegetable needs as possible from the rural areas lying immediately adjacent to the built-up areas under their administration. This reliance on the peri-urban zones marked a continuation of the traditional pattern of production. Over many generations the peasants surrounding large cities collected night soil and other urban wastes to use as manure and produced vegetables for urban consumption. The result was a concentration of fertile land for vegetable production in the areas surrounding large cities. The policy reduced transport and storage costs.

According to Skinner (1978), the system worked reasonably successfully. The vegetable production areas around cities could be divided into an inner and outer zone. The inner zone coincided with the area of most productive vegetable land and concentrated on vegetable production throughout the year. The outer zone produced vegetables on a seasonal basis, with the land often used for a grain crop for part of the year. Large cities were commonly 70–90 per cent self-sufficient. Those in the north, like Beijing, had to bring in some extra supplies for slack seasons and the cold winter. Those in the south, like Shanghai, could be virtually self-sufficient. There was also some inter-urban trade in easily transported pickled or processed vegetables.

In practice, there were many local variations in how the system operated. Units of urban government, specialised vegetable production and marketing organisations, the commercial bureau and others, managed different parts of the marketing process. Urban governments issued sown-acreage, production and sales quotas to the communes in the surrounding areas and channelled supplies of inputs to producers through the supply and marketing co-operative system. Often producers were also provided with grain at base prices in return for vegetables. The prices paid to the producers for vegetables were also set by the government, with controls focusing on the main types for each season. Producers usually delivered their vegetables to stations run by the urban vegetable marketing authorities who transferred products to state shops for sale to consumers or to urban units with their own canteens. In some cities, producers delivered directly to retail centres.

The overall trend during the 1960s and 1970s was for a concentration of vegetable and fruit marketing in state shops. The selling price was also determined by the government and kept low and stable for long periods of time. In the 1970s the reported mark-up between procurement price and consumer price varied between 10 and 40 per cent. The system often involved subsidies, either by the government providing incentives to producers or by the government bearing the costs of the commercial distribution. If supply was less than demand, some form of rationing limiting the amount sold to each consumer was used.

A typical example of the system at work is the production of Chinese cabbage for the Beijing winter, often known as 'patriotic cabbage' (aiguo baicai). This has long been a staple vegetable for winter consumption. Commonly, the urban authorities mobilised the peasants around the city to plant the cabbage in July and August. After harvesting in late October, large quantities were brought into the cities and sold to urban households. These were then stored outside houses in the cold weather. As the winter progressed, the outside of the cabbage froze and helped preserve the inside. The outer layers were then peeled off and thrown away, leaving the heart of the cabbage for eating. A good stock lasted most of the winter, though the diet was monotonous.

Sometimes, urban governments also invested in modern technology for vegetable production. By November 1979, for example, the Sijiqing commune on the outskirts of Beijing had installed a large and expensive computer-controlled hothouse, where the total environment was managed and vegetables could be grown out of season. The costs of production were well above the selling prices but the commune was subsidised by the government and was experimenting with technologies for vegetable production.

The net result of this system was the guarantee of a stable supply of basic vegetables in season. Fine vegetables and out-of-season vegetables were neglected. Products from other areas were also rarely seen. The lack of economic incentives in the system also meant that there was not much attention to quality, and consumers had to buy what they were offered.

The impact of reform on demand

After 1978 the economic reforms affected all aspects of the established production system. Steady improvements in income meant that there was increased demand for better food. Within food budgets, there was a shift from staples towards consumption of more expensive foods, including vegetables and fruit. Within the structure of vegetable and fruit consumption there was a shift towards consumption of better quality and out-of-season products. These changes might not have been expected so early in a country with the low levels of income reported officially for China, where improvements in income might be expected to lead, in the first instance, to a rise in total consumption rather than to improvements in quality. That this is less evident in China is a reflection of the fact that the rationing system for staples and the subsidies for housing and other services have tended to provide most of the basic requirements and have allowed consumers to shift new income to quality improvements. It also reflects underestimation of Chinese per capita income in the official data (Garnaut and Ma 1993a).

This growth in demand inevitably put pressures on production. The change in urban consumption patterns was reflected in a shift away from direct grain consumption towards meat, poultry and fish (Garnaut and Ma, chapter 4).

From 1981 to 1983 per capita purchases of vegetables in urban areas rose quickly. They then declined to below 1981 levels. To some extent this may have reflected the shift to greater meat, poultry and fish consumption, and the substitution of quality and variety for monotonous quantity. It is also possible that this pattern reflected both problems with variations in vegetable supplies and responses to the substantial increases in food prices. The rise in vegetable prices after 1984 was a large contributor to inflation.

The changing pattern of purchases by urban consumers may have been influenced by these higher prices. It is also not clear whether all vegetables sold directly by peasants to consumers are captured by the per capita series, which may thus understate the actual amount bought. Improvements in quality may also mean that consumers are actually eating a larger proportion of the vegetables bought and thus have to purchase less. In general, the aim of government policy is to ensure a supply of 0.4–0.5 kilograms per day for all urban residents.

The impact of reform on supply

The reintroduction of household farming after 1978 meant that land was divided among households and that they became free to make their own decisions on production, subject to meeting state sales quotas. In the richer communes near cities, however, elements of coordinated production were often retained, with the collective managing inputs and marketing, or providing subsidies to producers from its non-agricultural income. The simultaneous introduction of free markets and the growth of price differentials between state and free market prices, however, meant that peasant producers rapidly became aware of the opportunity costs of their land and labour. There was a shift to producing crops which produced the highest return.

Being relatively profitable in favoured locations, total vegetable production has tended to increase. At times, however, there have been shortages, often related to weather problems, and there has been a marked increase in prices. Since 1984, production costs have been rising. There is thus a conflict between producers wanting higher prices, consumers wanting more and better products at stable prices, and local governments wanting to reduce their subsidies to both producers and consumers.

Non-agricultural employment is especially significant near cities, where peasants have been able to engage in manufacturing, commerce, transport and other activities. The returns to these undertakings are much higher than to agriculture and there has been a marked shift of land, labour and capital out of farming. This trend has been reinforced by the expansion of urban building and production. Much land in the inner zones has been taken over for non-agricultural uses in recent years. Less acreage is now being sown in the highly-productive inner zones, the peasants having become entrepreneurs or rentiers deriving income from land. In Beijing, for example, the vegetable acreage of the inner zone dropped from 15 thousand hectares in 1984 to 11 thousand in 1988 (*Jingji cankao* [Economic Reference News], 27 April 1988: 1). A further effect of this change was that remaining vegetable producers in the inner zones tended to shift towards the production of finer quality vegetables. These were then sold at higher prices through the free markets to urban consumers. This trend is reflected in the figures for vegetables handled by the Beijing Vegetable Company (table 11.1).

The development of new intensive vegetable production areas takes time, and the initial phase was characterised by lower yields from poorer quality land. Some large cities have been forced to seek more sources of supply outside their administrative area, which can also provide supplies during low seasons. This shift also reflects opportunity costs for peasants in more distant areas having moved in favour of producing vegetables for urban consumption. By the early 1990s, for example, Beijing was planning to develop five base areas in other parts of China as sources of supply to balance seasonal and climatic factors (Interview with Beijing officials,

Table 11.1 *Beijing Vegetable Company supplies, 1981–9*

	Sown area (mu)	Output (mt)	Purchases (mt)			
			Total	Inner	Outer	Transfers
1981	449,264	0.98	1.16	0.97	0.07	0.12
1982	472,365	1.10	1.43	1.09	0.13	0.13
1983	478,708	1.02	1.30	1.05	0.12	0.13
1984	474,488	1.10	1.36	1.09	0.09	0.18
1985	322,668	0.47	0.92	0.52	0.11	0.26
1986	345,391	0.66	0.94	0.58	0.13	0.23
1987	312,799	0.43	0.97	0.44	0.15	0.32
1988	282,423	0.44	1.15	0.42	0.26	0.39
1989	288,508	0.50	1.15	0.51	0.35	0.24

Source: Beijing Vegetable Company, Interview, November 1990.

December 1990). These bases were: the winter base in six south coast provinces; the spring slack season base in counties in Jiangsu and Anhui; the autumn slack season bases in areas along the Great Wall (one in counties around Zhangjiakou and one in Gansu); and the winter cabbage base area in Hebei and Shandong.

These developments will inevitably lead to further increases in inter-regional trade in vegetables. Officials in the Ministry of Commerce reported that the proportion of urban vegetables that were locally produced had fallen from some 90 per cent in 1978 to around 80 per cent in 1990. In 1990 total urban demand was estimated to be around 30 million tonnes and some 5 million tonnes were supplied through inter-regional trade (of this, 3.5 million tonnes were moved by rail) (Interview with Beijing officials, December 1990). It was anticipated that by the year 2000, inter-regional trade would account for 7.5 million tonnes.

Transport is a major constraint on the rate of growth of this trade but extensive road improvements have occurred in the reform period both in cities and on long-distance routes. The railways have also expanded, although their capacity has continued to be inadequate. The possibilities for moving large quantities of perishables long distances are improving with relative costs moving in favour of road, relative to rail and water transport.

This trend, however, presents urban governments with a dilemma. To maintain stable supplies, they have commonly provided producers with both input and grain subsidies. Urban governments cannot use similar policies to encourage the growth of supply in areas outside their control.

The alternative is to pay the outsiders higher prices for vegetables delivered to the urban state markets. Although the prices paid by outside consumers may reduce the cost of subsidies for local production, the net balance of these forces will ultimately lead to higher consumer prices.

Apart from these administrative efforts, the main growth of vegetable supplies flowing into urban areas from outside has come through the free markets. Peasants in rural counties have been keen to develop vegetable production for cities. Areas distant from cities have much lower opportunity costs for their land and labour, and vegetable production is thus an attractive alternative. These producers are now also free to invest in local cold stores and transport to enable them to maximise value-added and to compete more effectively with urban producers. Fruit and vegetable supplies in the Beijing free markets now come from almost all provinces. There is often a difference in the type and quality of products supplied in this way, with the free markets predominating in the higher value and fine quality crops.

It is reasonable to assume, however, that the growth of the free market system is constrained by the fact that vegetable producers within the urban administrative areas are often still receiving subsidies from their local administration to produce crops that otherwise might not have priority. Outsiders have to bear all of the risks of their crops and are less likely to attempt to compete in crops where urban peasants are subsidised.

Changes in the pattern of production have led to considerable improvements in vegetable supplies and in quality (Coady *et al.* 1990). Nationally, there has been an increase in total acreage sown to vegetables over a period when farm acreage as a whole has been declining. Total sown acreage was reported to have risen from just over 6 million hectares in 1988 to 6.3 million hectares (SSB 1989b: 95, 1990: 90).

On the technical side, the changes in production have raised many new issues. The quality of new vegetable lands has to be improved, and peasants just beginning vegetable production have to develop new skills. The spread of production areas away from cities has also placed new requirements on transport, storage and marketing services. The demand for quality has meant that producers have to pay more attention to handling and packaging. Efforts to raise yields have required more investment in inputs, seeds and plastic sheeting. All of these in turn have placed pressures on a vegetable production and marketing system geared to the geographical boundaries of urban administrations.

The impact of reform on marketing

At the same time as the reforms transferred control over land and labour back to the households, peasants also gained the right to trade surplus and sideline production on the free markets. This right was subsequently extended to cover all categories of goods once contractual obligations to the state were fulfilled. Free market prices were substantially higher than state prices and were powerful incentives for peasants to produce those products with the highest relative profitability. These factors began to affect fruit and vegetable marketing as early as 1981. The rapid growth of free marketing was almost inevitable and eventually, large-scale liberalisation of the marketing system was sanctioned in early 1983. Markets were hastily established in villages and urban streets and both individual peasants and collective units began to trade on them. All fruit and vegetables produced outside of state contracts could now be sold on the markets and prices could be set by negotiation.

The net effect of these changes has been a proliferation of vegetable and fruit marketing systems. The state vegetable companies and shops remain in operation. Alongside these there are large numbers of private shops and peddlers. By 1987 these accounted for nearly 83 per cent of retail traders (Coady *et al.* 1990: 14). There are also direct sales from peasants to urban residents through street markets. The latter grew at around 35 per cent a year from 1978 to 1987 and by the end of that period accounted for 46 per cent of vegetable retail sales (Coady *et al.* 1990: 13). Nevertheless, the state system continued to play a significant role in wholesale activity and in the supply of key basic vegetables each season. These were produced through contracts made with growers and supplied at subsidised rates

The co-existence of the free and state marketing systems, however, has important implications. Better quality products tend to go through the free market system where they can attract higher prices, and subsidised products in the state system tend to affect the behaviour of producers and merchants in the private system.

Between 1978 and 1992 the total number of free retail markets more than doubled, while the number in urban areas grew from zero to around 18 per cent of the total (table 11.2). At the same time, there was a large increase in the value of market trade. The expansion of the free retail market system inevitably generated strong pressures for changes in wholesale marketing. Specialised production by households and regions for the market meant goods had to be aggregated in producing areas, moved to cities, and disaggregated for selling to consumers. At the same time, changes in the location of production also required new channels for transport and marketing. This required the development of wholesale merchants, transporters, wholesale markets with appropriate facilities, and the range of information, communications, financial and support services required to operate a wholesale system. The first new wholesale markets were established as early as 1980–1. After 1983 they entered a period of

Table 11.2 *The growth of the free market system, 1978–92*

	1978	1979	1980	1981	1982	1983	1984	1985
Number of markets	33,302	38,993	40,809	43,013	44,775	48,003	56,500	61,337
Urban	–	2,226	2,919	3,298	3,591	4,488	6,144	8,013
Rural	33,302	36,767	37,890	39,715	41,184	43,515	50,356	53,324
Value of trade (100 million yuan)	125	183	235	287	333	386	457	632
Urban	–	12	24	34	45	56	75	121
Rural	125	171	211	253	288	330	382	512
Of which:								
Grain and edible oils	20	29	34	36	39	43	46	50
Meat, poultry and eggs	21	33	42	51	58	73	92	140
Aquatic products	5	7	9	12	15	19	24	33
Vegetables	14	17	22	26	27	33	38	49
Dried and fresh fruits	4	6	8	9	10	13	19	26
Fodder and farm tools	10	12	7	8	11	12	13	14
Large animals	21	30	27	39	45	42	36	33

Table 11.2 *The growth of the free market system, 1978–92 (cont.)*

	1986	1987	1988	1989	1990	1991	1992
Number of markets	67,610	69,683	71,359	72,130	72,579	74,675	79,188
Urban	9,701	10,908	12,181	13,111	13,106	13,891	14,510
Rural	57,909	58,775	59,178	59,019	59,473	60,784	64,678
Value of trade							
(100 million yuan)	907	1,157	1,621	1,974	2,168	2,622	3,530
Urban	244	347	545	724	838	1,079	1,583
Rural	622	811	1,076	1,250	1,330	1,543	1,974
Of which:							
Grain and edible oils	71	85	108	143	147	165	213
Meat, poultry and eggs	247	320	460	571	619	706	859
Aquatic products	64	85	123	158	182	224	292
Vegetables	97	131	193	238	264	332	435
Dried and fresh fruits	59	83	123	161	184	233	291
Fodder and farm tools	15	16	18	22	23	25	30
Large animals	31	33	38	39	38	44	48

Sources: Watson (1988); SSB, ZTN (1990: 633; 1993: 625).

rapid growth, and their development accelerated with the reforms to marketing in 1984.

The process of development was often haphazard but by the early 1990s these markets had evolved into a complete system administered in various ways, including direct management by state agencies that also participated in the trade, by the railway authorities with other state organisations supervising, and by independent peasant organisations on the outskirts of cities (Ministry of Agriculture, Rural Research Centre 1992). The main participants are long-distance traders, wholesalers and retailers, the latter including private merchants, peddlers, government commercial units, factories, schools and hospitals. There are no restrictions on who may buy and sell, and prices are set through the market. In some cases, these markets maintain offices in other provinces and cities in order to collect and distribute information on markets conditions and to stimulate the flow of goods.

A significant result has been that many vegetables and fruits that formerly were only available during the short local growing season now appear on the market much earlier and are sold over a longer period because of trade from other parts of the country. There is an emphasis on handling quality fruit and vegetables from areas outside local administrative control and, often, goods out of season.

Until 1991 basic vegetables produced through state contracts (such as the Beijing cabbage) were handled through the state system and these still accounted for the bulk of vegetable supplies by weight. A further wave of market liberalisation begun in late 1991 and early 1992 meant that many large cities withdrew fully from vegetable production and distribution so that the proportions of vegetables flowing through the free market system were set to grow.

Prices in the wholesale markets generally reflect supply and demand and product quality, though there are administrative attempts to set upper limits and to control speculation. Consideration has been given to the use of state stocks as market buffers.

Wholesale markets are administered in three main ways. Some were established under the wing of the local Industrial and Commercial Bureaus. Others were set up by independent organisations such as the railways and local peasant bodies and are supervised by the Industrial and Commercial Bureaus to ensure that regulations and standards are met. In the former, the Bureaus act as both administrative and licensing bodies and as providers of marketing services. In the latter, their role is purely administrative. The third type of wholesale markets are those established by state commercial agencies using the warehouses and other facilities available to them. In these markets, the state agency both runs the market and participates in the trade.

Chinese surveys indicate that they are neither adequately staffed nor managed (Li Ji 1989; Ministry of Agriculture, Rural Research Centre 1992). There are many problems associated with the provision of facilities and services and a lack of standards and regulations and this generates many disputes. There are extensive opportunities to manipulate the market and make high profits. There is also confusion between the role of state agencies as supervisors of market regulations and providers of market services. Many Chinese observers argue that these functions should be separated in order to ensure that all the functions of the market become more efficient. They argue that the role of the Industrial and Commercial Bureaus and other commercial agencies should be purely administrative in terms of licensing and ensuring the rules are not broken.

Another range of problems facing the markets are the purely technical ones of building adequate facilities and transport connections, and improving communications and banking services. There are many adjustments to be made in moving from state control of marketing to an open market network. There are also concerns about the emergence of speculative dealing and large middleman profits.

The impact of reform on pricing

The pricing of vegetables in China since 1949 has passed through three main phases (Zhu and Zhou 1987: 61–3). From 1949 to 1956 prices were largely determined through free market sales. After 1957 vegetables were brought within the plan system and subject to unified purchase and sales, with the state setting prices. The emphasis was on quantity not quality, on bulk, 'heavy' vegetables rather than delicate perishables, and on the key vegetable for each season. Under this system, prices remained basically stable from the early 1960s to the late 1970s. After 1981 these controls were progressively relaxed. From 1981 to 1984, peasants produced by contract, with the freedom to sell surpluses on the market. In 1984 the state system restricted its controls to a few key vegetables per season and left the remainder to the market. In 1985 the remaining controls were further loosened and local cities were given the power to fix prices according to local supply and demand, within state guidelines. By 1986 only the large cities retained considerable price controls. After that time, however, fluctuations in supplies and prices forced many urban governments to reintroduce aspects of price or marketing control for some vegetables.

The changes after 1984 resulted in a sharp increase in vegetable prices to consumers and the difference between state selling prices and free market prices narrowed. The rising costs of production, the result of both increasing input costs and the higher opportunity costs of labour, also put pressure on prices. This process left the Chinese government with a dilemma. On the one hand, reform of the marketing system, relaxation of controls and increasing reliance on the free market led to inflationary pressures. On the other hand, intervention in the marketing system involved large subsidies to producers, the state commercial system and consumers. These subsidies were a burden on government budgets and led to distortions in production, consumption and marketing. At various times after 1984, policy shifted between phases of relaxation, with accompanying jumps in inflation, and phases of greater government intervention, with accompanying problems of subsidies. There was thus a cycle in the pattern of vegetable marketing and pricing. The nature of this cycle also varied considerably between regions, with some large cities (such as Guangzhou) and many smaller cities moving to a greater reliance on markets, and other cities (especially the major ones like Beijing, Tianjin and Shanghai) experiencing greater government intervention.

Efforts after 1988 to increase production in major cities and to control prices of key vegetables were reported to have had some success. In the 49 cities with a population of over 500 thousand in 1989, the vegetable-sown areas increased by 6.5 per cent, output by 11.7 per cent, sales by 15.7 per cent and state supplies by 6.7 per cent. Though this all involved an increase in state subsidies, prices in 1989 were reported to be much more stable, rising only marginally compared with previous years (Cheng 1989: 2–5). Nevertheless, the subsidy problem remained severe (*Jingji cankao* [Economic Reference News], 3 May 1988: 4).

The changes in pricing in recent years have also had an effect on relative prices for producers. In 1989, for example, one analysis reported that the ranking of returns per unit area in descending order were vegetables, fruits, grains, cotton (Kong *et al.* 1989: 55–7). Although this relationship could be expected to stimulate increased vegetable production, the central government was also concerned about the production of other crops and, at various times, attempted to adjust relative prices in order to encourage production of other crops and to prevent the transfer of land out of grain and cotton.

Issues in fruit production and marketing: the effect of complete reform

After 1984 the marketing and pricing of fruit was fully liberalised. This meant that government departments no longer had a monopoly in handling fruit and prices were essentially determined by supply and demand. This reform of the fruit production and marketing system has been reasonably successful. Fruit output in 1989 was 18.3 million tonnes, an increase of 160–70 per cent over 1978. Of this, the four major staple fruits, which account for 70 per cent of supply, were apples (4.5 million tonnes), oranges (4.6 million tonnes), pears (2.5 million tonnes) and bananas (1.4 million tonnes). Sown acreage was around 5.7 million hectares. This growth in output has led to an increase in market supply, variety and quality. The growth of inter-regional trade has also lengthened the supply time. Average per capita fruit consumption for China is estimated to be 16.5 kilograms but the figure is much higher in urban areas. Beijing per capita consumption, for example, rose from 31 kilograms in 1978 to 74 kilograms in 1989. Furthermore, these figures did not include melons, of which some 15 million tonnes are also produced and marketed.

Like vegetables, most of this fruit now passes through the free market system. Merchants in Beijing buy supplies from other provinces and transport them to the capital for distribution through wholesale markets. Much of the picking, packing, transport and handling is poor quality and entails much waste. Market forces, however, can be expected to encourage producers and dealers to improve quality. Nevertheless, equipment, services and market information are all in need of upgrading.

The solution to new problems: the 'vegetable basket plan' and government policy

Since 1986 the underlying strategy for vegetable production in China has been summed up by the phrase 'near suburbs as the base, outer suburbs as the supplement and other sources to help out' (Zhu and Zhou 1987: 61). This sustains some key elements of the previous strategy in a situation where changes in production and marketing have created a more complex overall structure. The 'vegetable basket project' evolved over 1987–8 to achieve this target (Liu 1988a: 2). This plan intended to increase supplies and stabilise prices, with rates of growth in production based on estimates of growth in demand. The plan involves meat, eggs, vegetables, fish and dairy products and is based on greater investments by urban governments. By 1991, at the central level, Liu Jiang (Vice-Minister of Agriculture) had overall direction of the policy but local implementation was through urban mayors with direct responsibility to develop production and marketing systems.

The main elements were presented in a speech by Li Peng in May 1988 (Li Peng 1988: 6–11). Li stressed that further reform of marketing and liberalisation of vegetable production was the ultimate goal. He also emphasised that cities should be free to develop their production and marketing systems in the light of local conditions.

Li saw a conflict between small-scale household production and large urban demand. He therefore called for economies of scale and specialised production by peasant households and teams in order to lower production costs, improve technology and help stabilise production. He set an acreage target of 2,700 hectares of vegetable land per million urban consumers, with variations from north to south China, depending on local seasonal production. He saw inner zones specialising in quality vegetables, outer zones specialising in basic vegetables and external areas supplementing supply during slack seasons. Urban administrations were to play a greater role in managing production and supplies. Supplies increased during 1989 (Cheng 1989: 2–5).

By and large, the main elements have remained in place. A State Council Circular on improving non-staple food supply (September 1990) stressed the relationship between inner and outer zones and external supplies (SWB, FE/0866/B2/1–2). It called for stabilising sown areas and raising yields and for integration of production and marketing systems. Nevertheless, it also acknowledged a major role for the free market system calling for greater urban investment in wholesale systems and in free market facilities. The long-term goals of the reforms are thus clearly focused on a declining role for the state planned system.

Wholesale marketing in Beijing

In 1987 the Beijing vegetable marketing system had to supply around 6.5 million people, with an annual requirement of 1.2 million tonnes based on 500 grams per person per day. According to a 1988 survey of wholesale marketing in Beijing, fruit and vegetables entered Beijing by two routes: the urban state-run vegetable company (70 per cent of supplies by volume) and the free market system (30 per cent by volume and 40 per cent by value) (Li Ji 1989: 59–61). The former were largely supplied by contracts between the vegetable company and producers with contracts subsidising supplies of such things as grain, edible oil, fertilisers and diesel to producers. In 1987 the free market system was served by 37 wholesale markets, selling fruit and vegetables to merchants and peddlers, and by peasants selling directly to the consumer.

These new wholesale markets take several forms. The first originated in 1979 when the Beijing Industrial and Commercial Bureau built two markets (Shui Duizi and Beitaipingzhuang) to facilitate wholesale trade by outside producers. It administered and serviced these markets and collected a levy of 2 per cent on transactions. The tax authorities also collected a turnover tax of around 3 per cent from sellers who did not have a certificate to show that they were producers selling their own product. The emergence of these markets led to a rapid expansion in the varieties offered (from 60 to 250) and in sources of supply (20 provinces and some 132 counties).

A second type of market was established by a peasant collective and the Industrial and Commercial Bureau, and tax authorities acted as supervisors. Fees for services went to the peasant company and the transaction fees were shared by the Bureau and the company. A similar market, and now one of the largest in Beijing, is the Dazhongshi Agricultural Wholesale Market in north Beijing. By 1992 this market supplied one-fifth of all vegetables consumed in Beijing.

A third type (Shazikou market) was set up by the railway authorities near Yongdingmen Station to facilitate the distribution of vegetables and fruits entering Beijing by rail. This market was again operated with supervision by the Industrial and Commercial Bureau and tax authorities and a sharing of some fees.

Some markets were run by the urban authorities at city and district levels, using their existing facilities catering for private merchants.

The markets can be divided into two types; those which purely provide a service to sellers and buyers and charge a fee, and those which involve the operator of the market participating in the trade. The first type also falls into two sub-sets: those where the Industrial and Commercial Bureau acts as both a supervisor of trade and a provider of services, and those where the Bureau supervises and other agencies provide the services. Some wholesale markets open all night, others operate at special times: they also tend to specialise in different types of products, depending on their location and the sources of the products they handle. The bulk of their fruit and vegetables (70–80 per cent) comes from outside the Beijing administrative area. There are complex linkages between merchants and peddlers (estimated to be around 60 thousand in Beijing). In some instances they have been associated with the emergence of 'forward' contracts where suppliers negotiate quantities and delivery times with purchasers.

The rapid growth of these markets has meant that little preparation has been made for future growth and, in some cases, facilities are already stretched. The fact that the functions of market operators, market supervisors and market participants sometimes overlap has also created problems for efficient operation.

The problems now facing the Beijing system include the need to improve facilities and the siting of wholesale markets and management; to separate out market operation from state supervision and controls so that it becomes more efficient; and to set up appropriate information and financial services to facilitate the role of merchants.

Li Ji (1989) suggested that Beijing should establish wholesale marketing laws to set standards and provide the parameters for merchant operation, a vegetable and fruit marketing information centre to forecast demand and supply and guide traders, and a proper site for forward trading.

The political economy of market reform

The economic power of urban governments to intervene in the vegetable production and marketing system is declining. Urban governments are also becoming more dependent on outside areas for supplies of food for urban inhabitants and are less able to assert authority over producers or to provide subsidies to their residents. They have to depend on supplies coming through commercial systems and they therefore have to dismantle obstacles to the transfer of products across urban administrative boundaries and to facilitate market growth and services. Failure to do so would threaten urban supplies and, thereby, urban stability.

The evolution of free market networks requires continuous improvements in transport, with greater flexibility in the flow of people, traffic and goods with further declines in bureaucratic controls over movement. It is inefficient to stop goods at administrative boundaries and require changes in ownership, packaging and transport. Quality and efficient movement of products requires the breaking down of administrative boundaries for economic activities.

The growth of the free market system has led to an increase in prices and a change in the distribution of economic benefits between town and countryside. Rural areas are seeking higher returns. Urban consumers face rising prices and, in the context of wage and employment reforms, greater economic uncertainty also. This issue was one of the factors behind the events of June 1989. The growth of the free marketing system will inevitably continue this process of redefining sets of economic interests and the division of economic returns between them. To a large extent, the key issue here is the way the government handles the other aspects of urban reform such as wages and employment.

Changes affect the nature and role of administrative units. The Ministry of Commerce formerly controlled all commerce and cold stores located in urban areas and monopolised such services as long-term storage of fruit. As producers move into these activities, the Ministry of Commerce finds itself increasingly redundant. There is also potential for a new alignment of functions between the Ministry of Agriculture, primarily concerned with production and producers, but now being drawn into marketing by the producers, and the Ministry of Commerce, primarily concerned with supplies for consumers but losing its marketing role to producers and private merchants.

There are a number of issues currently facing Chinese policy-makers. The process of institutional and managerial change occurring in the transition from a planned model based on local self-sufficiency to a model based on inter-regional dependency and free market interaction can be conceptualised in terms of the two models discussed earlier. As this transformation entails a change in the distribution of economic benefits between producers, commercial institutions and consumers, it also generates social conflicts and requires institutional adjustment. The extent to which and speed with which the Chinese food production and marketing system can shift from one model to the other will therefore be constrained by the rate of institutional reform and by the economic and technical constraints on the realisation of a regionally interlinked production, supply and marketing system.

The process of change in the past ten years has tended to improve fruit and vegetable production and to introduce much greater variety into urban diets. Nevertheless, the threat of inflation and of instability in supply has meant that many urban governments were for a long time reluctant to withdraw from the vegetable production and marketing systems. Such uncertainties have contributed to the cycle of reform and the reassertion of government intervention. Urban governments will continue to adjust their administrative methods to build more integrated production and marketing systems. They will also, however, be anxious to ensure basic supplies, especially to low income households. Until the social and institutional problems are resolved, the potential for intervention remains high. Nevertheless, economic forces will continue to force the reforms further towards the free market model. The economic costs of attempting to restore the former system are now much too high.

Internationalisation

12 The World Trade Organization and agricultural development

Ma Xiaohe

China was a founding member of the General Agreement on Tariffs and Trade (GATT) but its membership has been suspended for more than forty years. The Chinese government began discussions in 1986 with contracting parties to the GATT to regain its membership and, if successful, to enjoy the rights of a founding member. The formation of a new World Trade Organization from 1 January 1995, as a successor to the GATT, has heightened China's sense of urgency to regain membership. It will then be obliged to assume corresponding commitments that will have implications for Chinese agriculture.

Direct and indirect benefits from WTO membership

After regaining membership of the WTO, China will enjoy more secure access to international markets, tariff reduction by trading partners and an easing of non-tariff barriers. Importantly, acceptance as a developing country member would enable China to enjoy preferential treatment in its trade with industrial countries, including more time to liberalise imports from them, and preferential tariffs on exports to them. These preferences would stimulate the expansion of cooperation in agricultural production between China and the rest of the world. In addition, the implementation of the Uruguay Round will see freer trade in agricultural products and enhance the power of the WTO to maintain open international trade. This will provide a better climate for agricultural trade in the world market.

Membership of the WTO will provide new opportunities for the development of Chinese agriculture, including expanded opportunities for the export of some agricultural products and processed goods based on them. China numbers some raw and processed agricultural products among its main export items.

There will be favourable developments in the textiles trade. Importing countries will be more strictly bound in relation to restrictions on textile imports. As a consequence, raw materials such as cotton, wool and flax may enjoy increased production opportunities in China.

Membership of the WTO will facilitate foreign investment, the introduction of new techniques and reform of traditional agriculture in China. The scope of the WTO is being extended from traditional commodity trade to service trade, intellectual property and relevant investment arrangements, and this will prove advantageous for China. The 1990s are especially important for China given the large amount of capital and technology required to support the fast growth of Chinese agricultural production. China's domestic resources are hardly sufficient to meet the needs of a country in the early stages of industrialisation. By returning to the WTO, China will be qualified to enjoy unconditional most-favoured-nation status and the privileges available to developing countries. China's position will be strengthened by technical and financial assistance for agricultural development provided by international financial organisations. At present, many industrial countries and international economic and trade organisations are bestowing greater attention on agriculture and the environment in developing countries.

China is now undergoing reform from a planned to a socialist market economy, and is moving towards the middle stage of industrialisation. The Chinese government now needs experience in managing and developing agriculture under these rapidly changing circumstances. As a member of the WTO, China would benefit from the experience of other contracting parties, especially the industrial countries, in relation to policies relevant to the middle stage of industrialisation in market economies, and in particular to the formulation of suitable policies for its own agricultural development.

WTO membership could facilitate China's agricultural imports, especially grain. China in fact has scarce farming resources relative to its population. The relationship between supply and demand for agricultural products in China will be increasingly tight, due to its high economic growth and huge population. China has been a net grain importer since the 1960s. As the third peak in China's birth rate nears and the economy continues to grow strongly, demand for agricultural products will increase significantly. Given limited domestic production, China may have to expand its imports steadily. Under the free trade principles and the reciprocal and mutually advantageous arrangements embodied in the WTO, such as the schedule of concessions, China will be able to enjoy equal rights on agricultural imports from all contracting countries.

Here it is relevant that many industrial countries maintain financial subsidies on agricultural production and exports, which serve to keep international prices, especially for grains, below what they otherwise would be.

This lowers the cost of importing grains. These agricultural subsidies will be gradually reduced following the Uruguay Round.

Challenges

WTO members will require that China reduces its tariffs and non-tariff barriers and further opens up its domestic markets. This will be helpful to China over the long run but may create some short-term problems for agricultural development.

First, as China fulfils the requirements of WTO membership, there will be openings for some agricultural products from other contracting parties in the Chinese market because of low cost and better quality. This competition with Chinese domestic products will reduce the profitability of Chinese farm producers – the other side of the coin to the greater access given China by WTO membership into other countries' markets. High-cost producers of some relatively uncompetitive products such as edible and inedible vegetable oils, rubber, timber, sugar, tobacco, soybeans, dairy products, tropical fruits and perhaps wheat are likely to be hardest hit. Domestic production of goods with higher prices or lower quality will have to be scaled back as new suppliers arrive on the scene. A sagging market will mean less employment or less income for farmers who continue to grow these products.

Second, after the Uruguay Round negotiations, all the contracting parties of the GATT are required to open up more of their domestic agricultural markets. China will be asked to change its present import management rules, for example, to lower tariff rates and to reduce non-tariff barriers. These will affect some sub-sectors of Chinese agriculture.

China has a huge population but it is poorly endowed with agricultural resources. The natural foundations of agriculture are extremely weak and the burden for meeting the needs of industrialisation is heavy. With successful economic growth in China, there will be a tendency for the relative importance of agricultural production to decline quite quickly. The reason is very simple: for a given pool of resources, if more is devoted to one sector, less will be available to other sectors, and many resources will be used more productively outside agriculture. Some people will use the relative decline to argue for government protection of agriculture. There is, indeed, a case for government provision of some services, such as extension and infrastructure, that are not adequately provided by private markets. On the other hand, if agricultural protectionism raised Chinese prices above world prices, this would keep resources out of their most productive uses, create a burden for China's export-oriented industrialisation, and slow down the development of China's economy.

Some protective policies may be necessary to improve relations between rural and urban areas and to maintain social stability in the countryside. These may conflict with some WTO principles, but such is the reality of China. The Uruguay Round agreement seeks freer agricultural trade than the previous seven rounds and foreshadows stronger rules to make entry into the international market easier. If the domestic market is opened too widely and various forms of assistance are removed, the present price advantage of Chinese agricultural production will soon disappear. At the same time, it must be recognised that protectionist policy itself can lead to high costs and difficulties in becoming internationally competitive.

The first sector immediately to be affected by outside competitors will be grain. The cost of Chinese grain production has increased by 10 per cent annually since the commencement of reform fifteen years ago. This has quickly pushed domestic grain prices towards average prices in the world market. It will not be long before Chinese prices catch up with and exceed world prices. When this time comes, in a relatively open domestic market with little protection, China will have no way of preventing foreign grain from entering the Chinese market and threatening its producers.

Third, when supply and demand are suddenly affected by changing prices as the WTO requirements are met, domestic shortfalls of supply of some agricultural products will become more serious. Many prices for Chinese agricultural products are below world market prices. As China rejoins the WTO, sales prices and output of some agricultural products may suddenly boom due to greater initial exports. This will mean a decline in the supplies available in the domestic market and a rise in domestic prices. These developments will generate tension.

Fourth, of the many measures designed to achieve free trade in agricultural products in the Uruguay Round, one of the most important is the reduction in subsidies on production and exports, raising prices in the world market. A rising trend in prices would raise the terms of trade of net exporters. But net importers will have to pay more for the same amount of imports. China is an exporter of many agricultural products but a net importer of grain – now, and more so in the future. A rise in grain prices in the world market would force China to spend more foreign currency on grain imports.

Selected policies for Chinese agriculture

A number of policies should be adopted now to maximise the benefits and minimise the costs of rejoining the WTO:

China needs to adjust its structure of economic organisation and reform its management systems in preparation for entering the WTO. The most serious problems in agriculture and related industries relate to fragmentation of the Chinese national administration system and a lack of mechanisms for adjusting management structures. It is first of all necessary for policy to ensure that the market works efficiently. This will require the central departments of state responsible for agricultural policy to be well equipped professionally and administratively to make decisions on production and trade in agricultural products and goods processed from them, and administrative arrangements in, and policy on, the use of foreign capital and technology.

There is a need to formulate plans and policies that will allow China to make full use of opportunities flowing from membership of the WTO and to move into more competitive agricultural industries. These include programs to support the export of agricultural products with competitive advantage through the use of foreign capital and technology and through smooth arrangements for importing other agricultural products.

It is important to formulate measures to moderate the possibly negative effects on some agricultural industries of re-entry into the WTO. The Chinese government needs to prepare for the provision of moderate financial and technical support, as allowed within WTO rules.

In addition, China should educate agricultural producers and business people to save labour, reduce production costs, improve product quality and search for competitive advantages. Two practical early steps might be to utilise opportunities for raising productivity through economies of scale in farm production, and to accelerate the transfer of redundant workers to non-farm activities. Labour markets in urban areas should be opened up to speed up the development of non-agricultural industries and to attract more workers from the agricultural sector.

Considering China's limited land resources, emphasis on a domestic balance between the supply of and demand for all agricultural products would be misplaced. The strategic consideration must be to encourage the production of items with competitive advantage and to scale down the production of products that lack competitive advantage.

There is no doubt that China needs to lower its import tariffs on agricultural products and reduce some non-tariff barriers. China's tariff rates on most agricultural products, including in processed form, are about 50–70 per cent. Some are lower, at 15–18 per cent. These rates are too high.

Tariff reduction is a prerequisite of China's rejoining the WTO. To minimise the shocks to agriculture, China may start with less important products and reduce their tariffs by a relatively large amount. The timing and degree of reductions on 'bread and butter' items needs to be managed carefully. Among the many non-tariff barriers on imports of agricultural products, it is necessary to lift administrative barriers related to licences, inspection and approvals for imports, and to simplify procedures for technical, hygienic or sanitary inspection.

13 Comparative advantage and the internationalisation of China's agriculture

Fang Cai

The experience of many economies shows that, with economic development, the share of agriculture in production and employment tends to fall. This is related to Engel's Law, which says that the ratio of food expenditure to total living expenditure declines as incomes rise. In other words, income elasticity of demand for food is less than unity. For grain, this relationship is especially strong. In a large economy (and in the world as a whole), foreign trade is not (and cannot be) large enough to prevent changes in demand being closely linked to changes in production. Consequently, as incomes grow, non-agricultural sectors employ a larger share of the total labour force, and produce a larger share of GDP. In the meantime, smaller shares of production and employment of agriculture would be enough to meet the needs of the national economy, especially with higher agricultural productivity. More of the social production capacity is therefore used to produce non-agricultural goods and services.

China's economic development strategy from the 1950s gave top priority to the development of heavy industry. Because heavy industry is highly capital intensive, the implementation of this strategy slowed the decline in the agricultural share, and lowered the pace of economic structural change.

Reform in rural China in the 1980s has resulted not only in increases in agricultural production but also in rapid changes in the industrial structure. Decline in the agricultural share became significant in the process of China's economic growth. Between 1952 and 1979 the share of farm labour in the total labour force fell from 83.5 per cent to 69.8 per cent, while the agricultural share of national income fell from 57.7 per cent to 36.6 per cent. During the period 1979–92 these two shares fell to 59.8 per cent and 32.7 per cent, respectively.

In the course of falling agricultural shares, the terms of trade for China's agricultural products have been unfavourable, lowering returns to resources engaged in agriculture and causing them to flow away from the

Table 13.1 *China's export specialisation index, selected sectors, 1965–92*

	Agriculture	Other primary products	Textiles	Other manufacturers
1965–9	2.08	0.33	3.08	0.44
1970–4	2.33	0.33	3.16	0.47
1975–9	2.10	0.71	3.83	0.47
1980–4	1.61	0.99	4.68	0.45
1985–9	1.39	0.99	4.59	0.52
1990–1	0.92	0.54	4.48	0.71
1992	0.78	0.43	4.40	0.74

Source: International Economic Databank, The Australian National University, Canberra.

agricultural sector. The speed of resource movement depends on supply and demand elasticities. Economies with an abundance of arable land and capital but a shortage of labour can achieve an expansion of farm size and promotion of farm productivity, and thus achieve a comparative advantage in agriculture, through substituting capital for labour. The United States, Australia and Canada are typical examples in this aspect. Generally speaking, the faster an economy grows and the less per capita arable land it has, the more quickly comparative advantage in agriculture is lost (Garnaut and Anderson 1980). Japan, South Korea and Taiwan belong to the group of East Asian-style economies that share these characteristics.

Per capita arable land in China is much less than the world average, and China has experienced very fast economic growth since 1980. Naturally, its comparative advantage in agriculture has fallen rapidly. Statistics show that in China, while comparative advantage in manufactured goods has increased, that in agriculture has fallen steadily. Here we can make use of an index of the strength of a country's export specialisation in a commodity, relative to the whole world's export specialisation in the commodity – the index that Balassa (1965) referred to loosely as the index of 'revealed comparative advantage'. China's index of 'revealed comparative advantage' (export specialisation) in farm commodities fell from 2.1 in the late 1960s to 1.4 in the late 1980s and to 0.8 in 1992 (table 13.1).

Distortionary agricultural policies

Distortionary agricultural policies exist in most parts of the world. Agricultural policy is distortionary when the prices of farm products or

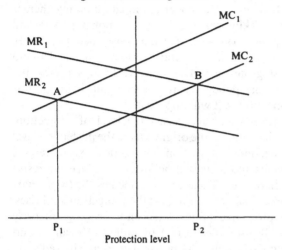

Figure 13.1 The level of protection

inputs consistently differ from their equilibrium levels due to government intervention through policy measures such as taxation, quantitative restrictions, licenses for import and export, as well as price intervention, overvaluation of the domestic currency, and subsidies.

If policies are introduced to lower agricultural prices below their equilibrium levels, they can be regarded as taxing agriculture. If they aim to push up agricultural prices above their equilibrium levels, they can be regarded as assisting or protecting agriculture. Both taxation and protection on agriculture are distortionary.

Agricultural distortion has a long history and is associated with stages of economic development and structural change. Empirical evidence of agricultural distortion in both time series and cross section data points to a similar path in many countries. At a low level of per capita income, agriculture tends to be taxed. By contrast, when an economy is more developed, it tends to be protected or subsidised.

The analytical framework of 'political market' provides insights into the formation of agricultural protection (figure 13.1). It describes the typical relationship between development stages and protection rates, and factors that determine the transformation from negative protection (taxation) to positive protection.

In a political market of agricultural protection, farmers are on the demand side (wanting more protection) and the government is on the supply side (making more of it available). The government decides whether or not and to what extent to provide (supply) protection by weighing its political costs and benefits. For a modern political economy, there is an hypothesis about policy-making which suggests that policy-makers and politicians usually offer policy packages that maximise their popularity and avoid policies that could cost them political support. On the demand side, the more an interest group expects to receive from a policy, the stronger is its demand for that policy. On the other hand, if an interest group expects to lose from a policy, it will oppose it.

In figure 13.1 the horizontal axis represents the level of protection, increasing from the left to the right. At the origin, where the protection level is zero, there is neither protection nor taxation. The vertical axis represents the marginal political benefits and costs that policy-makers face as a result of implementing protection policies. These are described by the (MR) marginal revenue and (MC) marginal cost curves. As the protection level rises, lobbying intensity for a protective policy falls, and lobbying intensity against it rises. These are shown in figure 13.1 by falling MR curves and rising MC curves. The political benefit of policy-makers is maximised at an equilibrium point where marginal revenues are equal to marginal costs.

In the early stage of development, when most of the labour force in a nation is engaged in agriculture, it is costly to organise the lobbying activities of peasants, and their political pressure is weak. People engaged in industry and commerce, however, have considerable power to influence policy-making by the government. Under these circumstances, there are higher costs and lower benefits for the government in carrying out an agricultural protection policy. Therefore, for most economies in their early development stage, agricultural distortionary policies mean taxation or negative protection (as shown at P_1 in figure 13.1).

With economic growth and greater income, the situation changes. First, the proportion of expenditure on food declines and consumers now have much greater capability to sustain increasing food prices. This lowers the costs of a protection policy. Second, the agricultural shares of both production and employment decline, and the fiscal cost of protecting a smaller part of the economy decreases. Third, with the reduction in the proportion of the agricultural population, improvement in farmers' education and development of rural transportation and communication, the transaction costs of organising the agricultural population become less significant, and farmers become more powerful in influencing policy-making. For these reasons, both demand for agricultural protection and the political costs of agricultural taxation policy have increased considerably in China. Fourth, since agriculture is being taxed or exploited, when conditions arise to change the traditional policy orientation, moral perceptions can lower lobbying costs for protection. This tends to lead to a policy transformation that is more than should be appropriate. Finally, the fact that comparative advantage in agriculture has been lost turns the economy into a net importer of farm products. This provides a congenial environment to press for protectionist policies. Naturally, the upholding of food security is often an influential argument for the introduction of a protectionist policy.

It is for these reasons that during an economy's loss of comparative advantage in agriculture, policy is often transformed from taxing to protecting agriculture (P_2 in figure 13.1). According to worldwide experience, the turning point of policy orientation typically occurs at a per capita GNP level of between US$1,000 and US$2,000 (Johnson 1991). Garnaut and Ma (1993a) estimate that by 1992 China's per capita GDP, measured on the same basis as other developing countries, reached a level of around US$1,300, suggesting that China is entering a stage of transformation.

The welfare loss due to agricultural protection

Although any policy package usually produces some political benefits for government, a given policy also has its costs, not only for government but also in terms of social welfare. In the past decades of China's economic development, distortionary agricultural policies that exploit agriculture have brought substantial efficiency loss. Giving up these policies has gradually become the mainstream view of economists in China. Many Chinese economists view agricultural protectionism as a good thing however, and even suggest transforming the taxing orientation of agricultural policy to a positive protection level.

There are some negative effects of a protection policy in China's circumstances.

First of all, agricultural protection increases the burden on consumers and taxpayers. The essence of an agricultural protection policy is to keep the domestic price of food above that of the international market, through a variety of policy distortion measures. Domestic consumers therefore have to pay higher prices than they otherwise would. Also, taxpayers have to pay for the costs of price-supporting and income-supporting programmes that are components of a protection policy package.

The low wage policy has been an important precondition of traditional development strategy in China. It will eventually change as a result of economic reform. But if increases in food prices are large, as they will be if China adopts a protectionist policy as its income rises, there will be a conflict between low wage rates and high living costs. This will create some obstacles for further reform.

Second, agricultural protectionism creates and intensifies trade friction.

In an economy with a high growth rate, economic growth is associated with expanding international trade. It is necessary for an economy to maintain a reasonable balance in external payments. Many industrial countries in particular are large food exporters, so if an economy carries out an agricultural protection policy, trade friction will follow, affecting the expansion of international trade. Japan exemplifies the problem. Whether or not China can maintain a high rate of growth in the 1990s depends to a great extent on its export expansion. If China does not give up its food 'self-sufficiency' policy, which implies agricultural protectionism, trade friction has the potential to become a serious constraint on growth.

Third, an agricultural protection policy distorts price signals in both commodity and factor markets. Consumer prices and producer prices of farm products differ from their equilibrium levels if the market is distorted. The distorted commodity prices in turn induce a distortion of factor prices, because demand for a factor is influenced by the corresponding demand for the goods in the production of which the factor is used intensively. Farm producers will respond to higher farm prices by increasing the use of production inputs, which raises demand for related production factors and causes an increase in prices of the related factors.

An initial goal of a protection policy is to raise incomes of agricultural labour and to stabilise farmers' incomes through these mechanisms. This policy, however, overlooks the role played by the supply of factors in the process of price formation of factors. According to economic theory, if supply of a production factor is elastic in response to expanding demand, more of the factor will be used, and increases in the price of this factor are likely to be small. By contrast, if supply of a factor is less elastic, its price will increase proportionally more. In most economies with agricultural protection, farm labour is fairly elastic. But arable land, being restrained by the resource endowment, has low elasticity. Because of this, an agricultural protection policy usually brings about an unreasonable increase in the land price (rent), while increases in returns to the farm worker are limited (Johnson 1991). For example, in Japan in 1934–80, the price of paddy land in Japan went up by 9,617 times, while farm surplus from paddy production increased only by 828 times. As a result, the rate of return on paddy rice production declined from 6.8 per cent to 0.6 per cent (Hayami 1988: 87). Once rises in the land price exceed increases in farm income, it can become more difficult to encourage the reallocation of farm land among producers in order to improve efficiency.

China has a large amount of labour but only a relatively small amount of available agricultural land, similar to Japan. Therefore, a protection policy in China is likely to have similar effects as in Japan, which defeats its purpose of protecting income to farm labour.

Fourth, a distortionary policy is usually associated with economic inefficiency and political corruption. On the one hand, an agricultural protection policy distorts prices of commodities and factors, establishing a policy environment in which the government is responsible for allocation of resources in all sectors of the economy. Such a system, as the experiences of many countries including China have shown, is inefficient. In addition, this system or environment encourages 'rent seeking' behaviour, which is costly both economically and politically.

When there are distortionary policies, interest groups mushroom and exercise their lobbying power. They try to influence the policy-making process through harmful political activities such as 'vote trading', 'logrolling' (Buchanan and Tullock 1962) and bribery, with the particular form of corruption depending on the political system. Those who benefit from an agricultural protection policy form vested interest groups, closely organised and fighting for higher protection. Reversing the existing protectionist stance is very difficult.

Chinese farmers have not yet exerted a major influence on policy-making and have suffered low producer prices. Agricultural policy has been changing in the direction of greater economic liberalisation. Since agricultural protectionism, once established, is a rigid institution which hinders further reform, policy-makers should be careful to choose the correct agricultural policy, so as to avoid the formation of special interest groups.

The protectionist trend in China's agricultural policies

Recently, Chinese and foreign economists have undertaken many studies of China's agricultural policies, and have examined several indicators that reflect the level of protection in China's agricultural sector. Gunasekera et al. (1992) estimated the producer subsidy equivalents (PSEs) related to some major crops in 1986. They show that cotton has the highest real protection level in terms of PSE (14 per cent), followed by poultry (7 per cent). The protection levels of pork, beef and mutton are among the lowest at −77 per cent, −15 per cent and −27 per cent, respectively.

Garnaut and Ma (1992a) estimate that the protection levels for rice are sharply negative (−46 per cent in 1988 and −22 per cent in 1991). Protection levels are heading towards being positive for other grains (wheat at −7 per cent in 1988 rising to +5 per cent in 1991; soybean fluctuating widely from −41 per cent in 1988 to −36 per cent in 1991; and corn being positive at times but −26 per cent in 1991). Gunasekera et al. (1992) indicate that producer subsidy equivalents are higher, though they are still negative: −9 per cent for wheat, −6 per cent for soybeans, and zero for coarse grains. Garnaut, Fang and Huang (chapter 14) show that there has been a powerful recent trend towards protection of agriculture. From these studies, although we cannot conclude that China's agriculture as a whole has already enjoyed positive protection in absolute terms, it is clear that the protection levels of some commodities such as cotton and poultry are positive, while others such as sugar and most grains are tending to shift from a negative protection regime to a positive one. This trend has been related to the changes in comparative advantage in China's agriculture.

Judging by the above findings and worldwide experience, there are signs that China may be shifting from taxing to protecting agriculture. In particular, it seems that grain protectionism is likely to be an important component of future agricultural policy in China. There are three reasons for this likely policy change. First, grain has historically been considered a key commodity in the national economy and is perceived as a symbol of state security. Therefore, policy is formulated on every government level to ensure self-sufficiency in grain. Second, Chinese politicians think of social stability in the countryside as being based on a steady income of farm households. Many think that maintaining a higher relative price of grain can keep farmers' income stable. For this reason, no one dares to ignore the voices of officials urging more attention to agriculture, the countryside economy and the situation of farmers. This is equivalent to increasing farmers' lobbying power. Third, urban residents do not care as much about increases in grain prices as they did a few years ago, since their incomes have been rising rapidly in recent years.

Maintaining self-sufficiency in grain has negative effects on resource allocation in Chinese agriculture (Lardy 1984: 426–7). China's size means that great variety exists throughout the country with respect to comparative advantage in agriculture (table 13.2). Here we examine the change in the regional specialisation level in the country's agriculture, using the correlation co-efficients between the comparative advantage index in a given year and the ratio of sown area of cash crops to that of grain in the following year. The 'comparative advantage index' is computed as cash crop output value per hectare in each province with the national average as 100. It is generally believed that a high correlation co-efficient implies regional specialisation according to comparative advantage.

There was comparatively high regional specialisation in Chinese agriculture before 1985. The relationship between the comparative advantage index for cash crops in 1983 and the ratio of sown area in 1984 was positive and high, reflected by a correlation co-efficient of 0.594 (table 13.2). In 1984–5 it was 0.416. It fell significantly after 1985, dropping to 0.182 in 1985–6, 0.145 in 1986–7, 0.136 in 1987–8, only 0.038 in 1988–9 and 0.138 in 1990–1, which represents a declining trend in regional specialisation in agriculture.

Table 13.2 *Comparative advantage index of cash crops, by province, 1991*

Beijing	0.79	Zhejiang	0.81	Sichuan	0.94
Tianjin	0.79	Anhui	0.80	Guizhou	0.82
Hebei	1.03	Fujian	1.34	Yunnan	1.60
Shanxi	1.14	Jiangxi	0.55	Xizang	0.46
Neimeng	0.86	Shandong	1.06	Shaanxi	1.17
Liaoning	0.75	Henan	1.20	Gansu	1.20
Jilin	0.84	Hubei	0.89	Qinghai	0.44
Heilongjiang	0.70	Hunan	0.60	Ningxia	0.65
Shanghai	0.63	Guandong	1.36	Xinjiang	1.67
Jiangsu	0.97	Guangxi	1.23	Hainan	1.12

Source: SSB, ZTN (1992).

When specialisation occurs according to regional comparative advantage, the ratio of cash crop yield to grain yield should be similar across provinces. On the other hand, the difference in ratios of cash crop sown area to grain sown area among regions should be relatively large. These tendencies can be observed only before 1985. Since then, China has moved away from the positions suggested in these generalisations, pointing to a serious inhibition of specialisation in agriculture in the second half of the 1980s (table 13.3).

To explain the change in specialisation levels of agriculture before and after 1985, account must be taken of the changes in state grain policy during this period. The household responsibility system for agriculture spread throughout the country and brought about substantial increases in farm production in the early 1980s. Rapidly increased output alleviated the longstanding grain shortage. The government then called for an adjustment of the rural production structure, and eased control over the distribution system for agricultural products. For the first time in the history of rural China, free markets of commodities and factors were active, and provided effective signals to guide farmers' reallocation of production resources according to comparative advantage. This gave rise to the existence of relatively strong specialisation in agriculture and a relative abundance of grain around 1983–4.

The serious reduction in grain output in 1985, however, precipitated change. Afraid of a grain shortage, the central government restored a series of restrictive policies to control the sown area of grain and grain distribution all over the country, inducing a lower specialisation level in agriculture.

The government has employed two related policy measures in its

Table 13.3 *Change in specialisation in Chinese agriculture, by province*

	1983	1984	1985	1986	1987	1988	1989
(1)	0.484	0.525	0.478	0.507	0.574	0.802	0.614
(2)	0.069	0.070	0.078	0.074	0.085	0.085	0.082

Notes:
(1) Standard deviation of ratios of yields
(2) Standard deviation of ratios of sown areas.
Source: Fang Cai (1992).

attempt to enhance grain production since 1985. One is geared towards strengthening administrative control over production of grain through each level of the government, and the other towards increasing grain prices so as to stimulate the expansion of the grain sown area. The state procurement price index for grain has increased faster than that for cash crops since 1985. This may have distorted the relative price of grain to cash crops, though the bias of procurement price against cash crops has been weakened because an increasingly large share of their prices has been determined through the market mechanism. It is reasonable to say therefore that the decline in specialisation after 1985 has been related to the tight domestic supply of grain, and to related government responses.

Marketisation and internationalisation of Chinese agriculture

The distortionary agricultural policy aimed at solving problems of farmers' income and grain supply has proven costly in terms of social welfare. It was not helpful in raising farmers' income, and it has impeded the development of market systems.

It is necessary to find a more workable policy. Trade liberalisation based on the principle of comparative advantage is better than trade protectionism. Specialisation in production should be based on the principle of comparative advantage.

According to trade theory, differences in comparative advantage among countries arise from differences in the relative productivity of resources in different industries, as well as from differences in their resource endowments. The more populated the country and the more scarce its arable land, the faster its comparative advantage declines in agriculture. Every country can benefit from producing and exporting goods in which it has comparative advantage and importing goods in which it has comparative disadvantage.

Taking advantage of trade liberalisation produces different results from implementing protectionist policies. With liberal trade policies, if domestic costs of agricultural goods are higher than those on the international market, imports of agricultural products can help to develop a more efficient industry structure and use of resources. Industries which rely on agricultural raw materials can obtain them at competitive prices from abroad. In the process of rapid economic growth and structural change, the basic conditions for increases in farmers' income – rising human capital of farmers, increasing off-farm wage rates and employment (Johnson 1991) – can only be created through structural adjustment under free trade, not through agricultural protectionism.

There are three ways for China to utilise its comparative advantage through international trade. The first involves changing its export composition on the basis of comparative advantage and market competition. As a developing country, China's total exports have long included a large portion of agricultural goods, though this declined from about 25 per cent in 1985 to less than 11 per cent in 1992. This percentage will drop further as a result of a higher proportion of labour-intensive manufactured goods in Chinese exports. This is a consequence of diminishing comparative advantage in China's agriculture. In contrast, there is great potential in exporting textiles and clothing. Export specialisation indexes in these products went up from 3.1 in the second half of the 1960s to 4.68 in the first half of the 1980s, thereafter remaining constant (table 13.1). With capital accumulation and increasing labour cost, the shares of Hong Kong, Korea and Taiwan in world textiles and clothing exports are being replaced by those of China. This provides opportunities for China's industry in rural areas to expand. In 1982, Hong Kong, Korea and Taiwan accounted for 39.7 per cent of world exports of clothing and textiles, much higher than mainland China's 11.7 per cent. By 1992, China's 28.1 per cent was much closer to the other three economies 30.2 per cent.

The second way for China to utilise its comparative advantage in international trade is through adjustment of its agricultural structure in accordance with its resource endowments and commodity characteristics. China's land-to-labour ratio is low by world standards. According to economic theory, other things being equal, increases in input of a factor results in a reduction in its marginal return. When farmers have the opportunity to plant crops which utilise more labour and less land, the marginal return to labour should be smaller than it would be otherwise. Based on analysis of labour input and land productivity of 17 crops in China, the higher the labour share in total cost, the larger is the net value of production per hectare. The correlation co-efficient is 0.235. Generally speaking, grain production is more land intensive and cash crops are more labour intensive. On average, in 1989 the number of work days per *mu* 7.6 hectares for rice, wheat, corn, sorghum and 'other' coarse grains was 16.9, compared with 40.5 for cotton, 45.0 for jute and 54.8 for tobacco. This suggests that there would be advantages in China's agriculture producing more cash crops and less grain. An implication of such a strategy would be a greater amount of grain import, and part of the necessary foreign exchange could be earned by exporting more cash crops and their processed products.

The third way for China to utilise its comparative advantages is to ensure that regional agricultural production specialises along lines that conform to local comparative advantage. As a large economy, there are substantial differences among regions, in initial resource endowments and in development levels, and each region has its own comparative advantage. The emergence of different production structures in different regions according to their advantages can result in a convergence of factor returns. This would allow resources to be used where they are most productive.

14 A turning point in China's agricultural development

Ross Garnaut, Fang Cai and Yiping Huang

China faces important policy choices

After fifteen years of economic reform, China's agricultural policy is coming to a turning point – the ending of the policies discriminating against agriculture. The government now faces a policy choice between agricultural protection and free trade. This decision will, to a large extent, determine China's future patterns of agricultural production, consumption and trade. It will also affect welfare in China's major trading partners.

Although Chinese economic history and institutions are distinctive, the policy choice is similar to other densely populated countries that have experienced sustained, rapid economic growth. These conditions cause demand for agricultural products to rise more rapidly than economically efficient domestic supply. Britain, the first modern industrial economy, responded to the policy choice first by introducing two protectionist Corn Laws in 1773 and 1815, and then by reversing the policies, abolishing the Corn Laws and opting for free trade in 1846. In East Asia, the tendency so far has been to opt for agricultural protection, favoured in Japan since the 1950s and 1960s and in Taiwan and Korea over the past quarter century. These policies have been costly to domestic welfare and to co-operative relations with international trading partners. Singapore and Hong Kong have benefited from truncated policy choice, with their economic modernisation supported by free access to food at international prices.

Agricultural policies in the pre-reform China had three major components (Lin, Cai and Li 1994; in chapter 2; Huang, chapter 3). First, agricultural production was set by economic plans and carried out through the collective commune or production-team system. Second, purchase and marketing of agricultural products were monopolised by state institutions and there was, virtually, no free agricultural trade.[1] And, third, state agricultural prices were kept below market equilibrium levels to maintain low (wage and raw materials) costs for industrialisation (Huang Yiping 1993).

Recent changes in prices signal an important turning point in China's agricultural development: the previous policies discriminating against agriculture are coming to an end. But it is not yet clear which future direction the Chinese government will pursue. One option, consistent with the on-going process of economic liberalisation, is for China to introduce a free trade regime for agricultural products and to allow domestic agricultural prices to be determined by interaction with the international market. Another is to follow other high income Northeast Asian economies into protective measures.

The turning point

Incentive distortions to agricultural production in pre-reform China were due both to purchase policy and to border policy. The first is reflected in differences between state and market prices, and the second is represented by gaps between domestic and international prices. Reforms so far have initially targeted elimination of the first type of distortion, through adjustment of state prices, and introduction of free markets have so far also had the effect of reducing the second type of distortion.

China's economic reform started in 1979 when the government decided to raise state purchase prices for agricultural products (by 20 per cent on average) to encourage agricultural production – the first attempt to reduce domestic incentive distortions to agriculture (Lardy 1983a).[2] In the following years, agricultural prices were raised successively, although the increase in domestic market prices was not particularly high before 1985. On the one hand, the abolition of the commune system and the increases in state purchase prices significantly raised agricultural output (table 14.1). Of the 42 per cent increase in crop output (it was 70 per cent for all agricultural output) between 1979 and 1984, Lin (1992a) finds about half was driven by productivity changes directly linked to reform.[3] On the other hand, since economic reform had not been widely extended beyond the agricultural sector by 1984, non-agricultural income did not rise rapidly. Income growth only generated moderate demand pressure on agricultural markets during that period. In 1983 and 1984, a temporary grain surplus occurred and free market prices in many regions were close to or lower than state purchase prices.

From 1984, the government started to extend reforms to other sectors of the economy. In the rural economy, free markets were introduced for non-agricultural and most agricultural products. These changes produced upward pressures on agricultural prices from both the supply and demand sides. As farmers were able to participate in a wider range of production activities, resources were re-allocated from agriculture to high-return non-agricultural output, although total rural output rose rapidly (Huang

Table 14.1 *Economic growth and agricultural prices, 1978–93*

	GNP growth (%)	Agricultural growth (%)	Grain output (mt)	GNP per capita (yuan) (1985 prices)	Price indices Agricultural purchases[a]	Food markets[b]
1978	12.3	3.9	304.8	398	59.9	81.4
1979	7.0	6.4	332.1	420	73.2	83.4
1980	6.4	−1.8	320.6	442	78.4	88.4
1981	4.9	7.1	325.0	457	83.0	90.0
1982	8.2	11.8	354.5	487	84.8	91.5
1983	10.0	8.5	387.3	529	88.5	91.9
1984	13.6	12.9	407.3	593	92.1	92.9
1985	13.5	2.7	379.1	663	100.0	100.0
1986	7.7	3.0	391.5	703	106.4	106.1
1987	10.2	4.5	403.0	762	119.2	112.6
1988	11.3	2.3	394.1	835	146.6	132.1
1989	3.7	3.2	407.6	853	168.6	156.7
1990	5.1	7.5	446.2	881	164.2	160.9
1991	7.7	2.3	435.3	936	160.9	163.7
1992	12.8	5.0	442.7	1047	166.4	170.2
1993	13.4	4.0	456.4	1174	182.5	182.1

Notes:
[a] Agricultural purchase prices are weighted average prices of both state and market purchases
[b] food price are prices in rural markets.
Source: SSB, ZTN (1993 and 1994).

Yiping 1993). Grain output dropped sharply in 1985 and did not recover its 1984 record level until 1989. Income growth in both rural and urban areas then created an increasing demand for agricultural products. The annual inflation rate of food prices reached 12 per cent during 1984–8 (table 14.1).

The austerity program implemented in 1989 and the following years caused a slowdown of economic growth, especially in non-agricultural production. In rural areas agricultural production, particularly of grain, recovered because many resources (labour and investment) returned from rural non-agricultural sectors (Huang Yiping 1993). Agricultural prices only rose slowly in 1990 and 1991.

In 1992, 1993 and 1994, the Chinese economy experienced another period of fast growth, with an average growth rate of 12 per cent per annum. At the same time, China had a succession of good harvests. Agricultural prices at first grew slowly during this period. At the end of 1993, however, grain shortages in a number of southern provinces (including Guangdong and Fujian) caused significant increases in grain market prices within a very short period, although this movement was quickly stabilised by government's administrative measures.[4] To encourage grain production further, the government adjusted grain prices upward by 20 per cent on average in 1994 (Huang 1994b).

One problem with grain price reform was that while state purchase prices and free market prices continued to rise, state marketing prices hardly changed. In order to reduce domestic distortions and to encourage grain production, every increase in the purchase price had to be subsidised by the government and was therefore directly transformed into a burden on the state budget. This became an important constraint on further reform of grain policies. In 1992, the government took a substantial step to unify state purchase and market prices so that the gap between state and market prices (the first type of distortion) for agricultural products was virtually eliminated. As most of the economy is now marketised, the government finds it extremely difficult to purchase agricultural products at prices substantially below market equilibrium levels.

Incentive distortions between domestic and international agricultural markets (due to border policies) have also been declining significantly in recent years. China had large negative nominal protection rates for most agricultural products in the pre-reform period.[5] These negative numbers decreased in the process of economic reform (Guo Shutian et al. 1993; Ke Bingsheng 1993). Guo Shutian et al. (1993) suggest that by 1988 the nominal protection rate had been raised to –48 per cent for rice, –26 per cent for maize, –4 per cent for wheat, –16 per cent for soybean, and between –30 and –50 per cent for pork, beef and lamb. The gap between domestic and international prices narrowed more quickly after 1989, with some agricultural products being positively protected in 1989 and 1990 (Guo Shutian et al. 1993).

In 1993, domestic market prices of wheat, rice and maize ranged from about 20 to 50 per cent below their international counterparts. By mid-1994 domestic prices exceeded international prices for wheat and maize, and by September 1994 for rice, despite the large rise in world prices following Japanese entry into the market as an importer (figures 14.1, 14.2, 14.3). In 1994, domestic prices of wheat, maize and rice moved above international prices. These three products are among the most important agricultural commodities for both the government and farmers. Their domestic prices are usually more strictly controlled or more heavily influenced by the government.

A more comprehensive measure of incentive distortion, taking into account subsidies and other non-border assistance measures, is the Producer Subsidy Equivalent (PSE). We have calculated PSEs based on

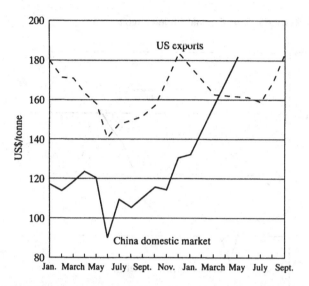

Figure 14.1   China's domestic market price and US export price: wheat, January 1993 to September 1994 (US$/tonne)
Note: China domestic prices are market prices in rural and urban fairs converted using the swap exchange rate and US export prices are f.o.b. Gulf of No. 1 hard red winter (ordinary protein).
Sources: International Monetary Fund (various issues).

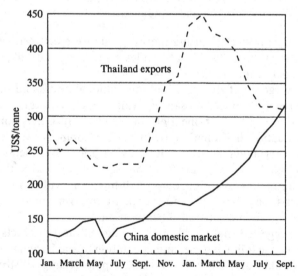

Figure 14.2   China's domestic market price and US export price: rice, January 1993 to September 1994 (US$/tonne)
Note: China domestic prices are market prices in rural and urban fairs converted using the swap and exchange rate and Thai export prices are f.o.b. Bangkok, white milled 5 per cent broken.
Sources: International Monetary Fund (various issues).

Figure 14.3   China's domestic market price and US export price: maize, January 1993 to September 1994 (US$/tonne)
Note: China domestic prices are market prices in rural and urban fairs converted using the swap exchange rate and US exports are f.o.b. Gulf of No. 2 yellow.
Sources: International Monetary Fund (various issues).

the swap exchange rate. PSEs using the swap rate were between –40 and –65 per cent in the mid-1980s. The PSE index came to around –20 per cent in 1993 and –2 per cent in 1993 (table 14.2).

Was the convergence of domestic and international prices and the substantial reduction in producer subsidy equivalents for agricultural production through the first half of the 1990s a historical turning point or a temporary fluctuation in China's agricultural development? While there were some short-term factors behind the speed of price adjustments in late 1993 and through 1994, the underlying pressures associated with rising domestic demand and constraints on growth in supply will continue and strengthen over time. They will tend eventually to push domestic prices much higher in the absence of trade liberalisation.

It has been suggested that world prices for agricultural products, especially grains, will rise following the implementation of the Uruguay Round settlement (Brandão and Martin 1993 and Yiping Huang 1994b). One simulation based on the Dunkel proposal, by Brandão and Martin (1993) using the RUNS model, predicts increases in international prices resulting from implementation of the Uruguay Round – by 6 per cent for wheat and meat, 4 per cent for rice and coarse grain, and 10 per cent for sugar during

Table 14.2 Producer subsidy equivalent (PSE) for China's agriculture, 1978–94 (billion yuan, per cent)

	1986	1987	1988	1989	1990	1991	1992	1993	1994
Producer value	401	467	587	654	766	816	909	1030	1280
Income transfer due to border policy	-190.6	-260.3	-414.6	-157.5	-245.2	-168.2	-209.9	-251.4	-96.5
(exchange rate)	5.0	5.7	6.3	5.9	5.8	5.8	6.5	8.6	8.7
Agricultural taxes	4.5	5.2	7.4	8.5	8.8	9.1	9.0	9.6	9.6
Budget on agriculture	18.4	19.6	21.4	26.6	30.8	34.8	37.9	44.1	44.1
Disaster subsidy	1.1	1.0	1.1	1.3	1.3	1.6	1.6	1.6	1.6
Welfare subsidy	0.3	0.3	0.3	0.3	0.3	0.3	0.3	0.4	0.4
Input subsidy	1.0	1.1	1.2	1.5	1.4	1.3	1.4	1.5	1.5
Interest difference	7.9	9.5	11.3	13.2	14.9	17.4	20.8	24.7	24.7
(Agricultural loans)	(28.3)	(33.7)	(40.4)	(47.1)	(53.1)	(61.8)	(74.0)	(87.8)	(87.8)
PSE value	-162	-229	-379	-115	-197	-113	-148	-179	-24
Share (%)	-40	-49	-65	-18	-26	-14	-16	-17	-2

Notes:
The exchange rates used in this table are swap rates. For the years before 1896, we fail to define an acceptable exchange rate.
Sources: SSS, ZTN (1993); Food and Agricultural Organisation (various years).

the implementation period. This will tend to reverse the long-term declining trend of agricultural prices in the past several decades (Tyers and Anderson 1992). Upward movement of world agricultural prices may precede the implementation period and may exceed the expected Uruguay Round effects because of supply developments in important agricultural producing countries. Much will depend on policy and institutional developments in Russia and India, economies with the large capacity to expand output under favourable economic conditions.

Increases in agricultural prices in China are likely to be faster than in international prices if domestic agricultural markets remain largely isolated from international markets. As a rapidly growing agricultural resource-scarce (per capita) economy, domestic agricultural prices will have to rise rapidly because of rising marginal costs of production and increasing demand for consumption. Garnaut and Ma (1992a; chapter 4) project that, while China's demand for grain will rise quickly before the turn of the century (due to the expected rapid increase in per capita income and steady growth of population), grain output can only increase slowly because of the escalating competition for agricultural resources. Slowdown of agricultural growth has been observed in China's most dynamic regions (including Guangdong, Fujian, Jiangsu and Zhejiang) where resources were quickly attracted out of grain and other important parts of agriculture to higher-return activities. Rapid increases in food prices occurred between 1984 and 1988 because the economy was growing rapidly and fewer constraints were imposed on farmers' production decisions and on free markets.

China's domestic food prices grew faster than international prices during the reform period (figure 14.4). World food prices were relatively stable during 1978–83 before they jumped in 1984. Fluctuations in world food prices were significant after 1984 with several peaks (1984, 1986 and 1990) and valleys (1985 and 1988). Looking at the trend over the whole period, however, world food prices did not change much in nominal terms between 1978 and 1992.[6] Domestic food prices, on the other hand, experienced a dramatic increase over the period (especially between 1987 and 1989), registering an average growth rate of 5.4 per cent.

The experience of other East Asian economies suggests that the turning point comes sooner the less agricultural resources an economy has and the faster the economy grows (Anderson and Hayami 1986).

China's population density (121 persons per/km^2) is not high compared to many countries in Western Europe and East Asia, although it is much higher than the world average (Table 14.3). China's agricultural area, including arable land, forestry and pastoral areas, howevei, is very small on a per capita basis. China has about 22 per cent of world's total population, but only 7 per cent of world's arable land area. At the margin, China

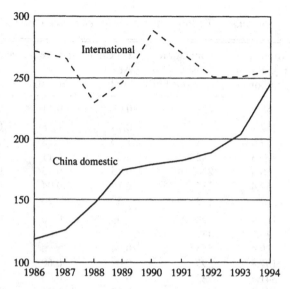

Figure 14.4   Changes in international and domestic food prices, 1986–94
(aggregate price: US$/tonne)
Notes: The international food price is an aggregate of international prices
weighted by value shares in total world trade. The commodities included in the
calculation are beef, lamb, pork, eggs, wheat, rice, maize, oranges, apples and tea.
The domestic price is the rural market food price.
Sources: SSB, ZTN (1993); International Monetary Fund (various issues).

cannot be expected to have a comparative advantage in agricultural production as its incomes rise towards those in industrial countries.

The Chinese economy has now reached a stage of development similar
to that in Japan, Korea and Taiwan when these countries turned from
taxing to subsidising agriculture. China's GNP per capita in 1993, adjusted
to a reasonable basis for international comparison, was around US$1300
(1987 prices). This is close to the income levels of Korea and Taiwan in the
1960s and 1970s and similar to Japan's income levels in the pre- and post-
war years. This suggests at least that this may be a time when China might
face pressures to turn from taxing to subsidising agriculture.

Not all the indicators convey the same message. The relative importance
of agriculture in total output and employment is higher in China in the
early 1990s than in other East Asian countries at the turning point.
Agriculture's share in the Chinese economy rose in the early stage of economic reform and fell after 1985. Its share in GDP was 35 per cent in
China in 1990. This compares with 18 per cent and 21 per cent, respectively, in 1935 and 1955 in Japan, 30 per cent in Korea in 1970 and 32 per

Table 14.3 *Population and agricultural resources in selected countries*

	Total population (million)	Population density (persons/km^2)	Per capita land areas (hectare) Arable land	Forestry	Pastoral areas
China	1,158.2	121	0.08	0.11	0.19
United States	252.7	27	0.74	1.16	0.96
Canada	27.0	3	1.70	13.28	1.04
Australia	17.3	2	2.81	6.11	24.09
Germany	80.3	226	0.15	0.13	0.07
Britain	57.4	235	0.12	0.04	0.19
France	57.1	103	0.32	0.26	0.20
Japan	123.9	328	0.03	0.20	0.01
Korea	43.3	437	..	..	..
Taiwan	20.4	565	0.04	..	..
Indonesia	187.8	99	0.09	0.60	0.06
India	841.7	283	0.20	0.08	0.01
Philippines	62.9	210	0.07	0.16	0.02
Thailand	56.9	111	0.33	0.25	0.01
Malaysia	18.3	56	0.06	1.05	0.00
Pakistan	115.5	145	0.18	0.03	0.04
Bangladesh	118.7	825	0.07	0.02	0.01
Mexico	87.8	45	0.26	0.48	0.85
Argentina	32.7	12	0.76	1.81	4.35
Brazil	153.3	18	0.33	3.22	1.20
World	5389.2	40	0.25	0.75	0.63

Sources: SSB, ZTN (1993); Food and Agricultural Organisation (1993).

cent in Taiwan in 1960. China's share of agricultural labour in the total labour force is high, perhaps reflecting earlier policies restricting labour movements between rural and urban areas, especially in the pre-reform period. At 60 per cent in 1990 it was higher than that in Japan in years before and after the Second World War, but is, in fact, very close to the share in Korea in 1960 (61 per cent).

The best policy choice

Recent changes in both nominal protection rates and PSEs indicate that China's agricultural development is coming to a turning point with the Chinese government facing a critical and historical policy choice. An appropriate decision will not only increase the probability of China's growth at high rates over a longer period, but will also contribute to welfare improvement in other countries.

There are two avenues ahead of China. It can follow some other East Asian economies introducing agricultural protection or it can go beyond the Uruguay Round agreement to internationalise its agricultural sector.

There is already a powerful lobby for agricultural protection in China, although not mainly by farmers' organisations. The agricultural economists and agricultural bureaucrats, with very few exceptions, strongly favour protection. It is argued that, because past policies disadvantaged farmers and made the agricultural sector a bottleneck for overall economic growth, China's growth, China should learn its lessons and protect agriculture and farmers (Chen Jiyuan and Deng Yiming 1993).

China's policy objective to maintain self-sufficiency in major agricultural products such as grains, oilseeds and cotton, lends strong support to agricultural protectionism. According to studies by Garnaut and Ma (1992a; chapter 4) and Huang (1994b), China's total grain demand will rise by a big margin before the end of the century. Its grain supply, however, can only increase slowly (at the most at the same rate as the population) if a free trade regime is adopted. If the Chinese government chooses to maintain self-sufficiency in grain, the domestic grain market will have to be protected, with the associated higher prices, discouragement of domestic demand and incentives to expand domestic production.[7]

But agricultural protection cannot deliver food security. The degree of food security in a closed domestic market is much lower than in a wider global food market. Japan's experience in 1993 clearly demonstrated that, without access to international imports, it would not have had food security. It is much easier for larger international markets to accommodate production fluctuations than smaller, closed domestic markets. Isolation of the Chinese grain market would also increase instability in international markets. High levels of agricultural self-sufficiency are likely to be associated with larger risks of environmental damage. They would also be associated with higher levels of dependence on imported inputs and therefore are unlikely to deliver higher levels of security in any fundamental sense.

Fang (chapter 13) has described problems that will arise if China opts for agricultural protection. Agricultural protection creates adverse effects on production consumption, trade and welfare (Vousden 1990). Distorting domestic terms of trade by artificially raising agricultural prices prevents the economy from fully exercising its comparative advantage and draws resources away from more efficient uses. Efficiency losses in resource allocation lead to reductions in aggregate output, reducing the economy's (especially urban consumers') income and welfare. Often, agricultural protection also results in heavy burdens on government budget.

Agricultural protection not only reduces an economy's domestic welfare, but also affects the welfare of its trading partners with agricultural protection policies often a source of trade conflicts.

Policies protecting agriculture in China may not have the income re-distribution function that have been claimed for them in Western Europe, North America and East Asia. Because of the characteristics of rural industrialisation in China, most farmers derive their income from rural non-agricultural sectors as well as from agriculture. In the early 1990s, agricultural production contributed to about 60 per cent of farmers' total net income. This share is expected to rise steadily as the rural township, village and private enterprises are just gathering momentum. Agricultural protection may raise agricultural income but depress non-agricultural income.

China's current comparative advantage lies in labour-intensive manufacturing, with labour-intensive exports crucial to its rapid economic growth. If China integrates with the world economy, with dynamic labour-intensive sectors producing increasingly more employment opportunities to absorb surplus farmers, this growth can probably be sustained or even accelerated for another decade or two.

Rural China has already developed a township, village and private sector employing about 100 million rural labourers. If the relative returns to agriculture decline because of trade liberalisation, farmers will move to the rural industrial and service sectors within their township or village.

If the government chooses this critical time, when China's domestic prices for wheat, rice and maize are very close to international prices, to liberalise domestic grain markets, the immediate adjustment costs will be minimal. Since international prices can be expected to remain fairly steady and perhaps increase moderately in the next decade, adjustment costs incurred by wheat and maize farmers will be gradual allowing farmers either to pursue alternative crops or to find jobs in non-agricultural sectors. Adjustment costs to internationalisation later, after domestic prices have risen well above world levels, would be much greater.

The choice China makes will be affected by the international political economy. China's fear that continuing to open up to the international food economy may increase its domestic instability has some basis in market behaviour. Agricultural protectionism in the 1980s made international markets residual, and therefore very vulnerable to relatively small fluctuations in demand or supply in major countries. China's worry that it may not be able to buy grain on international markets comes from its memory of embargoes imposed by the United States and other western countries at times of political conflict. And China's concern that it may not be able to secure export markets to earn sufficient foreign exchange comes from restrictions it faces in foreign markets (such as MFA on China's textile exports). China requires the co-operation of the international community in overcoming these inhibitions to integration into the world food economy.

It is in the interests of the international community to work cooperatively with China to help it to build confidence in an open international trading regime. Chinese accession to the WTO, and the implementation of the Uruguay Round trade negotiation are crucial to China's effective integration into the international system, and therefore to China's own acceptance of intimate linkages between domestic and international grain markets. Asia-Pacific leaders' commitment to Asia-Pacific free trade in Indonesia in November 1994, if it were implemented in the years ahead, would provide useful additional support.

Notes

1 Agricultural commodities accounted for large proportions in total exports in the pre-reform period in China. Those exports, however, were not based on assessment of comparative advantages and were planned by the government for the purpose of foreign exchange earnings (Huang Yiping 1993).
2 Quota prices were increased by 20.9 per cent for grain, 23.9 per cent for oil crops, 17 per cent for cotton, 21.9 per cent for sugar crops and 24.3 per cent for hog meat. The average increase for the quota prices was 17.1 per cent and premiums paid on above-quota delivery of grain and oil crops were raised from 30 per cent to 50 per cent of the quote prices. At the same time, retail prices of some agricultural products, excluding basic necessities as grains and edible oils, were also raised. A lump-sum of 5–8 yuan per month was paid to each urban resident as compensation (Lardy 1983a).
3 Lin (1992a), using a production function approach, concludes that the institutional reform – the shift from the production team system to the household responsibility system – alone produced 49 per cent of the farming output growth during 1978–84. Increases in purchase prices, on the other hand, contributed to 16 per cent of output growth. McMillan, Whalley and Zhu (1989) also find that 22 per cent of the increase in productivity in Chinese agriculture during 1978–84 was due to higher prices and 78 per cent to changes in the incentive scheme. In addition, they suggest that the incentive effects of the change from the pre-1978 communal system to the post-1978 responsibility system resulted in a 32 per cent increase in total factor productivity in agriculture. Similarly, Fan (1991) finds that institutional change contributed 27 per cent of agricultural growth during 1965–85.
4 To stabilise the grain market, the government sold some stocks at low prices and set an upper limit for grain sales by other marketing organisations.

5 According to one estimate by China's Ministry of Agriculture, farmers contributed 71 per cent of government revenue in 1957 and 76 per cent in 1965. This share fell over time, but it was still as high as 44 per cent in the late 1980s (information provided by Guo Shutian, Beijing).
6 World food prices in 1992 were, on average, only 3.6 per cent higher than those of 1978.
7 The likely distortion to domestic agricultural incentives would be particularly large, if China maintained self-sufficiency for grain, considering the fact that the greatest potential for grain output growth exists in the regions where economies are already well developed and where the opportunity costs for increasing grain output are high (Garnaut and Ma 1992a).

Regional issues

15　The grain economy of Guangdong: internationalisation or East Asian style protectionism?

Ross Garnaut and Ma Guonan

China is the largest grain consumer and producer in the world. It has 22 per cent of the world's population and produces 21 per cent of the world's cereal output. China is also the largest trading nation in the world grain market. Between 1985 and 1991 China's wheat imports averaged 13 per cent of the world's total traded volumes. The future direction of China's grain demand, supply and trade will have a profound influence on the international grain market.

The early liberalisation of the grain sector led to large increases in the volume of production, but was not problem free (Sicular 1988a). Guangdong province has been in the vanguard of China's reforms and open policies, including in agriculture. Guangdong's experiences in the past decade have served as something of a testing ground and inspiration for economy-wide reform (Lardy 1992a; Vogel 1989). It was among the first provinces to undertake major reforms on vegetable, fish, pork, grain and edible oil prices. Market forces have a much greater role in Guangdong's economy than elsewhere in China.

Guangdong is among the four highest-income provinces, although not yet the highest, and the fifth most populous province. It is by far the largest provincial economy in terms of GDP, and the nation's largest exporter. It is only eclipsed in openness and rate of growth by the small island province of Hainan, which was separated from Guangdong in 1987. Zhejiang and Jiangsu provinces in east China have had similar rates of growth but less international orientation over the whole reform period, and have not grown quite as rapidly as Guangdong in recent years.

Guangdong's economy has been increasingly integrated with the dynamic East Asian economies, especially Hong Kong. It is reported that one-quarter of Guangdong's GNP is realised through the international market and 80 per cent of its exports comprise manufactured goods (*Renmin ribao* [People's Daily] 6 March 1992).

Table 15.1 *Guangdong's share in the national economy (per cent), 1985 and 1991*

	1985[a]	1991
Population	5.4	5.6
Land area	1.9	1.9
Cultivated land	2.7	2.6
Fixed investment	7.6	9.2
GDP	7.0	9.0
Industrial output	6.1	8.9
Agricultural output	3.9	8.0
Retail sales	7.4	9.1
Exports	10.8	19.0
Imports	5.7	13.3
Grain output	4.2	4.3
Meat output[b]	5.6	6.0
Aquatic products output	15.5	16.7
Egg output	2.4	2.4

Notes:
[a] Adjusted to exclude Hainan before its separation in 1987.
[b] 'Meat output' refers to the sum of pork, beef and mutton.
Sources: Guangdong Statistical Department (1986 and 1992); SSB, ZTN (various issues).

Grain supply and demand in the reform period

Guangdong is a major grain-deficit province. In per capita terms, grain output is less than 80 per cent of the national average (table 15.2). It does, however, have the highest per capita physical potential for increasing grain production.[1]

Grain crops are predominantly paddy rice. Guangdong's grain yield during 1991 and 1992 averaged 4.8 tonnes per hectare, much higher than the nation's average of 3.9 tonnes per hectare (SSB, ZTN 1992). Per capita outputs of grain-intensive farm products were generally higher than the national average (table 15.2).

Guangdong's per capita food grain consumption is below the national average, and declined slightly between 1985 and 1992. Consumers have turned increasingly to high-quality rice, some of which is imported. More importantly, growth in indirect demand for grain has been strong.

Table 15.2 *Per capita output and consumption in Guangdong relative to China (national average = 1.00), 1985, 1986–9, 1990 and 1992*

	1985	Average 1986–9	1990	1992
Output				
Grain	0.79	0.78	0.76	0.72
Pork, beef and mutton	1.14	1.13	1.06	1.05
Poultry	3.67	3.23	2.75	2.74
Eggs	0.43	0.45	0.43	4.20
Aquatic products	2.90	3.07	3.00	2.87
Consumption				
Food grain	0.87	0.86	0.84	0.82
Pork, beef and mutton	1.04	1.07	1.08	1.06
Poultry	2.58	2.90	3.53	3.50
Eggs	0.39	0.40	0.45	0.49
Aquatic products	2.25	2.10	1.72	1.70

Source: Garnaut and Ma (1992a); SSB, ZTN (1993).

Guangdong's per capita consumption of meat and fish, as well as other animal products, is higher than the national average (table 15.2), and increasing rapidly. Between 1978 and 1991 pork consumption more than doubled, poultry more than trebled, and eggs increased by almost 500 per cent. These increases occurred despite the fact that Guangdong was the first province in the nation to remove most government price subsidies on meat, eggs, fish and vegetables. Stagnant or even falling direct human consumption of grain, together with sharp increases in the consumption of meat, fish and eggs, testify to the changing food demand of the increasingly affluent Guangdong consumers, and the dominant influence of income growth on higher-value food consumption.

Guangdong's rural food consumption is similar to 'urban' patterns in China's inland areas. This is related to the rapid industrialisation of rural Guangdong. Rural peasants in Guangdong consume more animal products than urban Shanxi (table 15.3). The one exception is eggs, reflecting different local dietary preferences. Average urban consumption of eggs in Guangdong was also below the national urban average.

This broad perspective on overall grain demand indicates some trends that may be important to the composition of grain demand growth in the future, and foreshadows the future pattern of grain demand for China as a whole.

The most important element of grain demand growth in Guangdong is

Table 15.3 *Comparison of consumption patterns, rural Guangdong and urban Shanxi, per capita per annum (kg), 1985 and 1989*

		Grain	Pork, beef and mutton	Poultry	Fresh eggs	Aquatic
1985	Rural Guangdong	256.1	12.6	3.4	1.2	8.4
	Urban Shanxi	200.4	11.1	0.5	6.3	1.4
1989	Rural Guangdong	260.2	15.2	4.1	1.7	9.0
	Urban Shanxi	195.7	13.4	1.1	7.8	2.8

Notes:
Unmilled grain.
Source: Guangdong Statistical Department (various issues); SSB, ZTN (various issues).

Table 15.4 *Sources of grain demand in Guangdong (per cent), 1980–9*

	1980	1983	1985	1988	1989
Human consumption	78.9	79.4	76.9	73.0	73.2
Feed use	14.6	15.7	18.3	22.4	22.4
Other uses	6.5	4.9	4.8	4.6	4.4

Source: Guangdong Statistical Department, Commerce Section (1990).

animal feed, the share of which in the province's total grain use rose from 14.6 per cent to 22.4 per cent between 1980 and 1989 (table 15.4). The relative importance of feed use in Guangdong's overall grain consumption is underestimated because Guangdong is a large net importer of grain-intensive products such as pork and eggs from other provinces (table 15.4). The strong growth in indirect grain consumption has important implications for projections of future demand as the whole of China becomes more affluent. The emphasis no longer lies in praising the success of feeding 1.2 billion people at the subsistence level. The questions have become: what is the quality of diet in relation to consumer preferences, and how much of the food that is demanded by consumers is efficiently and sensibly produced from domestic sources?

Guangdong's grain production increased rapidly in the early reform years, from 15 to 18 million tonnes between 1978 and 1984 (unmilled grain). But this strong momentum disappeared in the mid-1980s. The output level fell to, and fluctuated around, 16 to 17 million tonnes between 1984 and 1988 before it rebounded to 18 to 19 million tonnes during 1989

Table 15.5 *Grain production in Guangdong, 1978–92*

	1978	1984	1986	1988	1989	1991	1992
Output (million tonnes)	15.1	18.2	15.7	16.4	18.3	18.7	17.7
Areas sown to grain crops (million hectares)	5.1	4.2	3.8	3.7	4.0	3.8	3.6
Yields (kilograms/hectare)	2,980	4.350	4,100	4,380	4,620	4,970	4,874

Notes:
Unmilled grain.
Source: Guangdong Statistical Department (varous issues); SSB, ZTN (various issues).

Table 15.6 *Grain balance sheet in Guangdong province (million tonnes), 1980–9*

	1980	1985	1988	1989
(1) Human consumption	13.5	15.0	15.0	15.5
(2) Feed use	2.5	3.6	4.6	4.7
(3) Other uses	1.1	0.9	0.9	0.9
(4) Total consumption	17.1	19.5	20.6	21.2
(5) Grain output	16.8	16.0	16.4	18.3
(6) Minimum deficit	0.2	3.5	4.2	2.9
(7) Self-sufficiency rate (%)	98.2	82.1	79.6	86.3

Notes:
(4) = (1) + (2) + (3); (6) = (4)–(5); (7) = (5)/(4). All figures in this table are unmilled grain. 'Other uses' includes seed grain, industrial use and waste.
Source: Guangdong Statistical Department, Commerce Section (1990).

and 1991 (table 15.5). Grain output increases had their origins primarily in higher yields. Guangdong's area sown to grain crops fell by more than 20 per cent in the 1980s. In 1992, however, grain output, sown areas and yields all fell significantly from their 1991 peak levels, with output down by about 9 per cent (table 15.5). There were indications in early 1994 that there had been another sharp fall in output in 1993 by as much as 10 per cent from the 1992 level.

Guangdong's grain self-sufficiency rate dropped from 99 per cent in 1980 to around 80 per cent during 1985–8, implying an annual deficit of 3 to 4 million tonnes of unmilled grain (table 15.6). This amounts to about one-third of China's net grain imports during 1987–9. Note that this calculation fails to reflect the true size of the underlying grain deficit, as Guangdong has also been a major pork and egg deficit province. It has been estimated elsewhere that Guangdong's actual grain self-sufficiency, adjusted for inter-provincial animal product purchases, was about 75 per cent during 1989–90 (Garnaut and Ma 1992a). The ratio was much lower by 1993.

Responses to the grain deficit

Four strategies are available to the provincial government to close the gap between grain supply and demand in the province
   curtail overall grain demand
   increase output by artificially injecting more resources into the grain
      sector
   purchase more grain from grain surplus provinces through domestic
      trade
   reduce net exports or increase net imports of grain via international
      trade.
The first option is rarely adopted due to the dominant market role in Guangdong's economy. The second option of an autarkic policy is discussed in more detail later in the chapter. The third option has been exercised considerably. During the late 1980s more than 20 per cent of the province's total pork and egg consumption was supplied by other provinces. The fourth option was relied upon heavily through most of the 1980s.

In response to grain shortfalls, Guangdong's rice exports abroad fell from 200 thousand tonnes in 1980 to about 22 thousand tonnes in 1990 and 1991 (table 15.7). At the same time grain imports soared. In less than ten years, Guangdong has moved from being a net exporter to a net importer of grain. This occurred in a period when Guangdong's export of labour-intensive manufactured goods took off, leading the nation. But centralised controls over grain trade had a considerable effect on Guangdong's grain imports.

The deficits in grain and other farm products (mainly pork and eggs) were increasingly bridged through greater inflows from other surplus provinces, induced by Guangdong's higher market price levels. Net inflow via inter-provincial trade rose from 1.1 million tonnes of unmilled grain in 1980 to 3 million tonnes between 1985 and 1988, and 2 million tonnes in 1989.

Larger inter-provincial grain flows to Guangdong drove up market prices in the surplus provinces, raising the costs of procuring grain (and pork). If these costs had been passed on as higher negotiated transfer

Table 15.7 Guangdong's international exports and imports of grain (thousand tonnes), 1980–94

	1980	1985	1986	1987	1988	1989	1990	1991	1992	1993	1994
Grain imports	–	–	–	229	171	154	91	271	11750	7520	5500
Rice exports	204	119	89	78	35	58	22	23	950	1430	7530
Net import	–204	–119	–89	151	136	96	69	248	800	6090	–2030

Note:
Trade grain.
Source: Guangdong Statistical Department (various issues).

prices for additional purchases by Guangdong, inter-provincial trade would have expanded naturally.[2]

The higher grain costs in the surplus regions associated with sales to Guangdong at centrally controlled prices increased the fiscal burden for local governments (Lardy 1990). These governments sought to maintain a stable supply of low-priced grain to their local urban constituents and industries. Therefore, local governments had an interest in reducing the margin between market and state procurement prices by depressing market prices when grain supply was tight. They had the ability to do so because grain trade was largely monopolised by the state: large-scale grain trade across regions had to go through specialised grain trade departments before 1991.

Price distortion and the government's ability to monopolise and manipulate the grain market has caused 'chaos' in the marketplace in a number of dramatic episodes through the reform period. The strained transportation system and the associated high (including opportunity) costs of transport also adversely affected inter-regional trade in grain, and pushed some of the more internationally oriented coastal regions, notably Guangdong, increasingly towards the world market.

This is the context of reports about the 'grain wars': the closing of grain markets and the establishment of road blocks when there were poor harvests, as in 1988. State monopoly enabled the surplus regions to demand unrealistically high prices from grain-deficit regions such as Guangdong, or simply to refuse to sell. In 1988 a 4 per cent drop in Guangdong's grain output, coupled with the difficulties of securing grain through inter-regional trade, and rising demand caused by incomes growth and an accumulated influx of 5 million peasants into Guangdong from other provinces, raised market grain prices to unprecedented levels in the province. The overall grain retail price increased by 40 per cent in Guangdong in 1988. The market rice price doubled between January and December of 1988, reaching 1.05 yuan per kilogram. In October of the same year, the market rice price in Guangzhou shot above 4.0 yuan per kilogram. Yet, in the neighbouring province of Hunan, the market price for rice was only 0.37 yuan per kilogram (*Guangdong Price* No.2, 1989: 47–50; *China Price* No.2, 1990: 32).

Similar events also occurred in late 1993 when Guangdong's grain output fell for the second year in a row. This reduced high-quality grain stocks and drove up local grain prices by 30–40 per cent in November and December 1993. The province also encountered some difficulties in purchasing and transporting grain across provinces.

Even intervention by the central government failed to solve Guangdong's 'grain crisis'. Under intense pressure, the state in late 1988

Table 15.8 *Structural changes in Guangdong's economy (per cent), 1980, 1985 and 1992*

	1980	1985	1992
Grain share in total sown areas	77.1	71.6	66.3
Agricultural share in rural labour force	94.3	77.3	63.3
Agricultural share in GDP	33.8	31.1	23.4

Source: Guangdong Statistical Department (various issues).

permitted Guangdong to import grain, provided that Guangdong had the foreign exchange to pay for the imports. Guangdong's grain imports more than doubled and rice exports halved in 1988–9 (table 15.7). In 1991, Guangdong again increased its net grain imports substantially, to an historical high.

Some of Guangdong's authority to import grain was passed on to decentralised industrial areas within the province. Now that a pattern of provincial access to international markets has been established, it will not easily be withdrawn, at least in circumstances of high prices in China's grain-surplus provinces. Nevertheless, central government policies will remain a crucial factor in affecting the future process of internationalising the grain sector for Guangdong in particular and for China as a whole.

Autarky or free trade?

The option of autarky or self-sufficiency also ran into a wall created by the powerful trends in the province's economy. Over time, a larger share of resources has been attracted to the non-grain sectors of the Guangdong economy. An increasing proportion of Guangdong peasants have switched into cash crop production and non-farm employment. In ten years the share of the agricultural labour force in the total rural labour force fell by about 30 percentage points. The portion of Guangdong's sown areas devoted to grain crops dropped from 77 per cent in 1980 to 66 per cent in 1992 (table 15.8).

Market forces unleashed by economic reform worked on relative factor endowments to move Guangdong's economy towards a comparative advantage in producing sub-tropical crops (notably sugar cane and fruits) and certain live animal products (aquatic and poultry), as well as labour-intensive manufactured products. As a result, the agricultural share in Guangdong's GDP declined from 34 per cent to 23 per cent between 1980 and 1991, a process of rapid structural changes induced by market-oriented resource reallocation and by greater openness of the Guangdong economy. A high saving rate and strong capital formation were part of the process attracting people away from agriculture.

These are the fundamental economic forces behind the slowdown of grain output growth in the 1980s and early 1990s. A lower grain self-sufficiency ratio in Guangdong reflected not failures of the economic reforms or government policies, but a more efficient allocation of resources in the province's economy. As a result faster economic growth was promoted. Such an assessment is decisively at variance with the conventional views in the Chinese and international literature.

Faced by sluggish growth in grain output during the mid-1980s, the Guangdong government realised that choices had to be made as to the allocation of scarce resources across different sectors. It had to choose between pushing up the growth rate of grain output by manipulating prices and quantities of inputs, and allowing market forces to guide resource flows.

In the mid-1980s the strategy adopted by the Guangdong government was largely market oriented. Government controls and subsidies affecting the prices of most agricultural products other than grain and sugar were removed by the mid-1980s. For grain production, cash substitution for mandatory quota requirements for grain procurement was quietly accepted to allow peasants to decide on their own whether to withdraw from grain production. A targeted grain self-sufficiency ratio of around 70 to 75 per cent was formally proposed and integrated into the province's economic and social development strategy (Research Centre of Guangdong Provincial Government 1988).

Amidst Guangdong's grain crisis in late 1988 and early 1989, international market prices for rice increased significantly from the 1987 level. In response to regional trade barriers, political influence from the central government, and higher international prices, the Guangdong government raised the urban retail price of rice and the procurement prices of paddy rice, by 114 per cent and 30 per cent respectively (*Guangdong Price* No.2, 1989: 47). This was an attempt to limit the fiscal spill-over by reducing grain price subsidies to urban consumers, discouraging consumption and encouraging grain production. To raise the province's grain self-sufficiency rate, the practice of cash substitution for grain taxes was discontinued. The total sown areas for grain in Guangdong increased by 7 per cent between 1988 and 1990, reversing the earlier trend.

This injection of both resources and command controls, together with strong but distorted market signals in the form of high rice prices, raised Guangdong's grain self-sufficiency rate above 85 per cent during 1989 and 1990. With excessive stocks and a good grain harvest, Guangdong even tried to limit the grain inflow and delay acceptance of the planned grain transfer from the surplus regions where harvests were exceptionally good. Market prices plunged in 1989–90. Grain imports fell substantially in 1990. The opportunity costs of the higher self-sufficiency, in terms of foregone cash crops and industrial growth, was high.

The retreat into controls was revised again as part of the national grain market liberalisation and acceleration of price reform in 1991 and 1992. The declaration of Guangdong as a successful model of market-oriented reform by senior leader Deng Xiaoping in early 1992 makes the return to agricultural controls of the kind employed in 1989–90 unlikely while current political conditions prevail. Indeed, Guangdong, with Hainan, was held up as the case of irreversible movement to a free grain market in 1992. The more influential role of market forces was one cause of the divergent trends between grain production in Guangdong and the nation: a decline of 10 per cent in the province and a rise of 3 per cent in China in 1993. Nevertheless, the grain price surge at the end of 1993 again tested the provincial government's willingness and determination to remain on the path of a market-oriented grain policy. At the National People's Congress meeting in Beijing in March 1994, there were calls by senior officials for Guangdong to lift its grain output. And the provincial government is again under pressure to inject more resources into the grain sector due to limited access to international grain markets and higher world rice prices caused by Japanese imports.

Comparative advantage

The policy swings reflect, at least in part, a lack of clear understanding of the economic costs associated with grain self-sufficiency and of the benefits of allocating scarce economic resources according to comparative advantage.

In the literature, unfavourable prices are often blamed for the stagnation of grain output in China during the second half of the 1980s. Different views on the causes of stagnation have very different policy implications. If indeed low prices were the main factor, then it might at first sight, and in isolation from other economic considerations, seem desirable to raise grain prices. This would induce more resources into the grain sector. But the important questions are whether all regions should try to achieve higher grain self-sufficiency, and whether domestic prices should reflect the opportunity costs of using resources in rice production.

An attempt is made here to shed some light on these important issues by analysing the regional and international comparative advantages of grain production in Guangdong. The central idea is that given market allocation

Table 15.9 *Indexes of regional crop comparative advantages for major rice-producing provinces[a] (national average = 1)*

	Rate of return on rice production[b]	Ratio of per hectare output values of cash crops to grain crops[c]
Guangdong	0.2	1.4
Jiangsu	1.0	0.9
Zhejiang	0.7	0.8
Anhui	2.3	0.6
Fujian	0.4	1.5
Jiangxi	0.9	0.6
Hubei	1.0	0.7
Hunan	0.6	0.7
Guangxi	0.3	1.5
Sichuan	1.3	1.1

Notes:
[a] Both indicies are normalised by national averages.
[b] Rate of return is defined as the ratio of gross profit to total variable cost. The latter excludes rents accruing to land and part of the interest cost on capital. The former is the difference between gross receipt and total variable cost (1988 figure).
[c] 1989 figures.
Sources: Almanac of China's Agriculture (1990); Fang (1992).

and different relative resource endowments, economies are better off from trade through specialisation according to their comparative advantage. Here the economic potential – rather than technical potential through expanded use of irrigation, fertiliser, machine and seed varieties – is stressed.

Guangdong's rate of return on rice production is the lowest among the major rice-producing provinces in China (table 15.9). Rice production is quite labour intensive. Rates of return are strongly influenced by the costs of labour which are lowest in provinces where alternative employment opportunities are least developed, such as Anhui and Sichuan.

Guangdong's comparative advantages lie not in grain crops but in cash crops, at least within the crop-growing sub-sector of agriculture. The ratio of output values of cash to grain crops in Guangdong is considerably higher than most of the listed provinces and also the nation's average (table 15.9).

Production of paddy rice in Guangdong earns the lowest returns among all major farm products, in terms of both gross profit per hectare and the ratio of profits to costs (table 15.10).

Table 15.10 *Returns to different farm crops in Guangdong, 1988 (national average = 1)*

	Profit per hectare	Rate of return
Paddy rice	0.1	0.2
Peanuts	0.8	0.6
Sugar cane	0.8	0.5
Oranges	2.3	1.2
Mandarin oranges	1.5	0.8
Tea	0.7	0.4
Pond fish farming	2.1	1.0
Pig raising	n.a.	0.4
Chicken farming	n.a.	0.7
Milk	n.a.	1.0

Note:
See table 13.9 for definitions.
Source:Almanac of China's Agriculture (1990).

That is to say, even if prices for paddy rices were artificially propped-up relative to other crops in all provinces, Guangdong still would not enjoy regional comparative advantage in producing paddy rice. It would still gain from shifting its resources out of rice production at the margin. This is not surprising as Guangdong's relative land endowment, as measured by cultivated land per capita, is only half of the nation's average, and grain generally is more land intensive than other crops and economic activities. The higher opportunity cost of labour, due to more off-farm employment opportunities adds to the argument.

Therefore, the relative stagnation of grain output for Guangdong during the mid-1980s was mainly a result of more efficient resource reallocation across sectors, taking account of Guangdong's factor endowment, of greater internationalisation in resource allocation, and greater allocation of resources by market forces. It was not a failure of economic reforms. On the contrary, it was part of the story of Guangdong's fast and export-oriented economic growth.

Trade theory suggests that rapid industrialisation competes for labour and capital resources with the traditional sectors. Guangdong has been embarking on rapid export-oriented industrialisation, and aims to narrow the gap in incomes between itself and other East Asian newly industrialising economies. Will Guangdong, as one of China's front-runners in market reforms and in opening up to the outside world, internationalise its grain sector further or repeat the past experiences of East Asian-style agricultural protectionism? This raises the issue of comparative advantage in the world market.

International comparative advantage is not static. It changes with relative income levels (labour costs), and the relative pace of capital accumulation. There are a number of standard methods for empirical analysis of comparative advantage, but these often demand large data requirements. The simple approach employed here compares the experiences of Taiwan in the 1960s and 1970s and Guangdong in the 1980s and early 1990s.

The comparison is likely to be very fruitful because, during Taiwan's rapid growth and industrialisation period of the 1970s, agricultural protectionism gradually became one of the key features of its economy. The nominal rate of protection for rice in Taiwan changed from negative in the 1960s to positive in the early 1970s, and rose rapidly afterwards. It was –8 per cent during 1960–4, and –13 per cent in 1965–9, then 4 per cent in 1970–4, 58 per cent in 1975–9, and 144 per cent in 1980–2 (Anderson and Hayami 1986: 22). The switch from taxing to subsidising agriculture was quite swift.

Assuming that both Guangdong and Taiwan have similar factor endowments and access to the same underlying technology in paddy rice production, it is interesting to compare chemical fertiliser application intensities and rice yields in the two economies (table 15.11). Guangdong's average fertiliser application intensity rose swiftly, from 117 kilograms per hectare in 1978 to 192 kilograms per hectare in 1985, and further to 309 kilograms per hectare in 1991, reaching Taiwan's level of application intensity during the early 1970s when agricultural protectionism in the latter began to set in. As increased use of fertiliser has been found to be an important source of agricultural growth in China since the second half of the 1980s (Lin 1992a), the pursuit of higher grain output by substantially greater fertiliser application intensity may be profitable only if the Guangdong grain sector is protected either by a tariff or by government subsidy, as was the case in Taiwan from the point in its economic history that corresponds to Guangdong today.

Guangdong's rice yield in 1991 had already reached the level of Taiwan in the mid-1980s (table 15.11). The relatively high yield in Guangdong is partly explained by the now-defunct government strategy to increase grain output by adopting high-yield but low-quality hybrid rice varieties at the expense of value-added. Another possible reason is Guangdong's higher labour intensity in rice production compared with Taiwan.

Assuming that rice production has the same average fertiliser application intensities as the crop sectors in both Guangdong and Taiwan, rice to

Table 15.11 *Rice yields and fertiliser application: comparison of Guangdong (1978–91) and Taiwan (1969–90)*

| | Guangdong | | | Taiwan | |
Year	Fertiliser application (kg/hectare)	Rice yield (tonne/hectare)	Year	Fertiliser application (kg/hectare)	Rice yield (tonne/hectare)
1978	117	2.47	1960	162	2.49
1980	160	2.94	1965	238	3.04
1985	192	3.26	1970	295	3.17
1988	257	3.15	1975	404	3.16
1989	282	3.69	1980	480	3.69
1990	286	3.82	1985	490	3.86
1991	309	3.88	1990	468	3.92

Note:
Rice is measured as brown rice.
Sources: Guangdong Statistical Department (various issues); SSB, ZTN (various issues).

fertiliser ratios in the two economies can be calculated by dividing rice yield by average fertiliser application intensity. Guangdong's ratio was 12.6 in 1990, a sharp fall from 17.0 in 1985, whereas in Taiwan the ratio was 12.8 in 1965 and 11.0 in 1970. Falling rice to fertiliser ratios are evidence of diminishing returns in fertiliser use. Taking into consideration that high-yield and low-quality hybrid rice varieties account for about 20 per cent of Guangdong's rice production output, Guangdong's rice to fertiliser ratio is not much higher than the 1970 level in Taiwan. Also, Guangdong may be more labour intensive in applying fertiliser, implying a higher fertiliser to rice ratio than in Taiwan.

Taiwan's current low rice to fertiliser ratio is supported by its protection policy in grain trade. The comparison suggests that in the early 1990s Guangdong is at a critical crossroad of either achieving a higher grain self-sufficiency ratio by government protection or opting for free grain trade in both domestic and international markets.

Resisting protectionism, the next five years

The Guangdong case provides a number of insights which are helpful to projections of future paths of policy, supply and demand in the Chinese grain economy.

First, Guangdong's total grain demand has continued to grow strongly, despite relatively high incomes, and despite large increases in the relative price of grain. Income effects have overwhelmed price effects, but mainly through demand for animal-feed use of grain. Growth in grain demand was more differentiated in type and quality of grain, and realised through a wider range of institutions, than the established pattern of demand in Guangdong or in China as a whole. Increases in demand were enhanced by inter-provincial migration to Guangdong's dynamic industrial economy.

Second, on the supply side, despite Guangdong having a high physical potential for raising grain yields and production, greater exposure to the international economy, market-oriented reform and the reduction in price distortions tended to reduce grain production. The principal agent of this reduction in production was the diversion of rural land and labour into alternative uses. High savings in Guangdong flowed through market mechanisms into highly profitable service and industrial invest-ments, with disproportionately little into grain production, further siphoning labour away from the grain sector. These powerful forces, with their logic of internationalisation, reached their apex in 1993, when GDP growth of 20 per cent was associated with a fall of 10 per cent in grain production.

It has been shown that Guangdong's relative returns to grain production are among the lowest in China's major rice producing provinces, implying that Guangdong does not enjoy a regional comparative advantage in grain production. The stagnation of grain output growth and the declining grain self-sufficiency ratio in Guangdong during the late 1980s were not consequences of 'errors' of the Chinese economic reforms, but a reflection of a very promising start in more efficient resource allocation through market mechanisms and according to Guangdong's comparative advantage. Improved resource allocation in turn stimulated strong overall growth of the province's economy.

Third, disconcertingly, the Guangdong experience shows that the logic of reform and internationalisation, at least in circumstances of rapidly increasing domestic grain deficits and rising international prices, can be challenged effectively by grain protectionism, even in the most outward-looking of China's large provinces. The Guangdong retreat into grain protectionism during 1989–90 may have been a reflection of the weakness of political commitment on the part of the national leadership to reform during the macroeconomic contractions of 1988 and 1989. More likely, it indicates that the political economy of Chinese grain policy is not immune from pressures towards East Asian-style inward orientation. This reality must be assimilated into the international comprehension of the Chinese grain outlook. It is too soon to know the outcome of the challenge to market-oriented grain policies that emerged in December 1993.

The comparative study of Taiwan and Guangdong reveals that if Guangdong intends to achieve higher self-sufficiency in grain, it needs substantially to boost its grain production through government protection. As Taiwan's experiences in the early 1970s indicate, the time span between taxing agriculture to protecting agriculture was quite short. Guangdong in the 1990s is growing more rapidly than Taiwan in the 1970s, so the time from taxation to protection of agriculture, if this were Guangdong's course, would be even more compressed. Guangdong is currently at an important crossroads of heading towards either free trade or grain protectionism. What is happening in Guangdong is likely to provide an important leading indicator of what will happen in China's grain sector as a whole.

The East Asian experiences in the 1960s and 1970s show that often when there were problems in the grain sector, grain protectionism was introduced first tentatively, and then became institutionalised. Once grain protectionism set in, it would be likely to persist for a long time, mainly owing to vested interest groups (Anderson and Hayami 1986). The grain price-hike in late 1993 and the government reaction to the price change could test the will of the government in advancing market reforms. The next five years in Guangdong will reveal the answer to the fateful question: will China opt for open, market-oriented agriculture, or will it follow Japan, Taiwan and Korea into agricultural protectionism?

Notes

1 Measured as a ratio of actual to theoretical physical maximum grain yields, Guangdong was ranked by Chinese agricultural engineers as having the second highest potential for increasing its grain yields. In 1988 this ratio for Guangdong was only 26 per cent (Food Study Group 1991).
2 The surplus provinces were always unhappy about the low state-set prices for fixed quota, inter-regional grain transfers.

16 Grain production and regional economic change

Li Qingzeng, Andrew Watson and Christopher Findlay

Grain transfer between provinces and regions has long been a major issue in China's agricultural policy (Lardy 1990). Grain has to be transferred from the major producing areas to the large urban centres and it has always been necessary to adjust for varietal composition in regional supplies and to compensate for the vagaries of weather and local fluctuations in output. The appropriate balance between grain for human consumption and for animals has been an important issue with priority consistently given to human consumption.

Since 1978, the structure of grain production, pricing and marketing has passed through several phases of reform (Lin, chapter 2; Huang, chapter 3). Economic growth, by transforming both demand and supply, has added a different dimension of change. In terms of demand, increases in income have encouraged a change in consumer's diets (Garnaut and Ma, chapter 4). As a consequence, the proportion of grain consumed directly is declining and that consumed through animal products is increasing. This change has consequences for both regional transfers within China and for the structure of China's international grain trade.

In terms of supply, peasant households are now sharply aware of their opportunity costs. Fluctuations in grain production since 1984 have, in part, reflected producer's desire to move to higher-value crops. The management of grain production now has to take into account producer incentives, and, given the problems of handling this issue successfully in a semi-reformed economy, it is not surprising, after a brief period of relaxation, that governments throughout China in the late 1980s again shifted towards greater coercion in grain production through the system of fixed contracts. These supply-side effects have been most marked in the more developed coastal regions, where the people-to-land ratio is lowest and the opportunity costs of labour and other inputs are highest (Ministry of Agriculture 1989a: 459–73). It was not until 1991–2 when grain

220   Li Qingzeng, A. Watson and C. Findlay

production was once more stable that policy-makers again began experimenting with radical reforms to the grain marketing system.

Inevitably, these changes have had a major impact on grain relationships between provinces and regions. The regional structure of output and demand has changed, there have been shifts in the variety of grain output, and the central government's ability to manage grain flows has weakened. Furthermore, fluctuations in output and problems with transport have generated significant practical problems for grain handling. Understanding and solving these problems requires a study of the structure of grain production and demand by different varieties and regions and an analysis of the production-marketing regions of China and the inter-regional grain transfer system.

Most analyses of these issues in the past have focused on provincial data. Given that statistics are collected at a provincial level, this approach is in many ways inevitable. Furthermore, grain transfers have important implications for provincial budgets and thence for regional political relationships. Nevertheless, the broader regional relationships beyond provincial boundaries are also of concern, as these can be used to illustrate some of the fundamental processes taking place in China as economic growth occurs. In effect, differential rates of growth across China are transforming local supply and demand. This has a knock-on effect on the structure of the rural economy.

For simplicity of analysis, the economic regions defined in China's Seventh Five-Year Plan (1986–90) are adopted. The country is divided into the eastern, western and middle regions, according to the economic and technical development level of each region, its geographical conditions and resources (map 16.1).

The changing structure of grain production

Since the mid-1970s particularly in the period following the start of reforms in 1978 the total area sown to grain has fallen (figure 16.1).

The rate of growth of grain output declined slightly in the period leading up to commencement of the reforms, then grew rapidly between 1978 and 1985, slowed again thereafter and then recovered in 1991. The causes of the slowdown in the growth of grain output in the second half of the 1980s have attracted considerable research interest (Lin 1989a; Fan 1991). Output growth is a combination of input growth and productivity changes. Contributors to productivity growth in the period to 1984 included the introduction of the household responsibility system in conjunction with price reforms and the increased scope for regional specialisation. The most important contributor to input growth was fertiliser.

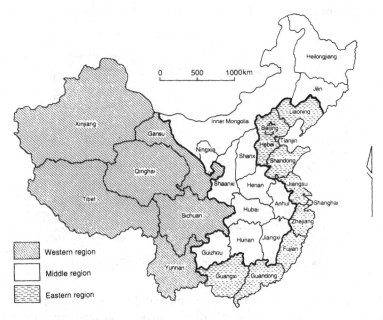

Map 16.1   Economic regions in China

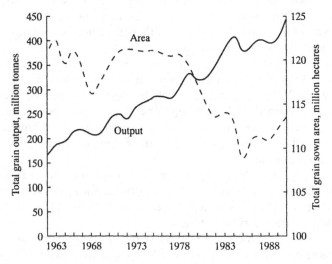

Figure 16.1   **Total grain output** (LHS) and total grain sown area (RHS), 1963–90

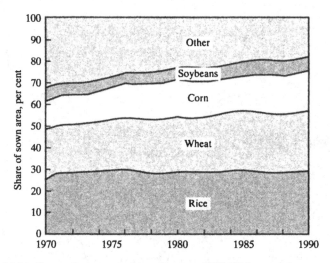

Figure 16.2   Share of sown area by grain type, 1970–90 (per cent)

After 1984 the introduction of the household responsibility system was completed so there was no scope for it to make a further contribution to productivity growth. Labour and land inputs into crop production fell and the use of fertiliser increased, but more slowly than in the previous five years. Price changes and the scope for regional specialisation continued to make a contribution to output growth. In addition to these changes in total grain output and total sown area, there have been important changes in the composition of grain output.

From the early 1950s through to the 1970s, areas sown with rice and wheat were broadly similar but the productivity of rice was far higher than that of wheat.[1] This is an indication of the greater land intensity of wheat production. Given the relatively small per capita land endowment, especially in the coastal provinces, the land intensity of wheat represents an important influence on the likely pattern of China's comparative advantage in various grains.

By the early 1970s, the composition of grain production had started to change. The importance of wheat and corn in sown area had increased and that of coarse grains (except for corn) had declined (figure 16.2). Of these, the reduction was largest for millet.

During the 1980s the sown acreage shares (output shares) of rice and soybeans remained at the levels of the 1970s, and were around 29 per cent (43 per cent) and 7 per cent (3 per cent) respectively (figures 16.2 and 16.3). Corn area sown (output) increased to 19 per cent (20 per cent) from about 15 per cent (17 per cent). Wheat area sown (output) also increased rapidly,

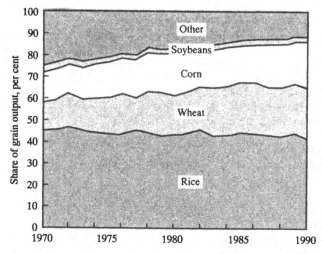

Figure 16.3   Share of total grain output by type, 1970–90 (per cent)

rising to more than more than 26 per cent (22 per cent) from less than 22 per cent (13 per cent) during the 1970s. Over the decade of the 1980s, therefore, the structure of sown area and output of the various grain crops continued to change.

These changes are consistent with expected changes in the pattern of household spending that occur with rising income levels. In an open economy, these shifts in demand would have been accommodated by changes in trade patterns. However, barriers to trade in grain and price regulation within China mean that world prices do not rule automatically in all markets. Domestic demand factors therefore have a closer association with changes in the output mix.

Overall, the long-term processes of economic growth in China have generated consistent change in the structure of national grain production. The changing structure reflects the dynamic economic relationships between the grains involved, the priorities of government policy and planned inputs and the changing nature of technology. The national picture, however, inevitably disguises the extent to which the aggregate changes have been brought about by marked variations in the provincial and regional structure of grain production (Crook 1991).

Under the collective system, such change was driven by the priorities of the plan system. Since the reforms, the impact of new relative prices, new marketing arrangements, provincial preferences and greater freedoms for producers can be expected to have added new layers of complexity to this issue.

Table 16.1 *Resource endowments by region, 1987*

	Eastern	Middle	Western
Grassland area per head (*mu* per thousand)	438	3,758	14,856
Arable land area per head (*mu* per thousand)	1,058	1,644	1,372
Irrigated area (% of arable area)	62	38	43
Index of machine power per *mu* of arable land (Eastern = 100)	100	54	42
Fertiliser use (tonnes per *mu*)	0.086	0.048	0.040
Index of per capita income (Eastern = 100)	100	60	48
Total population (M)	443	383	248

Source: Ministry of Agriculture (1989b).

The geographical distribution of major grain crops

The relative economic importance of agriculture usually declines with growth (Anderson 1990; Martin and Warr 1991). The focus here is on regional differences in the performance of the agricultural sector and their implications for domestic and international trade. Regional differences in factor endowments and their impact on grain production and trade are therefore of interest. Clearly, for example, rates of regional capital accumulation vary, and the extent of this variation will increase as the pace of structural economic change in the major regions diverges. This will inevitably influence production choices.

There were significant differences in key factor endowments by region in the latter half of the 1980s (table 16.1, map 16.1). Endowments per capita of grassland in western China were four times those in eastern China. The endowment of arable land per head was also relatively low in eastern China. Agricultural production technology is similar in middle and western China, in terms of irrigated area, use of machine power and fertiliser. In eastern China, these indicators are about twice as high. A greater degree of capital intensity in production is reflected in an index of average per capita incomes for the three regions. This index is about 66 per cent higher in the eastern region than in the middle region and twice as high as in western China. Income disparities of this size (given the land endowments per head) indicate substantial differences in capital endowments. Differential capital endowments, in turn, reflect the different capital intensities of agricultural production.

The eastern region had a much larger rural industry sector during the 1980s and experienced more rapid structural change (table 16.2). The agricultural share of output fell by 44 per cent compared with 22-9 per cent in the other two regions between 1980 and 1991.

Regional grain sown acreage and output

Data on changes in the regional shares of sown area and grain output illustrate two points: changes have been small, and to the extent that changes have occurred, the shift is slightly in favour of the middle region (appendix tables 16.4 and 16.5).

While the extent of change has been small, however, the direction of those changes is of interest and may be an indicator of future events. The general decline in total sown acreage has been more marked in the eastern region. The western region was the only region to experience long-term growth in grain sown acreage but this trend has apparently been reversed since reforms began.

The geographical distribution of grain crops inevitably influences the distribution of grain output. In the period 1978 to 1987 output in all three regions tended to increase although the relative speed of increase varied across regions. Growth was fastest in the middle region, where total output increased by 40.3 per cent between 1978 and 1987.

In effect, the decline in sown acreage did not result in a decline in output. Rather, improvements in productivity per unit area ensured increases in total output. Growth was not experienced evenly in each of the regions. The eastern region's share in total output fell by 1.7 percentage points and the western region's declined by 1.5 percentage points. By contrast, the middle region's share in total output rose by 3.2 percentage points.

In the western region the long-term increase in grain sown area was closely linked to a huge amount of land reclamation. The grain yield per unit area is not very high, however, and natural and climatic conditions are comparatively bad. In 1987 the grain area share of the region was 22.5 per cent of the entire country, but the output share was only 19.6 per cent. In the eastern region, the grain area in 1987 was 35.1 per cent of whole country and yet the output was 39.4 per cent (Ministry of Agriculture, Policy and Law Department 1989: 322-7).

While the eastern region was able to achieve major increases in land

Table 16.2 Changes in the composition of rural gross value of output, 1980, 1987 and 1991 (per cent)

	Eastern region			Middle region			Western region		
	1980	1987	1991	1980	1987	1991	1980	1987	1991
Agriculture	61.2	40.4	34.1	74.3	53.1	59.1	80.3	66.9	62.3
Rural industry	26.4	44.3	53.7	14.1	30.5	24.1	10.1	18.8	23.7
Rural building	6.7	8.2	6.1	6.7	6.2	7.4	5.1	6.1	5.2
Rural transport	1.7	3.0	2.5	1.8	5.2	4.0	1.3	3.6	4.3
Rural commerce	4.0	4.1	3.6	3.1	4.9	4.8	3.2	4.6	4.4
Gross value of output (billion yuan)	137.9	543.5	142.8	93.4	501.3	276.5	47.9	132.1	256.3

Source: SSB (1988: 27–8; 1992: 59).

productivity, the shift out of grain production tended to reduce its aggregate role. The growth in output in the west was much lower and its aggregate role tended to decline. The gains made in the middle region were thus vital for China's grain economy. This structural change reflects the economic forces at work in the different regions. A particular issue, in the longer term, is the increasing pressure associated with economic growth in eastern China to divert inputs out of grain production into industrial and other commercial activity.

In 1985 China's grain production decreased considerably. The decline in the middle region was biggest, at 7 per cent, and accounted for 42.6 per cent of the national fall. Unlike the eastern and western regions, which remained below their previous highest production levels of 1984, however, by 1987 the middle region had surpassed its 1984 high. This region therefore has a significant grain supply resilience and occupies a pivotal position in China's grain production (Ministry of Agriculture 1989b: 327). This has important implications for China's regional grain trade.

While the focus so far on sown acreage and output has enabled the identification of some significant regional variations, the use of aggregate grain production has obscured some important elements of these changes. An example of this can be found in rice production. Although the south is the major rice production area, over the long term relative growth rates in the north have been higher than those in the south and the north's increase in the share of total output has also been larger (Chinese Academy of Agricultural Science 1989: 51).

Changes of this kind reflect both the national process of shifting from coarse to better grains and improvements in seeds, irrigation and technology. Many of these changes, however, were initiated during the plan period when resource allocation and acreage plans were driven by administrative decision rather than by prices and market forces. *A priori* it is reasonable to assume that the forces influencing this issue will change during the process of economic reform.

Supply behaviour was affected directly by the introduction of the production responsibility system, and the reforms to marketing which diversified the channels of distribution and created a mix of plan, negotiated and free market prices (Li Qingzeng, Zhou and Gao 1988). Given subsidised urban consumption and, in some areas, subsidised producers, and government attempts to enforce grain sales contracts at low prices, returns to grain producers have been relatively low. The effect has been to encourage diversification of production and a shift of resources towards non-agricultural activities.

These forces acted in different ways in different regions. Along the densely populated eastern coast, with its large urban populations, developed infrastructure and low people-to-land ratios, the effects were most strongly evident. It is in these areas that rural enterprises have developed most rapidly and the relative decline in the significance of grain production has been most marked. In the less-developed middle and western regions, the changes are taking place more slowly. To some extent, the declining relative importance of the western region may reflect the high costs of developing grain production at a time when the returns for grain are less attractive than those for animal husbandry.

The combination of changes in demand and supply has worked to bring about changes in both the varieties of grain produced and the regional distribution of production. And these changes, while accentuated by the reforms, have in some ways been occurring since 1949. In the current situation, however, they present new challenges to both central and local governments. In strategic terms, they require an evaluation of the relative importance of domestic production and imports. If the Chinese government recognises the nature of the economic forces at work and accepts that grain production in the eastern region has become increasingly constrained by the emergence of other economic uses for land, labour and capital, it may decide to develop policies to help the middle region. It will also have to consider the nature and problems of inter-regional transfers, some of which require the movement of different varieties of grain over long distances. Against these issues, it will have to balance the relative value of importing grain for consumption in the eastern regions. Even though the Chinese government has long been wary of reliance on imports for both strategic and economic reasons, such imports may save on transport and handling costs and may also help overcome any economic problems at the regional and provincial level caused by inter-regional transfers.

Regional grain transfers

In terms of regional grain supplies, at the start of the 1980s the eastern region was in deficit, the middle region in surplus and the western region self-sufficient.[2] Because grain production and marketing districts are different from general economic regions, however, their definition require further refinement. Furthermore, because provinces, cities and autonomous regions are the basic units in China's grain distribution, the classification of production and marketing regions cannot be separated from China's current administrative regions. Accordingly, the three general economic regions can be subdivided into various production-marketing districts as follows

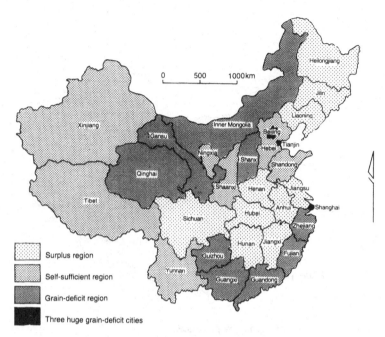

Map 16.2   Grain production and marketing regions in China

surplus provinces – three in the northeast and seven in the middle south
self-sufficient provinces – two in the east, two in the middle and three in
    the west
deficit regions – the three major cities plus five provinces in the south
    and south-east (four coastal provinces plus Guizhou) and four
    provinces in the north.

After 1981, with both the increase in grain production and growth in
demand, the volume of inter-provincial transfers increased greatly, leading
to increased pressures on transport capacity. Grain flows increased, but
transport capacity was far from adequate to meet total demand. Railway
transport accounted for most grain transfers, but normally only met 70 per
cent of planned movements, with the result that grain could not be transferred when required. When grain supplies were good and provinces were
looking for ways to export their surplus, they often encountered practical
difficulties. The extent to which these transfers occur, however, also
depends on the incentives facing provincial governments.

The changing pattern of regional production by grain type has become
a major issue in the domestic grain trade as the variations in regional economic growth and structural change work their way through the economy

Map 16.3   Rice self-sufficiency by province, 1988

and encourage still greater levels of specialisation and change in local production patterns.

The surplus, deficit and self-sufficient status of provinces for rice, wheat
and maize in 1988 are represented in maps 16.3, 16.4 and 16.5. This situation dictated the likely inter-provincial flows by grain type (Jiangsu,
Anhui, Hubei, Hunan and Jiangxi).

Inter-provincial grain flows are complex and the potential exists for significant changes in provincial relationships should the mix of provincial
output change. Clearly, this will also affect provincial financial flows and
inter-provincial economic relationships depending on the prices operating
in the market through which the grain transfers occur. The situation can
thus give rise to administrative intervention in market transfers in order to
protect local interests, such as occurred in the 'grain wars' of the late
1980s.

The 'grain wars'

Like the other commodity 'wars' of the 1980s in China, the so-called grain
war reflected the conflict between differing local needs and priorities and
the forces acting on the market. Inter-provincial grain transfers can have a

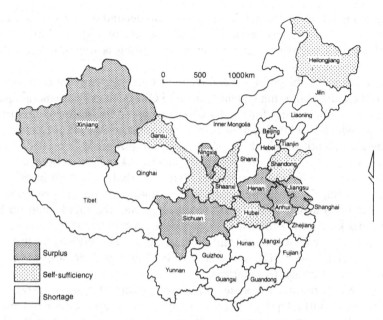

Map 16.4   Wheat self-sufficiency by province, 1988

Map 16.5   Maize self-sufficiency by province, 1988

strong impact on provincial finances and also depend on local infrastructure and other support services. The willingness of local authorities to facilitate and participate actively in grain trading is thus influenced by many factors.

The origins of the grain war and its impact on inter-regional grain flows lie in the grain marketing system reform. Li Qingzeng (1991) demonstrates that these reforms have followed a series of cycles. The state procurement system, which had lasted for 30 years, was abolished in 1985. At that time there were plentiful supplies of grain due to output growth post-1978 and a rapid increase in imports, averaging nearly 14 million tonnes a year between 1978 and 1984. It appeared, therefore, that the old problem of a 'grain shortage' had disappeared, and the state procurement system was dismantled. Further evidence of this change was the rapid build-up in grain stocks. Another force for reform was the commitment of the state to take all grain available at guaranteed state prices. This created a substantial financial burden. The solution was to allow a greater proportion of grain to flow through free markets.

In 1985, therefore, the state shifted to a contract system of buying grain, and contract prices were lower than previously. Grain not purchased through the contract system was sold through the market. The good harvest in 1984 and the drop in state guaranteed prices meant that more grain entered the market, and in 1985 free market prices for grain fell. This effect became more marked as the state tried to clear some of its stocks. Producers now had greater autonomy and they responded to the relative price changes. As a consequence, grain output fell rapidly (figure 16.3). As might be expected, the decline in grain supplies in subsequent years meant that market prices again started to rise. The perception among policy-makers was that grain was 'short' once more (imports had also fallen). Their response was to return to the old procurement system. Contracts were no longer negotiated and were replaced instead by fixed obligations.

This cycle in reform was made more likely because of the use of a double-track marketing system (Li Qingzeng 1991). The two components of the marketing system can be seen as the 'dead' part, grain purchased by the state through contract and mainly supplied to urban residents and industry, and the 'live' part, grain traded on the free market. The argument of the policy-makers was that grain was such a special commodity that some should be traded through a controlled marketing system, at least in the interim. The long-run ideal was to have the live part take over the dead part. But there were major problems in having the two systems operating side-by-side.

One problem was the ever-present incentive to divert supplies from the dead to the live part of the market, thereby encouraging 'corruption'. Another was that, as the central government tried to live up to its commitment to reform by reducing the amounts of grain purchased by contract, it was simultaneously concerned about the risk of not having access to all the grain required to satisfy urban and industrial demand. So it also assigned purchase obligations to local governments. They were supposed to buy grain according to local market conditions. But the local governments then became concerned about the risks of not meeting their targets and they turned their purchases into mandatory obligations. Central compulsory procurement of grain was replaced by systems of local compulsory procurement. Peasants tried to evade this new system and local governments responded by setting up road blocks in an attempt to restrict grain 'exports' (Lardy 1990). Provincial governments in grain surplus regions were also concerned (and their expectations would have been fulfilled) that increased trade in grain would push up local grain prices. This would have reduced the real incomes of local urban consumers and the profits of local industry which used grain as a raw material. These problems contributed to an apparent decline in inter-regional grain trade between 1986 and 1987 (Lardy 1990). The consequence was conflict between local governments anxious to control supplies and producers wishing to gain access to higher priced markets.

After 1985, documents issued by the central government repeatedly emphasised that, once state purchasing targets had been met, grain could be traded freely (Li Qingzeng 1991). They also required local governments to guarantee normal market trading in grain. Many provincial governments, however, especially those with grain surpluses, tried to prevent normal market flows. They established grain inspection stations in order to prevent grain flowing into neighbouring provinces and also tried to enforce maximum purchase prices. The result was conflict between inspectors and farmers dealing in grain.

Chuxian prefecture in Anhui, for example, is a grain-surplus area bordering Jiangsu.[3] In 1988 market prices were as much as 0.12–0.26 yuan per kilo higher in Jiangsu than in Anhui. The Anhui farmers thus preferred to sell their surplus in Jiangsu. In order to stem the outflow, the Anhui authorities established 55 grain checkpoints on the roads leading into Jiangsu. The farmers tried to avoid the checkpoints by sending their trucks through during the night. On 19 December 1988, for example, more than one hundred trucks forced their way through the checkpoints, and only six agreed to stop for inspection. Two days later another truck drove at speed through a checkpoint and, when it was chased by inspectors, it forced a motorcycle off the road and several people were injured. Although the authorities in Chuxian prefecture made an annual agreement with their neighbours to fix the grain purchasing price, the conflict of interests meant that the price was never implemented. The conflict was then expressed through the scramble to control the market. A truck-load of grain sold in Jiangsu could bring a profit of 1,000 yuan. The same truck stopped by a checkpoint and forced to sell at the local fixed purchase price made a loss of 3,000 yuan, a total price gap of 4,000 yuan. Farmers trading in grain were willing to risk their lives for the profit involved.

The pricing formula for inter-provincial transfers also had an effect on the size of such trade. In 1982 the government permitted the sale of grain between provinces outside the plan at negotiated prices. This contributed to the growth in inter-provincial transfers but a large part of this trade still took place at planned prices. Exporting regions complained that they received too little for their grain under plan transfers, and the reforms appeared to have been insufficient to encourage participation in such transfers. The centre was reluctant to raise these plan transfer prices or to permit too rapid a growth in out-of-plan transfers because it was subsidising the purchase of grain by the deficit regions. By 1988 it appears the response of the state to this situation was to reinstate many of its controls over grain marketing.

Overall, therefore, the 'grain war' was essentially caused by changes in prices and market supply. Nevertheless, the intervention by local governments also reflected the administrative pressures felt by local budgets and the requirement to guarantee quotas set from above.

Next steps in reform

The main production areas for different types of grain are relatively concentrated, but demand growth has been widely distributed. Since 1949 many efforts have been made to change the grain distribution system in order to cope with this feature of the economy. Major changes undertaken in the mid-1980s during the rural reforms had the effect of inhibiting inter-regional trade rather than promoting it.

The resolution of these regional contradictions has had important implications for China's international grain trade. China's international transactions are the outcome of many factors, including some special features of the Chinese grain distribution system. In future, international transactions will depend on

  long-run supply and demand factors, which are likely to operate in the direction of reducing China's self-sufficiency in grain

  the balance between the varieties of grain produced and the varieties demanded at current relative prices. Imbalances can be resolved by exporting rice and importing wheat.

In addition, in the Chinese case there have been some other special features of the marketing system which affect international transactions, including

logistical constraints on the internal movement of grain, leading to dealings in the world market instead (both exporting and importing)

locally imposed barriers to inter-regional trade, which will have the same effect.

The policy-imposed barriers to inter-regional trade were the outcome of attempts to promote inter-regional grain transfers in a partially reformed system. The experience of this period has led to policy-makers considering a more comprehensive set of reforms. In 1992 and 1993, for example, there were large steps towards free internal markets for grain, and there was discussion about linking domestic prices to international prices. That is, inter-regional transfers would be determined in the marketplace and the prices in those markets would be related to prices in the world market. The government could then withdraw from the distribution of grain between regions of China.

The experience of previous attempts at partial reform to resolve the supply and demand gaps between regions in China has thus led to even more radical reforms. This is another example of the cycles in the reform process in the agricultural sector, but with a trend towards a greater degree of market orientation. The experiments of the early 1990s were facilitated by a couple of years of record harvests. Therefore, the perception that there was a 'grain shortage' was weakened. As those reforms proceed, the forces of demand and supply will have a greater influence on internal trade patterns.

The next issue will be the links between these domestic developments and the world markets. One problem in the reform process in previous years was the gap between world and domestic prices. By early 1994 these two sets of prices had moved close together so that the integration of the domestic market for grain and the world market would cause little change in domestic prices. This fact and the plentiful supplies of grain at the time led many Chinese commentators to argue that this was the 'right time' to take that further step in reform. Indeed, wheat and some other food prices had risen to well above world prices, suggesting that the 'right time' might be passing, and that China was already stepping down the established and costly path of East Asian agricultural protection (Garnaut, Fang and Huang, chapter 14).

The longer-run scenario in China is therefore one of rising consumption of some types of grain, but confronting supply constraints (that is, higher value uses for land, or the lack of comparative advantage in grain production). Whether this leads to rising domestic prices and 'protection' for China's grain sector or to an increased flow of imports of grain into China depends on the outcome of this debate and the next steps in grain marketing reform.

Appendix

Table 16.1A *Grain production and trade, China, 1949–92*

	Output (mt)	Population (m)	Output per head (kg)	Imports (mt)	Exports (mt)	Net imports (mt)
1949	113.2	541.7	209	–	–	–
1950	132.1	552.0	239	0.07	1.23	–1.16
1951	143.7	563.0	255	0.00	1.97	–1.97
1952	163.9	574.8	285	0.00	1.53	–1.53
1953	166.8	588.0	284	0.02	1.83	–1.81
1954	169.5	602.7	281	0.03	1.71	–1.68
1955	183.9	614.7	299	0.19	2.23	–2.04
1956	192.8	628.3	307	0.15	2.65	–2.50
1957	195.0	646.5	302	0.17	2.09	–1.92
1958	200.0	659.9	303	0.22	2.88	–2.66
1959	170.0	672.1	253	0.00	4.16	–4.16
1960	143.5	622.1	217	0.07	2.72	–2.65
1961	147.5	658.6	224	5.81	1.36	4.45
1962	160.0	673.0	238	4.92	1.03	3.89
1963	170.0	691.7	246	5.95	1.49	4.46
1964	187.5	705.0	266	6.57	1.82	4.75
1965	194.5	725.4	268	6.41	2.42	3.99
1966	214.0	745.4	287	6.44	2.89	3.55
1967	217.8	763.7	285	4.70	2.99	1.71
1968	209.1	785.3	266	4.60	2.60	2.00
1969	211.0	806.7	262	3.79	2.24	1.55
1970	240.0	829.9	289	5.36	2.12	3.24
1971	250.1	852.3	293	3.17	2.62	0.55
1972	240.5	871.8	276	4.76	2.93	1.83
1973	264.9	892.1	297	8.13	3.89	4.24
1974	275.3	908.6	303	8.12	3.64	4.48
1975	284.5	924.2	308	3.74	2.81	0.93
1976	286.3	937.2	305	2.37	1.77	0.60
1977	282.7	949.7	298	7.35	1.66	5.69
1978	304.8	962.6	317	8.83	1.88	6.95
1979	332.1	975.4	340	12.36	1.65	10.71
1980	320.6	987.1	325	13.43	1.62	11.81

Table 16.1A *(cont.)*

	Output (mt)	Population (m)	Output per head (kg)	Imports (mt)	Exports (mt)	Net imports (mt)
1981	325.0	1,000.7	325	14.81	1.26	13.55
1982	354.5	1,015.4	349	16.11	1.25	14.86
1983	387.3	1,025.0	378	13.43	1.96	11.47
1984	407.3	1,038.8	392	10.41	3.19	7.22
1985	379.1	1,050.4	361	5.79	9.33	−3.54
1986	391.5	1,065.3	368	7.73	9.42	−1.69
1987	403.0	1,080.7	373	16.28	7.37	8.91
1988	394.1	1,096.1	360	15.33	7.17	8.16
1989	407.6	1,111.9	367	16.58	6.56	10.02
1990	438.0	1,143.3	383	13.72	5.83	7.89
1991	435.3	1,158.2	376	12.37	10.86	1.51
1992	442.7	1,171.7	378	10.58	13.64	−3.06

Source: SSB, ZTN (various issues).

Table 16.2A Composition of grain sown area, percentage of total, 1949–90

	Rice	Wheat	Corn	Soybeans	Sorghum	Millet	Potatoes	Other	Total ('000 ha)
1949	23.381	19.566	..	7.566	..	..	6.375	..	109,959
1950	22.856	19.929	..	8.393	..	..	6.727	..	114,406
1951	22.869	19.576	..	9.171	..	..	7.036	..	117,769
1952	22.893	19.987	10.136	9.420	7.571	7.933	7.008	15.054	123,979
1953	22.364	20.244	10.371	9.762	7.548	7.791	7.120	14.801	126,637
1954	22.266	20.905	10.210	9.810	6.703	6.980	7.582	15.544	128,995
1955	22.469	20.594	11.275	8.812	6.208	6.877	7.743	16.022	129,839
1956	24.433	20.003	12.954	8.836	4.450	6.321	8.062	14.940	136,339
1957	24.127	20.610	11.182	9.540	4.964	6.268	7.854	15.455	133,633
1958	25.009	20.198	12.703	7.484	3.122	5.404	12.054	14.026	127,613
1959	25.024	20.319	11.206	8.501	4.089	5.957	10.592	14.311	116,023
1960	24.183	22.294	11.509	7.635	3.223	4.659	11.052	15.445	122,429
1961	21.638	21.059	11.201	8.200	4.585	5.183	9.903	18.232	121,433
1962	22.147	19.795	10.539	7.814	5.203	5.286	10.007	19.209	121,621
1963	22.954	19.688	12.735	7.978	5.562	5.832	9.855	15.396	120,741
1964	24.248	20.809	12.582	8.197	5.120	5.496	9.219	14.329	122,103
1965	24.932	20.655	13.100	7.183	5.141	5.485	9.342	14.162	119,627
1966	25.233	19.770	..	6.964	..	..	9.627	..	120,988
1967	25.527	21.219	..	7.132	..	..	8.988	..	119,230
1968	25.736	21.228	..	7.200	..	..	8.873	..	116,157
1969	25.877	21.396	..	7.082	..	..	8.883	..	117,604

1970	27.131	21.345	13.274	6.695	3.987	5.306	8.986	13.277	119,267
1971	28.895	21.216	13.841	6.447	4.128	5.215	8.610	11.649	120,846
1972	28.994	21.700	13.780	6.256	4.419	4.751	8.944	11.156	121,209
1973	28.963	21.822	13.677	6.114	4.314	4.877	9.332	10.901	121,156
1974	29.355	22.369	14.391	6.002	4.343	4.371	9.150	10.020	120,976
1975	29.513	22.849	15.362	5.781	3.858	5.164	9.061	8.413	121,062
1976	29.995	23.535	15.925	5.542	3.584	3.727	8.585	9.107	120,743
1977	29.507	23.310	16.327	5.685	3.122	3.718	9.326	9.004	120,400
1978	28.545	24.201	16.553	5.924	2.868	3.542	9.782	8.586	120,587
1979	28.402	24.615	16.881	6.076	2.660	3.499	9.183	8.683	119,263
1980	28.899	24.931	17.361	6.165	2.297	3.303	8.660	8.384	117,234
1981	28.693	24.624	16.897	6.979	2.270	3.383	8.368	8.515	114,958
1982	29.147	24.638	16.343	7.420	2.453	3.560	3.499	12.941	113,463
1983	29.056	25.472	16.505	6.635	2.374	3.584	8.244	8.131	114,047
1984	29.392	26.201	16.421	6.454	2.170	3.364	7.962	8.035	112,884
1985	29.464	26.844	16.256	7.091	1.779	3.049	7.875	7.642	108,845
1986	29.086	26.697	17.239	7.477	1.691	2.686	7.829	7.294	110,933
1987	28.947	25.894	18.157	7.563	1.676	2.417	7.974	7.373	111,215
1988	28.803	25.986	17.772	7.328	1.610	2.268	8.186	8.046	110,801
1989	29.144	26.596	18.139	7.181	1.452	2.136	8.107	7.245	112,205
1990	29.140	27.103	18.862	6.662	1.362	2.008	8.038	6.824	113,466

Source: USDA, *China Statistical Tape,* Washington, DC: USDA.

Table 16.3A Composition of grain production, percentage of total, 1949–90

	Rice	Wheat	Corn[b]	Soybeans	Sorghum	Millet	Potatoes[a]	Other	Total[a] ('000 tons)
1949	43.741	12.418	..	4.572	..	..	7.082	..	11,318
1950	42.500	11.180	..	5.739	..	..	7.645	..	129,647
1951	42.982	12.230	..	6.126	..	..	7.950	..	140,885
1952	42.593	11.282	10.489	5.926	6.909	7.190	8.132	7.479	160,649
1953	43.591	11.181	10.208	6.073	6.850	6.300	8.152	7.645	163,498
1954	42.650	14.047	10.318	5.466	5.418	5.568	8.177	8.355	166,119
1955	43.310	12.747	11.279	5.062	5.690	5.579	8.393	7.940	180,155
1956	43.785	13.165	12.236	5.436	3.477	4.539	9.279	8.082	188,375
1957	45.513	12.399	11.245	5.271	4.012	4.484	9.197	7.878	190,661
1958	41.793	11.675	..	4.482	..	..	13.535	..	193,454
1959	41.979	13.423	..	5.302	..	..	11.533	..	165,236
1960	42.839	15.900	..	4.583	..	..	11.676	..	139,430
1961	37.470	9.954	10.828	4.338	4.017	3.667	12.144	17.582	143,154
1962	40.554	10.730	10.463	4.192	3.928	3.413	12.079	14.642	155,310
1963	44.511	11.148	12.418	4.170	4.133	3.621	10.326	9.673	165,722
1964	44.267	11.115	12.101	4.197	3.573	3.653	10.736	10.357	187,500
1965	45.094	12.965	12.163	3.156	3.650	3.187	10.209	9.575	194,525
1966	44.575	11.813	..	3.864	..	..	10.528	..	214,000
1967	43.010	13.077	..	3.797	..	..	10.297	..	217,820
1968	45.218	13.133	..	3.846	..	..	10.662	..	209,055
1969	45.061	12.933	..	3.617	..	..	11.433	..	**210,970**

Year								
1970	45.838	12.163	13.765	3.630	3.417	3.667	11.119	6.401	239,955
1971	46.056	13.023	14.332	3.442	3.518	3.078	10.022	6.528	250,140
1972	47.137	14.964	13.348	2.682	3.347	2.474	10.196	5.851	240,480
1973	45.949	13.296	14.581	3.159	4.020	3.076	11.912	4.007	264,935
1974	45.012	14.845	15.592	2.714	4.123	2.543	10.259	4.912	275,270
1975	44.131	15.925	16.597	2.545	3.778	2.513	10.042	4.469	284,515
1976	43.943	17.598	16.821	2.319	3.039	1.938	9.312	5.030	286,305
1977	45.474	14.528	17.469	2.568	2.723	2.175	10.494	4.568	282,725
1978	44.930	17.666	18.357	2.482	2.645	2.154	10.415	1.352	304,765
1979	43.283	18.888	18.077	2.246	2.296	1.844	8.569	4.797	332,115
1980	43.645	17.223	19.528	2.477	2.113	1.699	8.962	4.352	320,560
1981	44.291	18.350	18.216	2.869	2.046	1.774	7.990	4.464	325,020
1982	45.584	19.315	17.083	2.547	1.966	1.856	7.526	4.123	354,000
1983	43.603	21.016	17.612	2.520	2.157	1.947	7.551	3.593	387,275
1984	43.764	21.560	18.023	2.380	1.894	1.725	6.991	3.663	407,310
1985	44.465	22.633	16.836	2.772	1.480	1.577	6.868	3.370	379,108
1986	43.989	22.998	18.098	2.966	1.375	1.162	6.472	2.939	391,512
1987	43.244	21.317	19.664	3.093	1.346	1.081	6.999	3.256	402,977
1988	42.912	21.679	19.628	2.955	1.420	1.120	6.843	3.445	394,081
1989	44.198	22.281	19.367	2.509	1.088	0.921	6.700	2.936	407,549
1990	42.428	22.012	21.696	2.465	1.272	1.025	6.147	2.954	446,243

Notes:

[a] Total grain and potatoes for 1949–63 are adjusted to the same 5:1 potato to grain conversion rate used in official statistics after 1963.

[b] Corn is on an unshelled basis.

Source: USDA, *China Statistical Tape*, Washington, DC: USDA.

Table 16.4A *Sown area by region, 1952–90*

	Eastern region (%)	Middle region (%)	Western region (%)	Total (1,000 ha)
1952	38.60	42.00	19.40	123,977
1957	37.90	44.40	20.70	133,633
1963	36.11	42.04	21.86	119,897
1964	35.19	43.14	21.67	123,213
1965	34.54	43.89	21.57	122,463
1966	34.82	41.42	23.76	121,118
1967	34.93	41.17	23.90	119,873
1968	35.69	41.67	22.64	115,752
1969	36.39	41.21	22.40	116,240
1970	36.11	41.37	22.51	119,556
1971	35.83	40.72	23.46	122,933
1972	36.40	41.04	22.56	121,437
1973	35.98	41.96	22.06	123,748
1974	35.96	42.12	21.92	124,258
1975	36.77	40.70	22.54	121,354
1976	36.84	40.54	22.62	121,171
1977	36.58	40.62	22.80	120,779
1978	36.14	40.51	23.34	121,022
1979	35.74	40.92	23.34	119,802
1980	35.91	40.74	23.35	117,070
1981	35.66	41.29	23.04	114,958
1982	35.35	41.59	23.06	113,462
1983	35.30	41.93	22.78	114,046
1984	35.16	42.11	22.73	112,884
1985	35.16	42.10	22.74	108,843
1986	35.40	42.26	22.35	110,933
1987	35.05	42.46	22.48	111,448
1988	35.41	41.83	22.76	110,307
1989	35.02	42.05	22.93	112,205
1990	34.70	42.25	23.05	113,466

Source: USDA, *China Statistical Tape*, Washington, DC: USDA.

Table 16.5A *Grain output by region, 1963–90*

	Eastern region (%)	Middle region (%)	Western region (%)	Total (1,000 t)
1963	39.208	37.649	23.143	160,720
1964	40.108	37.398	22.494	179,380
1965	40.061	37.350	22.589	201,645
1966	40.487	37.426	22.088	213,490
1967	39.725	38.497	21.778	216,665
1968	39.971	39.415	20.614	208,040
1969	42.228	36.271	21.500	209,065
1970	39.984	39.231	20.785	241,607
1971	40.153	38.895	20.952	254,325
1972	41.771	37.382	20.848	244,465
1973	40.561	38.859	20.579	269,640
1974	40.093	39.738	20.168	274,910
1975	40.698	39.260	20.043	291,355
1976	41.289	39.222	19.489	291,750
1977	40.216	38.418	21.366	287,115
1978	41.065	37.760	21.175	313,030
1979	41.397	38.309	20.294	333,720
1980	41.360	37.217	21.422	319,945
1981	40.204	38.936	20.860	325,020
1982	40.945	37.897	21.158	354,500
1983	39.823	39.790	20.387	387,275
1984	39.636	40.214	20.150	407,305
1985	39.702	40.159	20.139	379,108
1986	39.796	40.209	19.995	391,512
1987	39.438	40.983	19.579	404,733
1988	39.102	40.975	19.923	394,081
1989	38.414	40.873	20.713	407,549
1990	37.974	42.234	19.792	446,243

Source: USDA, *China Statistical Tape*, Washington, DC: USDA.

Notes

* The authors are grateful for the support of the University of Adelaide for the research reported in this chapter. The work also relied on assistance from the

Policy and Law Division of the Ministry of Agriculture in Beijing. Work on revising this study was supported by a grant from the Australian Research Council.

1 Grain in China is defined to include potatoes and sweet potatoes, using a conversion ratio of 5 kilograms of fresh potatoes to 1 kilogram of grain. Coarse grains include corn, sorghum, millet and barley. Sources apart from appendix table 16.3 include Chinese Academy of Agricultural Science (1988: 48) and State Statistical Bureau (SSB, ZTN 1984: 137, 138, 141).

2 The following discussion is based on Chinese Academy of Agricultural Science (1988: 76, 82–9).

3 The following account is based on *Nongmin ribao* [Peasants' Daily], 17 January 1989: 1.

17 Regional inequality in rural development

Ke Bingsheng

China aims to become a medium-income economy by the year 2000. For rural residents, unlike those in urban regions, this goal seems very distant, especially for those in the vast inland areas of central and western China. While in many coastal regions the rural population enjoys a standard of living comparable to that in urban areas, a large proportion of farmers in central and western China struggle hard to make ends meet. This regional development gap has continued to widen in the past decade.

Regional features of the rural economy

There are obvious differences in income and consumption levels among regions (Table 17.1). The most developed provinces are found along the eastern coast. Shanghai heads the list, with a per capita income level in 1991 of over 2,000 yuan for its rural resident population. It is followed by Beijing, Zhejiang, Tianjin and Guangdong, with income levels between 1,100 and 1,400 yuan. Other coastal provinces including Jiangsu, Liaoning, Fujian and Shandong also have income levels above the national average. Income levels in the inland regions are much lower. In the poorest provinces of Gansu, Anhui and Guizhou, incomes average around 500 yuan. Other lower-income regions are Inner Mongolia, Shaanxi, Henan, Qinghai, Shanxi and Yunnan, where per capita rural incomes in 1991 were less than 600 yuan.

Consumption levels are closely correlated with income levels. Per capita consumption of high-value food products and ownership rates for colour television sets, for instance, are much higher in the coastal regions than in the inland provinces. Ownership rates for colour television sets for rural households in Beijing, Tianjin and Shanghai are over 20 per cent, but only around 2 per cent in Anhui and Guizhou.

The picture for the consumption of animal products is similar. Rural residents in the wealthier coastal regions consumed 20–30 kilograms of meat

Table 17.1 *Indicators for regional disparity in rural areas of mainland China, 1991 (national average=1)*

	Per capita income	Possession of colour TV sets	Consumption of animal products	Engel's coefficient (%)
Shanghai	2.83	3.91	2.04	47.7
Beijing	2.01	6.48	1.14	48.6
Zhejiang	1.71	1.67	1.58	50.5
Tianjin	1.65	3.65	1.34	52.0
Guangdong	1.61	1.93	1.80	56.6
Jiangsu	1.30	1.27	1.36	55.5
Liaoning	1.27	2.14	1.22	51.8
Fujian	1.20	1.28	1.15	59.0
Shandong	1.08	1.48	0.72	53.4
Jilin	1.06	0.84	0.92	56.6
Heilongjiang	1.04	1.18	0.77	57.7
Hainan	1.03	0.91	1.40	64.1
Tibet	1.00	0.03	1.04	72.3
Xinjiang	0.99	1.20	0.67	53.7
Jiangxi	0.99	0.22	0.98	63.2
Hunan	0.97	0.20	1.28	62.3
Hebei	0.93	1.41	0.51	47.9
Guangxi	0.93	0.13	0.95	82.0
Hubei	0.88	0.23	1.22	59.1
Ninxia	0.83	3.34	0.68	57.4
Sichuan	0.83	0.25	1.43	62.3
Yunnan	0.81	0.49	1.27	62.8
Shanxi	0.78	0.87	0.95	60.3
Qinghai	0.78	0.67	0.95	60.3
Henan	0.76	0.58	0.46	53.4
Shaannxi	0.75	0.76	0.46	54.8
Inner Mongolia	0.73	0.96	1.21	56.2
Guizhou	0.66	0.14	0.93	67.5
Anhui	0.63	0.26	0.71	57.7
Gansu	0.63	1.19	0.57	59.0
National average	709 yuan	6.4 sets/100 households	18.4 kg/person	56.8

Note: Animal products include meat, fish and eggs
Source: SSB, ZTN (1992).

and other animal products annually, compared with only 10 kilograms for farmers in the poor inland provinces of Shaanxi, Shanxi and Henan.

In some low-income inland provinces, such as Sichuan, Hunan, Hubei and Yunnan, animal food consumption levels are above the national average, but ownership of industrial consumer goods is much lower. This in part indicates the special features of consumption patterns or preferences: food consumption enjoys a higher priority in household expenditure (the Engel coefficient is greater than 60 per cent). It is also indicative of local production patterns. All the provinces are major livestock (mainly pork) producers, and the price for pork in these regions is generally lower than elsewhere.

Other low-income provinces such as Ningxia, Shanxi and Gansu show much higher ownership of colour television sets with significantly lower consumption levels for animal products. Again, this has some correlation with local patterns of production. In a society with high subsistence levels and an undeveloped transport infrastructure, consumption patterns are to a large extent shaped by those of production.

The gap between coastal and inland provinces can also be measured by the Engel coefficient. Most coastal provinces have an Engel coefficient of less than 50-5 per cent, whereas the coefficient for many inland provinces is over 60 per cent (table 17.1).

Other indicators also show strong regional differentiation. A 1990 Ministry of Agriculture survey found that the eastern regions have higher levels of income, cash income, savings deposits, possession of cash and fixed capital, and use of agricultural inputs (table 17.2).

Chemical fertiliser input in the eastern provinces is 2–4 times greater that in the inland provinces. For example, chemical fertiliser input per hectare is above 600 kilograms in Guangdong, Fujian, Shanghai and Zhejiang, but only around 150 kilograms in Gansu, Ningxia, Qinghai, Xinjiang, Inner Mongolia and Shanxi. In the livestock sector, the compound feed input in the eastern regions is 1–2 times higher than in the central and western regions.

More important than the existing gap is widening regional disparity, in absolute and also relative terms. Per capita current income for the whole rural population in 1991 was 709 yuan, 3.7 times that of 1980, and 1.8 times that of 1985 (table 17.3). Growth rates differed sharply across regions, however, with the eastern region performing much better than the central and western regions.

Special attention should be paid to income growth since the mid-1980s. Total nominal growth of farmers' per capita income was 78 per cent with a real increase of 9 per cent during the period 1985–91. Again, the eastern regions enjoyed a much higher real growth rate, with Shanghai the highest at 42 per cent.

Table 17.2 *Development disparity in three economic regions, 1990*

	Unit	Eastern	Central	Western
Family size	persons	4.7	4.6	5.0
Productive fixed capital	yuan/person	1,664	1,386	1,381
Non-productive fixed capital	yuan/person	8,867	4,958	3,875
Productive income	yuan/person	1,482	1,046	864
of which: farm	yuan/person	775	746	618
off-farm	yuan/person	707	300	246
farm	%	52	71	72
off-farm	%	48	29	28
Net income	yuan/person	1,041	710	624
Cash income	yuan/person	1,529	914	714
Year end deposit	yuan/person	362	137	163
Year end cash on hand	yuan/person	396	244	255
Sown area	ha/person	0.10	0.15	0.13
Grain production	kg/person	464	692	526
Grain delivery quota	kg/person	81	132	64
Production of animal products	kg/person	23	24	25
Input of compound feed	kg/household	327	1,821	121

Source: Ministry of Agriculture (1990).

On the other hand, there was only a slow increase in the central and western regions. Eight provinces experienced a fall in real income. Anhui province suffered the largest fall. Heavy flooding in 1991 was an important factor but not a decisive one, as the real income in the province was falling before 1991; the average per capita real income in 1990 was 12 per cent lower than in 1985.

Based on provincial average current income, the standard deviation of farmers' income in China was 56 yuan in 1980, 126 yuan in 1985 and 127 yuan in 1991. The corresponding coefficient of variation was 0.27, 0.30 and 0.42, respectively. In real terms, the standard deviation of farmers' income was 56 yuan in 1980, 104 yuan in 1985 and 155 yuan in 1991. The corresponding co-efficient of variation was 0.27, 0.29 and 0.39, respectively. This is indicative of the widening income gap between provinces over the decade to 1991, both absolutely and relatively.

According to official targets, the national average level of farmers' income is to be raised from 686 yuan in 1990 to 1,200 yuan (in 1990 prices)

Table 17.3 *Development of farmers' income, by province, 1980, 1985 and 1991 (yuan)*

	Per capita income in current prices			Per capita income in 1980 yuan			Total increase, % (in 1980 yuan)	
	1980	1985	1991	1980	1985	1991	1980–91	1985–91
National average	191	398	709	191	344	374	96	9
Shanghai	397	806	2,003	397	691	979	147	42
Beijing	290	775	1,422	290	623	667	130	7
Zhejiang	219	549	1,211	219	461	601	174	30
Tianjin	278	565	1,169	278	490	638	129	30
Guangdong	274	495	1,143	274	418	531	94	27
Jiangsu	217	493	921	217	428	461	112	8
Liaoning	273	468	897	273	409	464	70	13
Fujian	172	396	850	172	341	429	149	26
Shandong	194	408	764	194	364	420	116	15
Jilin	236	414	748	236	356	386	64	8
Heilongjiang	205	398	735	205	324	368	80	14
Hainan	..	..	730	..	..	339	..	..
Tibet	..	353	707	..	307	367	..	20
Xinjiang	198	394	703	198	341	341	85	8
Jiangxi	181	377	703	181	322	364	101	13
Hunan	220	395	689	220	323	328	49	–2
Hebei	174	303	658	174	252	321	84	27
Guangxi	176	385	657	176	332	354	101	7
Hubei	170	421	627	170	378	342	101	–10
Ninxia	178	321	590	178	281	303	70	8

Table 17.3 (*cont.*)

	Per capita income in current prices			Per capita income in 1980 yuan			Total increase, % (in 1980 yuan)	
	1980	1985	1991	1980	1985	1991	1980–91	1985–91
Sichuan	188	315	590	188	280	321	71	15
Yunnan	150	338	573	150	302	300	100	–1
Shanxi	156	358	568	156	310	287	84	–7
Qinghai	..	343	556	..	305	289	..	–5
Henan	161	329	539	161	299	303	88	1
Shaanxi	142	295	534	142	256	277	95	8
Inner Mongolia	181	360	518	181	306	268	48	–12
Guizhou	161	288	466	161	259	257	60	–1
Anhui	184	369	446	184	334	233	27	–30
Gansu	153	255	446	153	223	236	54	6

Source: SSB, ZTN (1992).

by the end of the century. The regional target is 1,500 yuan for the eastern regions, 1500 yuan for the central regions and 1,000 yuan for the western regions. To accomplish this goal, the average annual growth rate should be at least 5.8 per cent for the whole rural population, 4.3 per cent for the eastern regions, and 6.0 per cent for the central and western regions.

The eastern regions will find achievement of the target somewhat easier. The 1,500 yuan target has been already met in Shanghai, and is close to being met in Beijing, Tianjin, Zhejiang and Guangdong. An annual growth rate of 3 per cent will be sufficient to accomplish this goal.

The outlook is not as promising for the inland provinces. For many poor provinces, an annual growth rate of over 7 per cent will be required to realise the 1,000 yuan goal. The acceleration of development in these poor and lagging inland provinces will be one of the most difficult tasks in China's modernisation process.

Reasons for the uneven development

There are many reasons for uneven economic development including natural resource endowment, access to major markets (both domestic and foreign), infrastructure, education and technological extension, development of rural industries, state procurement policy for farm products and regional development policy. Among these, the development of rural industries is the decisive factor.

This can be understood by analysing the structure of income. Farmers' income has two components: farm and off-farm. The eastern regions have higher levels of both farm and off-farm income than the other two regions (table 17.2). Non-farm income in the eastern regions is more than twice that in the central regions and almost three times that in the western regions. The income structure is quite different between the eastern regions and the other two regions: in the east, the off-farm share is about 50 per cent, while in the other two regions it is only about 30 per cent. The difference in off-farm income is the major reason for the total income disparity.

The three regions are similar in terms of per capita livestock production (table 17.2). Per capita grain production however, is larger in the central regions. Average grain output in the central regions is 50 per cent higher than in the eastern regions and 30 per cent higher than in the western regions. Accordingly, the delivery quota of grain to the state on a per capita basis in the central regions is much higher: 60 per cent above that in the western regions and twice that in the eastern regions. The high state procurement quota partly explains why income levels in the central regions are not significantly higher than in the western regions, though the former have a higher per capita farm production level.

The stronger growth of rural industries in the eastern regions largely explains the higher share of off-farm employment and incomes in these regions (table 17.4).

The share of off-farm employment in rural areas in coastal provinces is as high as 50 per cent compared with 10–20 per cent in most of the inland provinces. The labour productivity of off-farm employment in the eastern provinces is 2–3 times higher than in the inland provinces. As a result, per capita non-farm production in the coastal provinces is 5–10 times greater than in the inland provinces.

Labour productivity in agricultural production in the eastern regions is 2–3 times higher than in the inland provinces. This is not due to better natural resource endowment. Even taking the multi-cropping index into consideration, per capita cropping area in the coastal provinces is only 0.15 hectares, which is similar to the national average. The cultivated area per farm worker, however, is larger in the eastern provinces because rural industries have absorbed a large share of the rural labour force. Furthermore, the application of modern inputs such as chemical fertiliser and compound feed is more intensive in the coastal provinces than in other provinces.

What are the main reasons for the uneven development of rural non-farm sectors among these three regions? The fast development of rural industries in the coastal regions is not caused by better natural resource endowment. In per capita terms, the possession of arable land, and production of food and agricultural raw materials for industries are all lower in the east than in the other two regions. The dependence of the rural industries on natural raw materials is also lower in the coastal regions than in the inland regions. The share of mining and raw material industries in rural industries was 30 per cent in the western regions, 21 per cent in the central regions and only 11 per cent in the coastal regions.

The development of rural industries in the coastal regions is determined by factors outside the rural areas, such as opportunities with nearby cities and the higher degree of urbanisation. The eastern regions have a much higher density of industrial output, a larger non-agricultural population and a bigger share of non-agricultural population (table 17.5). In fact, the regions with the most developed rural industries are almost exclusively those with easy access to metropolitan areas, especially large and medium-sized cities. Examples include the environs of Beijing, Tianjin and the Yangtze and Zhu river deltas. Rural industries are normally heavily dependent on nearby cities for markets, information, raw materials, technical know-how and technicians.

It is notable that the urban–rural income disparity is smaller where farmers' income is higher, and vice versa (table 17.4). In Shanghai, Beijing

Table 17.4 *Income disparity and influencing factors by province, 1991*

	Per capita income	Productivity of non-agriculture	Agricultural productivity	Per capita off-farm output	Urban–rural income ratio	Off-farm share in rural employment
			National average = 1		R = 1	%
Shanghai	2.83	1.85	3.14	5.87	1.17	60.8
Beijing	2.01	2.01	3.26	4.35	1.43	59.2
Zhejiang	1.71	1.51	1.09	2.12	1.61	24.3
Tianjin	1.65	2.39	1.69	5.20	1.45	52.4
Guangdong	1.61	1.09	1.23	1.43	2.22	27.8
Jiangsu	1.30	1.56	1.42	2.52	1.76	32.1
Liaoning	1.27	1.45	1.99	1.87	1.72	36.7
Fujian	1.20	.92	1.25	1.01	1.96	27.6
Shandong	1.08	1.23	1.13	1.57	2.05	28.2
Yunnan	0.81	0.63	0.50	0.28	2.67	9.0
Shanxi	0.80	0.83	0.81	0.86	2.17	27.0
Quighai	0.78	0.44	0.88	0.19	2.35	10.8
Henan	0.76	0.73	0.75	0.84	2.32	25.8
Shaanxi	0.75	0.61	0.68	0.57	2.56	21.0
Inner Mongolia	0.73	0.56	1.34	0.37	2.27	18.2
Guizhou	0.66	0.40	0.47	0.15	2.79	7.6
Anhui	0.63	0.66	0.87	0.61	3.01	20.1
Gansu	0.63	0.54	0.69	0.35	3.07	15.7
National average	709	10,340	2.0t	1060	2.18	22.1
	yuan/ person	yuan/ person	grain equivalent/ person	yuan/ person		

Source: SSB, ZTN (1991).

Table 17.5 *Influencing factors for township enterprise development, 1988*

Zone	Industrial output density yuan/km²	Non-agricultural population density persons/km²	Share of non-agricultural population[a] %
Eastern	115	97	24
Central	24	40	19
Western	2	5	15

Note: [a] As a percentage of the national total.
Source: SSB, ZTN (1991).

and Tianjin the income of urban residents is some 20–40 per cent higher than that of the rural population, whereas in the poor provinces of Gansu, Anhui, Guizhou, Shaanxi, Yunnan and Ningxia, the corresponding figures are 150–200 per cent.

Uneven development and policy reform

How will the uneven rural economic development be influenced by economic reform, especially by the ongoing market liberalisation?

In the short run, farmers' income will increase with the abolition of state grain procurement. Farmers in the central regions will benefit most from the liberalisation of the grain market, as the state procurement quota is largest there. This liberalisation of product markets alone will not significantly change the regional income disparity patterns in rural areas for three reasons.

First, the income rise from market liberalisation will not be significant. The margin between the free market and the state quota prices for wheat, corn and some rice varieties is now slight. The per capita income gain of farmers from grain market liberalisation will be only about 1–2 per cent in the eastern and western regions and about 4 per cent in the central regions.

Second, the gain will most likely be nominal because state subsidies in the form of pay increases to urban consumers will also rise. The pay increases may drive up the inflation rate.

Third, the grain resale policy to poor and grain-deficit regions has also been terminated. Rural populations in those regions will have to pay higher prices to buy grain from the free market. Market liberalisation will mean a net loss to farmers in these regions.

In the long run, market liberalisation will enable more efficient resource allocation. Farmers will adjust production according to market demand

and local conditions. This will certainly bring about some income improvement.

Uneven economic development in China's rural areas will continue in the coming years, or even decades. The income level of residents in a rural community is determined by three factors: net income from the agricultural sector, income from non-agricultural sector, and the number of dependent persons in a family. The low-income regions are mostly disadvantaged in all three aspects. First, many low-income regions are populated disproportionately by national minorities, whose population growth rate is much higher due to their exemption from government birth control policy. Second, the low-income regions are often ecologically much more vulnerable. The resource potential for further intensifying agricultural production is rather limited. Third, the degree of urbanisation and industrialisation in low-income regions is very low. The long distance from major consumer markets, along with other factors, makes it very difficult for local rural industries in these regions to expand rapidly.

The liberalisation of product markets will not significantly change the tendency towards increasing regional income disparity. Only the liberalisation of factor markets will bring about fundamental changes: free mobility of capital and, especially, labour, and transferability of land. Without fundamental changes in factor markets, structural adjustment and transformation of agriculture will not proceed successfully. The reforms will require a range of fundamental changes in the urban sector, including in the resident registration (*hukou*) system, urban employment, housing, medical care and social security policies. On the other hand, during the process of market liberalisation, existing poverty alleviation programs should not be abandoned, but strengthened and targeted more effectively to the poor. It is an obligation of the community and therefore an objective of public policy to help the poor, especially under a market system.

Institutional change

18 China's rural property rights system under reform

Chen Fan

In 1992 China defined the end point of reform as establishing a 'socialist market economy'. One of the essential conditions for a market economy is clear definition of property rights. This chapter proposes a new property rights system in China's rural economy.

Chinese Vice-Premier Zhu Rongji defined the objectives of economic policy in a socialist market economy at the Opening Ceremony of the 11th Session of the Interaction Council on 13 May 1993: 'The essence of a socialist economy includes two points. One is to achieve high efficiency of resource allocation and high labour productivity; and the other is to safeguard social fairness and realise the common welfare'.

At the core of an economic system there are two fundamental institutional arrangements: the property rights system, and economic contracts determined by the corresponding property rights system. A property rights system requires that the whole society or some of its individuals possess the entire property of the society or a defined part of it. Property here includes natural resources, human capital, technology, fixed assets and financial assets.

A property rights system is better the lower the operation or transaction costs. Transaction costs include the costs incurred in reallocating and protecting property, and in contract design and enforcement. To reduce transaction costs in an economy, the property rights system should not hinder competitive resource allocation and utilisation in economic activities. Transaction costs can be reduced through market competition.

Individual, joint and collective property rights

In an economic system based on individual property rights, everyone is potentially the owner of property, however large or small, and enjoys

the right to decide how to use the property and to refuse others use of property (the use right) the right to transfer or sell property to anyone else (the disposal right) the right to benefit from utilising the property (the benefit right).

Although in an economic system based on individual property everyone can make production decisions utilising his or her talent, capabilities and resources according to the law of comparative advantage, it is difficult to reconcile individual ownership of the means of production with a complex social division of labour in which large-scale co-operation is required for many activities. To solve this problem, various business institutions develop, including joint stock companies and transnational corporations.

A joint stock company or joint stock system vests ownership rights in shareholders. But this kind of ownership is restricted in the sense that property is actually under the control of the board of directors. An owner of shares usually cannot withdraw shares, but he or she can sell shares, and use the proceeds for re-investment in other activities or consumption. A joint stock system safeguards the basis of individual property on the one hand and meets the need for socialised production on the other.

In a system based on individual property rights, the evolution of business organisations from individual to family business, partnerships, leasing and various kinds of joint stock enterprises for the purpose of lowering transaction costs maintains the competitiveness of economic activities and results in more efficient resource allocation. But these economic institutions alone cannot maximise welfare for the majority of the society. In this sense, it is not a complete economic system.

An alternative basis for property rights is ownership by all of the people or collective ownership, as introduced by the former Soviet Union under Stalin. This form of property rights was typical of many socialist countries for a long period. The principle of ownership by all of the people can be explained as follows. The nation prepays the production costs. The necessary labour value is paid to workers, while the surplus labour value is collected by the nation in the form of profits and taxes. The running of enterprises and labour is controlled by the nation's planning departments. In this system, means of production are in fact owned by the state representing all of the people, and managed by the government leaders.

Although each worker is nominally an equal owner of all means of production, he or she is not conscious of this in practice. First, the labourer is unable to benefit directly from the right of ownership of the means of production. Second, although the surplus labour value collected by the nation still serves all of the people, each worker hardly has the chance to participate in decision-making with respect to distribution and utilisation of value, let alone feel that he or she owns it.

A third type of property rights system is collective ownership. The total production value excluding material costs is divided into labour rewards paid to workers, and profits used for capital accumulation and collective welfare. Collective ownership is superior to ownership by all of the people in that it mobilises the concern of members of the collective for the collective properties. Members of different collectives are made conscious of their rights of ownership of means of production by income differences between them.

But the system of collective ownership of means of production still has many weaknesses. First, income gaps in the system of collective ownership of means of production reflect the performance of the whole collective and its distribution to the collective members according to their work. Each member is unable directly to draw his or her income from the production profit and cannot benefit directly from the increase in the value of the collective properties. The members of the collective have only a vague notion about their rights of ownership, so they care less for the collective properties than for their own. There is no mechanism ensuring that more investment leads to a larger increase in a member's future income. Second, although the members of the collective economy have democratic management rights in theory, there is no mechanism in place that stimulates their participation in management. Meanwhile, there are few rules to restrict the collective leaders' authority. As a result, the collective properties are actually controlled and handled by the leaders. Third, the collective members care more about their labour rewards than about the increase in value of the collective.

Ownership by all of the people is actually ownership by the nation's administration, while collective ownership is actually by the rural community's administration. The basic problem of both systems is that most of the nominal property owners do not enjoy real ownership rights. The leaders of the government and rural communities who have *de facto* use and benefit rights do not have legal ownership rights, however, and thus do not take economic responsibility. State and collective ownership increase transaction costs and reduce efficiency in resource allocation.

Property rights in rural China

The reconstruction of China's contemporary rural property rights system must meet several requirements. First, workers must have real ownership, disposal and benefit rights in their properties. The three rights cannot be separated from each other. Second, to overcome the conflict between the need for large-scale organisation and individual ownership of the means of production, a system that brings together an individual system of ownership and joint stock co-operation must be established. Third, within a property rights system that gives a large place to joint stock companies, the Chinese government must take responsibility for the welfare of the community at large through macro-economic policies and specific intervention to enhance the welfare of people who are not equipped to do well in the market economy.

The embryonic form of property rights that is emerging in China's contemporary rural economy differs not only from pure systems of individual property rights, but also from ownership by all of the people and collective ownership. Rather, it is a hybrid property rights system that seeks to satisfy both efficiency and welfare standards, and is best described as a 'joint stock co-operation system'.

A joint stock co-operation system

The joint stock co-operation system integrates social and individual elements of ownership. It allows individual ownership, disposal and benefit rights of property. It defines property rights over capital, labour, land and technology, and provides for workers to participate in ownership of the business. This system allows government effectively to use broad fiscal and macro-economic policies to achieve the goal of maximum common welfare for Chinese farmers.

The joint stock co-operation property system provides for all kinds of production factors, including capital, labour service, land, technology, and even management and information to be converted into equity shares according to certain rules. The principle of 'distribution according to work' is implied in the distribution of shares. Since no shareholder can withdraw shares, no matter how the shares are transferred, 'co-operation properties' will ultimately be controlled by the general meeting of the shareholders, so this business form also suits the needs of collective production.

If the rights to transfer and benefit from production factors are given to households or individuals, the production factors can be converted into 'shares', and benefits distributed according to ownership of shares. Meanwhile, the government can secure wider social objectives and maintain stability in the rural economy by implementing land tax, public expenditure and other economic policies.

The joint stock co-operation system can be compared with the responsibility system, which was adopted in 1979 and is now the dominant economic organisational form in China's rural areas. In the family production responsibility system, the right to use land is separated from its collective ownership. Farmers can take their own decisions on production, and on disposal of most of their agricultural products. This mobilises the enthusiasm of farmers. But the family responsibility system did not provide farmers with unified ownership, disposal and distribution rights, and was fundamentally no different from the system of collective ownership.

Some weaknesses of the system have become evident, and increasingly severe. Farmland is redivided frequently due to vagueness about property rights. Since farmland cannot be transferred, it is difficult to achieve scale economies in agricultural production. Also there are more and more land disputes. Finally, lack of clarity about property rights inhibits the development of rational taxation on farmland.

Resulting problems include delays in access to proceeds from sales of farm output, short-sightedness of economic behaviour, declining farm capital investment in farmland, and the destruction of hydro-electric facilities. Transaction costs in the agricultural economy are unnecessarily high. Farmers are now less enthusiastic about agricultural production.

The vigorous development of rural enterprises owned by collectives at township or village levels – township and village enterprises – over the past ten years has been one of the most important factors contributing to high growth in China's economy in the 1980s and 1990s. Township enterprises take their own decisions on production, supply and sales according to market needs. There is no egalitarian distribution. They are responsible for their own profits or losses. Their economic efficiency is much higher than state-owned enterprises. But the blurred ownership, disposal and distribution in relation to their assets remains a problem. The township enterprises themselves possess most of the disposal and distribution rights on their assets, while ownership in theory belongs to the collectives to which the enterprises are subordinate.

The result in practice is that, nominally owned by the collective, these rural enterprises are actually in the hands of their administrative departments. The majority of the non-enterprise collective members (farmers engaged in plant or animal production) do not understand the benefit which they can obtain from the enterprises. Since township and village enterprises are largely controlled by the township or village Party leaders, the responsibility of apportioning work falls to these leaders. This arouses complaints from workers, and also from managers of township enterprises.

These problems are deeply rooted in the development of China's township enterprises. Two external factors conceal the full extent of these problems. The first is that although township enterprises do not possess rational management mechanisms and distribution processes due to the confusing property rights arrangements, a large number of farmers tend to work for these enterprises because of comparative disadvantage in farming and higher pay in the enterprises compared with the farm. The second one is that large and medium-sized state-owned enterprises in urban areas are not operating nearly so well as township enterprises, which therefore are not subject to much competition.

South of Jiangsu, in the birthplace of township enterprises, local people say that 'township enterprises are worse than village enterprises, and the village ones are worse than the individual ones'.

Generally speaking, since its adoption of reform and an open door policy, China has experienced a significant change in forms of rural management. But the creation of a new rural property rights system still remains critical. The absence of such a system has become an obstacle to the further development of China's rural economy and is associated with the rise of many new problems in agriculture and rural areas. Since the Chinese government has defined its general aim as the creation of a socialist market economic system, reform plans and strategic measures for the deepening of reform in the rural economy must satisfy the basic requirements of a market economic system.

This chapter proposes a joint stock co-operation system. Much work needs to be done and many specific questions need to be answered before the theory of property rights based on a joint stock co-operation system can be fully defined for application in rural areas. How precisely should land and other production factors be converted into 'shares'? How precisely should contributions in labour, technological services and other resources be converted into 'shares'? How should funds accumulated by public institutions in the past, and the new earnings of farm households and township enterprises after reform, be converted into 'shares'? What kind of regional differences should be accepted when establishing the new joint stock co-operation property associated with different levels of economic development? These and other questions remain part of the agenda of future rural economic research in China.

Notes

* The views in this chapter were formed after discussions with Professor Guo Shutian, Standing Vice-Chairman of the Soft-Science Committee of the Ministry of Agriculture, and Mr Gao Kuanzhong of the Department of Policies, Laws and Regulations and System Reform of the Ministry of Agriculture.

19 'All the tea in China': the reformation and transformation of the tea industry

Dan Etherington and Keith Forster

Tea is an important rural industry that stands out for its low growth in the reform period, with production actually falling after 1988. Is it possible that this is a case in which the effects of reform have been unfavourable? Or is it economically efficient for tea not to expand?

Figure 19.1 reveals rapid growth in tea output between 1978 and 1988. This had very little to do with the post-1978 reform process. It takes about three years before a tea bush can be plucked. Bushes are generally considered to be mature from their eighth year onwards. Yields are typically highest between the ages of about 10 and 50 years and bushes can have a life of 100 years or more. Thus there is a substantial lag between planting and full production, linking the rapid output increases in the post-1978 period to preceding events.

Increases in recorded area planted during 1965–77, a period coinciding with the Cultural Revolution, averaged over 9 per cent per year. Over the five years to 1976 (figure 19.2), the planted area grew at the phenomenal rate of nearly 13 per cent per year. In 1973 and again the following year, 100 thousand hectares of tea were planted. This is equivalent to planting the total area under tea in South India, or Kenya, in just one year – or Sri Lanka's total tea area in two years!

The very rapid growth in the national tea area over the period 1965–77 was followed over the next twelve years (to 1989) by a total increase of only 5 per cent. The tea area appears to have now stabilised, and it is government policy not to enlarge it further.

Whether total or 'plucked-area' yields are considered, national yields are very low in relation to those reported for 1914–18 (about 900 kg/ha) (Perkins 1969). Considerable variation in yields between provinces is also recorded (table 19.2) (Etherington 1990).

International comparisons confirm the very low level of China's aggregate tea yields. The comparison with India, for example, is stark. In 1990 China's average yield was about 500 kg/ha while that of India was nearly

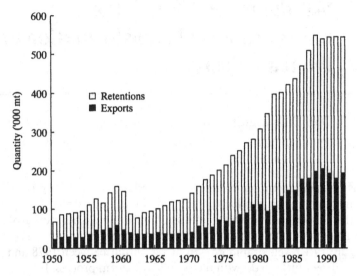

Figure 19.1   Retained production and exports, China, 1950–90
Source: Ministry of Agriculture (various issues).

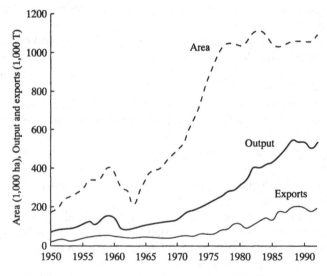

Figure 19.2   China's tea area, output and exports, 1950–92
Source: Ministry of Agriculture (various issues).

Table 19.1 *Mature area, output and tea yield, 1981–90*

Year	Area (1,000 ha) Total	Plucked	Output (1,000 tonnes)	Yields (kg/ha) Total	Plucked
1981	1,061	..	343	323	..
1982	1,097	752	397	362	528
1983	1,105	785	401	363	511
1984	1,077	778	414	384	532
1985	1,045	796	432	413	556
1986	1,024	804	463	452	573
1987	1,044	809	508	477	628
1988	1,056	812	545	516	664
1989	1,065	822	535	502	651
1990	1,065	823	540	507	656

Source: Editorial Board of China Agriculture Yearbook (various years).

2,000 kg/ha. With nearly half of the world's total tea gardens, China produces only about 20 per cent of world output.

Why are mature yields so low? There is a wide difference (243 thousand hectares in 1989) between the total area and the plucked area (table 19.1). In 1982 and 1989 official statistics included figures for new areas. These additional data allow calculation of the immature area as a residual: total area, less plucked area, less the new area. On this basis, in 1982 a total of 256 thousand hectares would be classed as 'immature'. By 1989 this area should have joined the plucked area. But the plucked area only increased by 70 thousand hectares. The implication is that this residual is not simply an immature area but includes abandoned and neglected areas of tea.

The production responsibility system and contracting tea fields

Enormous changes have taken place in the management of agricultural holdings since 1978 (Lin, chapter 2). In general, communes have been replaced by household-based farming. In this process, 70 per cent of land was allocated to each family on a per capita basis (Watson 1987: 9). By 1987, 80 per cent of the tea fields were contracted to households and the rest to specialised teams of households (Huang 1987: 5). Some villages have retained decision-making for tree crops. In others, all farming decisions have devolved upon individual households. Today, the size of tea gardens operated by each farmer is generally very small – typically about one-fifteenth of a hectare.

Table 19.2 *Provincial tea production statistics for China, 1979, 1984 and 1989*

Province	1979 Output (1,000 tonnes)	1979 Area (1,000 hectares)	1979 Yield (kg/ha)	1984 Output (1,000 tonnes)	1984 Area (1,000 hectares)	1984 Yield (kg/ha)	1989 Output (1,000 tonnes)	1989 Area (1,000 hectares)	1989 Yield (kg/ha)
National	277.15	1,050.33	264	414.14	1,077.40	384	534.88	1,064.00	502
Jiangsu	4.75	10.80	440	7.85	14.87	528	13.57	13.13	1,033
Zhejiang	65.45	164.60	398	95.55	178.40	536	117.78	167.13	705
Anhui	29.95	96.20	311	43.05	120.93	356	51.44	119.27	431
Fujian	22.80	99.73	229	35.25	126.40	279	55.38	118.53	467
Jiangxi	9.20	59.93	154	13.60	67.60	201	19.12	57.73	331
Shandong	1.05	5.40	194	0.80	2.80	286	0.62	1.33	468
Henan	1.15	12.87	89	1.80	17.20	105	3.21	15.00	214
Hubei	17.00	82.60	206	21.90	75.73	289	28.35	74.33	381
Hunan	57.35	167.47	342	74.80	124.00	603	79.96	102.13	783
Guangdong	10.55	42.00	251	20.00	46.33	432	23.51	42.73	550
Hainan	*a*	*a*	*a*	*a*	*a*	*a*	8.03	7.53	1,065
Guangxi	7.05	27.07	260	9.45	23.67	399	15.73	22.53	698
Sichuan	28.35	115.60	245	49.00	111.80	438	57.47	105.07	547
Guizhou	6.25	39.47	158	10.10	30.53	331	13.65	29.33	465
Yunnan	14.85	98.33	151	28.15	109.93	256	42.75	159.80	268
Tibet	—	—	—	.	.	375	.	.	579
Shaanxi	1.35	28.20	48	2.70	26.60	102	4.13	28.80	143
Gansu	.	.	750	.	.	182	.	.	251

Note:
a Prior to 1989 Hainan was included in Guangdong's figures.
Source: Editorial Board of China Agricultural Yearbook (various years).

Does a perennial crop like tea readily lend itself to the minute-scale farming now practised in much of China's tea gardens? Even if tea can be farmed in very small plots (and there is evidence from other countries and Chinese history that it can), is contracting of land feasible if the length of the contract is too short to encourage the contractor to do more than plunder the bush for short-term gain, and the size of the parcel of land is insufficiently large and concentrated to enable some degree of efficiency in the use of resources? The answer is no, but the reasons are not necessarily obvious.

Four features of the industry need to be borne in mind. First, tea tends to be grown on hillsides and 'reclaimed' land. This is how China found the land for the planting programs of the 1960s and 1970s. One implication of this is that tea fields are often some distance from the villages. Second, tea is usually considered to be a 'spare-time crop', or an optional extra. Third, in the major producing provinces, tea production is highly seasonal. The spring flush is by far the most important both in quantity and quality of output. In some regions, 80 per cent of revenue is earned over April–May (Etherington 1990; Etherington and Forster 1989a, 1989b). Finally, tea is a differentiated processed product. China produces in the major classifications of 'green' (unfermented), 'scented' (the infusion of flavours to green tea), Oolong (semi-fermented), 'black' (fermented) and compressed (post-fermented) tea (Forster 1990). Different environmental niches tend to specialise in the production of particular types of tea but switching between certain major varieties is possible.

These distinct features of the industry have led some Chinese scientists to urge a reform of the current household system to allow for greater specialisation. The specific reforms suggested include lengthening the contract period, increasing the size of plots allocated to farmers, and establishing voluntary farmers' associations. Some observers also argue that price controls should be dropped, and administrative controls relaxed in favour of the operation of market forces. In these ways it is hoped to encourage the establishment of a specialist tea farming sector in which farmers have a long-term commitment to the industry, resulting in improved management.

Despite the call in 1984 by the CCP Central Committee for contracts to be 15 years or more, and even longer for crops with a longer productive life, the length of contracts for tea fields remains well below the five to twenty years suggested (Xie 1989). A survey of tea fields in Hunan province in 1984 revealed that over 90 per cent of all contracts were written for a period of less than five years (Mao 1984). During a field visit to the extremely prosperous tobacco growing Yuxi district in Yunnan in 1990, we asked about the contrast between the excellent yields and quality of the local tobacco and those of tea. The immediate response from local officials related to the relative length of time required to get a return from the crops, and the inadequate length of contract period for perennial crops in general. The typical three-year contract for tea was recognised as being too short.

Hainan and Jiangsu provinces have the highest tea yields (table 19.2). The situation in Jiangsu province is of particular interest because of the decision not to subdivide the commune tea fields. Some districts of Jiangsu did divide the land among households, but recollectivised at the end of the initial contract (He and Qian 1990). According to Tan (1989), the reasons for this decision were that tea required an appropriate scale of business. At the end of the 1970s Jiangsu decided to concentrate large-scale tea production in four counties – Yixing, Piaoyang, Jintan and Jurong. In 1988 output from these counties made up 75 per cent of the provincial total. The province then developed a contract responsibility system called 'unified business, contract management, honouring bonuses and fines and farm head responsibility' in which tea fields were not divided up among households. Since 1983 output in Jiangsu has increased by 77 per cent, with mature yields increasing by 25 per cent. There has also been an emphasis on the integration of processing on a relatively large scale so as to promote efficiency. Finally, a systematic extension service network was established as a technical backup for the industry.

The household responsibility reforms have had a depressing effect on tea output at the national and local level in China. Notice needs to be taken by policymakers of the research findings of Chinese social scientists, and ways found to extend contract periods and bring some of the 'public good' scale economies that exist in tea production to the individual farmer.

Stress and strain within the market

In terms of China's agricultural sector, tea is an economically minor but culturally important crop. The 1990 edition of *Zhongguo tongji nianjiann* [China Statistical Yearbook] (SSB, ZTN 1990) gives the output value of tea, silk cocoons and fruit as 3.6 per cent of the value of agricultural output in 1988 and 3.4 per cent in 1989. Tea is not an important sector in the food processing industry either. In 1988 the tea industry contributed about 5 per cent to the output value of village and township food process-ing enterprises. Except in producing areas and the major urban centres of north and north-east China, tea is still a luxury consumer item. In 1986 retail sales of tea made up 0.54 per cent of the value of social retail sales, or 1.54 per cent of the value of sales of foodstuffs. Exports have accounted for an average of over 30 per cent of production since 1949, valued at around US$420 million.

Until 1984 the state procurement agencies (principally the National

Supply and Marketing Cooperative) held a virtual monopoly over the domestic marketing of tea and its procurement for export agencies. After the production reforms of the late 1970s contradictions between liberalised production activities and state monopoly marketing became apparent. The mentality of placing production first and neglecting marketing resulted in production for its own sake. The problem reached crisis proportions in 1983 with a huge build-up in stocks of unmarketable tea. This also suggested that the tea planted during the Cultural Revolution era was quantitatively impressive but was not suitable for market requirements.

In an attempt to solve this conflict, in 1984 the central authorities relaxed state control over the procurement and sale of tea (as well as other agricultural products). The State Council stipulated that negotiated buying and selling could take place, and supply and demand would play a role in determining prices and the supply of different varieties. Individuals, enterprises and other government departments were encouraged to enter the marketing system. The export market had also suffered because of the inability of the system to deliver the product on time and at a competitive price. From 1984, provincial governments and provincial state trading companies were permitted to export directly (in some cases they had possessed this power for several years), thus breaking the monopoly of the central Tea Import and Export Company.

The response of farmers, processors and private merchants to the liberalisation of tea marketing was immediate. In 1985, the first year of reform, output rose a modest 4.1 per cent, while exports fell. The share of tea procured by the state marketing agencies dropped precipitately from a previous average of about 90 per cent to 65 per cent. The mixed average procurement price per 100 kilograms of tea increased by 35.8 per cent, the highest rise ever, while for retail prices the increase was 10.4 per cent. Consumption rose by 10.1 per cent. Competition started among processors and procurers, state, collective and individual, to obtain tea leaf to supply the domestic and export markets.

Before the reforms had had time to consolidate, however, a conference in August 1985 of the principal companies from 12 sales provinces held by the Ministry of Commerce and other state agencies announced a retreat from the 1984 initiative. The notice from the above departments urged the strengthening of management over product quality and the market price of tea, and strongly suggested that the principal state marketing channel (that is, the National Supply and Marketing Cooperative) continue to play the predominant and leading role in the distribution of tea. In 1986 guiding prices were introduced for teas supplied to the domestic market. This policy regime remained in effect in the early 1990s. Thus, the authorities reacted instinctively to the problems thrown up by the semi-reformed market created by their reverting to the use of administrative controls. But, as events later illustrated, the reaction of the government merely exacerbated an already potentially disastrous situation. The result was the eruption of a full-scale tea war.

The tea war, which started in 1985 and continued in some provinces until 1989, was essentially a mad scramble by buyers and processors to secure supplies in the face of strong growth in demand. Tea had been in short supply since 1949, and the use of coupons and vouchers to ration its distribution was retained until 1982. Previously, government controls had contained prices and suppressed demand. Now, in a liberalised market, producers were besieged by buyers willing to pay enormous premiums for high-quality leaf.

Four key factors contributed to the tea war. First, fiscal contracting, in operation since 1980, encouraged local governments to develop processing industries as a means of raising taxation revenue and developing the local economy. In key tea producing counties, income from the crop comprises 30 to 40 per cent of the total income from agricultural products, and profits and taxes make up 50 to 70 per cent of county government budgetary revenues. It is the processor, not the producer, who pays the greatest amount of tax, thus encouraging local governments to ensure that the raw material stays at source under its own jurisdiction. The central government's policy of budgetary contracting thus revealed and intensified the parochialism of local interests.

During the 1980s both the crude and refining industry expanded very rapidly. In 1979 there were 14,000 crude tea factories in China and by 1989 the number had increased to over 70,000. In 1980 there were 120 state tea refineries and in 1989, the number of refineries of different types had more than doubled to 2,500.

This growth occurred while official government policy specifically forbade the expansion of refining capacity except where the situation required the building of new facilities. The final decision, however, was left in the hands of provincial planning commissions. Under collective agriculture, local refineries had been guaranteed supplies: decollectivisation uncoupled the producer from the processor.

In order to obtain crude tea, processors were forced to accept an inferior quality product at high prices. If state processors did not accept the tea they were offered, the village and town enterprises would snap it up. Although their facilities and technical standards were inferior, and the quality of their products often shoddy, this sector possessed the advantage of lower production costs and thus could afford to pay a higher price for tea.

Second, the devolution of export powers to the provinces in the mid-1980s further exacerbated the imbalance between supply and demand and the competition for tea supplies. Since the commencement of economic reform in the late 1970s, the power of provincial governments and their trading companies had grown. The original three ports monopolising export of tea (Shanghai – green tea, Fuzhou – Oolong and scented tea, and Guangzhou – black and speciality teas) had grown to 17 by 1988, with Shenzhen added in 1990.

Each province had its own foreign currency retention rate affecting the minimum price at which it could afford to export tea. Guangdong could retain 100 per cent, Jiangsu, Zhejiang and Shanghai 75 per cent to 80 per cent, while a backward inland province like Anhui could only retain 25 per cent of its export earnings. Because of the great difference then operating between the official and the market exchange rate, provinces with high retention rates could afford to pay a higher procurement price for tea, including in the markets of other localities.

Third, different tea varieties are supplied to quite distinct consumer markets, both domestically and overseas. In Yunnan, which produces teas for the different markets, black (export), green (domestic) and border (minority nationalities), the farcical situation which emerged was encapsulated in the phrase uttered by tea farmers: 'one bush, three policies and three departments in charge'.

Provincial governments, alarmed at their inability to fulfil centrally planned targets for export procurements and worried that the explosion in procurement prices would make exports unprofitable, moved to fix maximum prices and empower supply and marketing cooperatives to reassert their monopoly over the procurement of such teas. Such initiatives were implemented in 1986. All traders outside the state trading network were forbidden to enter the market, and many localities, from the village, county and provincial level, introduced protectionist measures. Thus, in Zhejiang and Yunnan, transport licences were introduced in 1986 to exclude buyers from other provinces.

Negotiated buying and selling was permitted for domestically consumed teas. But even in this, the most liberalised sector of the tea market, the localities acted to secure their own supplies. In 1986 the Ministry of Commerce and the State Prices Bureau had set guiding and floating prices. In the heat of the tea war, however, these prices were very quickly overwhelmed as buyers swarmed into a business in which they believed they could make a handsome profit. From 1984 to 1988 actual mixed average procurement prices per 100 kilograms of tea increased by 156 per cent. This figure should be set against an increase in the officially approved guiding procurement price of 50 per cent for the same period. The increase in the mixed average retail price of tea over the same period was 50 per cent (figure 19.3).

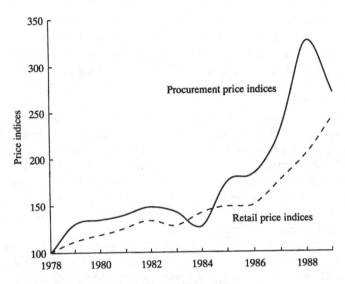

Figure 19.3   China's tea price indices (1978 = 100)
Source: Ministry of Agriculture (various issues).

Farmers shunned border tea and the export market. Where possible, black tea (export) processors switched to green, and green tea processors from roasted green (supplied to the international market) to toasted green (the base for scented tea) favoured by the major consumer markets in north China. This was a logical and direct consequence of the competition in different markets (domestic and foreign) and types of tea, partly created by the liberalisation policies of 1984.

The final factor was the blind pursuit of quantity to the neglect of quality. The tea war provided pressures for farmers to plunder their bushes and delay spring plucking so that they could pick larger and less fresh leaves in greater quantities. With higher-grade teas not being rewarded with an acceptable price differential, and buyers scrambling for fresh leaf and bidding up prices, quality came a distant second to immediate profit.

In statistical terms, the period from 1984 to 1988 when the tea war was being fought witnessed great quantitative achievements in the Chinese tea industry. National tea output increased by an annual average of 7 per cent, area decreased by an annual average of 0.5 per cent, while yields increased by an average of over 7 per cent per annum. Exports increased by an annual average of 9.1 per cent. Per capita tea consumption increased by over 25 per cent between 1984 and 1988.

In a period of high price inflation by Chinese standards, however, production costs in 1988 were 40 to 50 per cent above those for 1985. Thus, it was reported that the returns to producers from the tea war were largely eaten away by inflation and rising production costs, and tea was not as profitable as other agricultural commodities.

Administrative measures were not fully successful in regaining control over the industry in general and tea supplies in particular until the credit squeeze of late 1988. The fall in actual procurement prices in 1989 and 1990 and the stagnation in output growth for these two years reflected this squeeze. But output in 1991 recovered and reached an historical high in 1992.

Since the implementation of marketing reform, institutional sectoral responsibility in the tea industry has remained unchanged with three ministries involved in management. Each ministry supposedly has its own clearly defined area of authority, but co-ordination between the three is marked by squabbles over policy orientation and bureaucratic buckpassing. Jurisdictional conflict is rife. This institutional conflict is a major impediment to the efficient management of the industry, and contributed to the tea war.

Immediately after the economic retrenchment and political tightening-up of 1988–9, calls for the continuation of reform became much less frequent, although they increased again from 1991. One observer has described the government response to the disruption brought about by the tea war as aggravating the situation of the industry 'being controlled to death'. Although commentaries in 1991 recognised that the tea industry seemed to be caught in a no-man's land between the plan and the market, they tended to steer away from the kinds of radical reforms suggested only two or three years earlier.

Withdrawal from the international market

Raw tea is processed, traded, reprocessed, blended, packaged and traded again. There are economies of scale not only in processing and trading but in the provision of research and extension services to farmers. The most rapid expansion of the industry (during the Cultural Revolution) was undertaken with the provision of such services as public goods and on large blocks of land, although with such disregard for market requirements that much of the planted area now has little value. So far the process of reform of the tea industry in China has allocated pocket-handkerchief-sized parcels of land to farmers with short-term contracts and stripped smallholders of the provision of key services. The result is low levels of production relative to known potential: the 'yield gap' is large. Furthermore, the lag between the major plantings of the 1960s and 1970s and output have now worked themselves out. Production has reached a plateau.

Current per capita consumption of tea is estimated to be about 0.36 kilograms per person and grew at 7.5 per cent over the period 1965–88. Over the 11 years 1978–88 it grew at about 10 per cent per annum, implying an income elasticity of demand in excess of one. The state predicts a deceleration of demand growth to about 4 per cent per annum for the rest of the century. This in turn implies that the income elasticity of demand will drop well below one. This is considered to be a most unlikely outcome in the absence of major relative price changes. Such major price adjustments are likely, but would be less severe if foreign trade were liberalised. In this case, domestic consumption of tea would rise more rapidly, exports would fall and there would be upward pressure on world tea prices.

The struggle to strengthen the Chinese tea industry, both domestically and internationally, has been lengthy. There is much interest in the effects of reform and the adjustment policy to cater for the country's supply–demand imbalance. There is a possibility exists that over the next 20 years the mainland will withdraw from the international tea market.

Notes

* The authors are most grateful for the support given for this study by the Research School of Pacific and Asian Studies at the Australian National University, Canberra, and the Pacific Cultural Foundation, Taipei.

20 The growth of rural industry: the impact of fiscal contracting

Andrew Watson, Christopher Findlay and Chen Chunlai

Over the past ten years, the development of rural manufacturing, handicraft and commercial enterprises has become one of the cornerstones of China's economic reform policies. This process has absorbed surplus agricultural labour, raised incomes and transformed the structure of the rural economy. As a result, the Chinese countryside is embarking on a phase of development that is bringing an end to the economic dominance of agriculture. With the increasing commercialisation of rural production, growth of rural enterprises has accelerated the pace of urbanisation, playing a key role in a number of fundamental economic processes. The significance of the economic changes involved cannot be overstated.

Why has it been rural industry which has grown so rapidly? Reform and growth are likely to lead to economic transformation and a relative decline in the agricultural sector. But there are no expectations in this analytical structure about the location of industrial growth. Will it occur more rapidly in rural areas or in urban areas? One of our aims is to explain why industrialisation in China has had a rural bias.

The growth of rural industry has transformed the relationship between town and countryside and created some tensions in relations between the urban and rural economies. The growth of rural industry and the associated transformation has been greatest in the coastal provinces, especially from Hainan to Jiangsu, north of Shanghai, but its effects have been felt throughout the country.

Rural enterprises have their origins in the commune system. They are owned and operated by local government, collectives and co-operatives as well as individuals and any combination of these, and they are contributing to the diversification of China's economic system. But the main implication of their origins is that rural enterprises have important links with local governments and the attitudes of local governments play a key role in their development. Incentives created by a new form of fiscal relations between central and local governments, fiscal contracting, have contributed to local governments strong interest in promoting rural enterprises.

The introduction of fiscal contracting had two important consequences. First, it encouraged the expansion of industrial systems owned and operated by local government at provincial, prefectural and county levels, rather like small, local versions of the national state enterprise system but subject to local planning and budgets. Second, it meant that government at township and village levels had the incentive to support the growth of rural enterprises as the basis of their income. Furthermore, the parallel evolution of local and rural enterprises has fostered a close relationship between them, involving common activities and economic interests. County governments see rural enterprises as part of their local tax base and encourage links between such enterprises and their own industrial systems.

The definition of rural enterprises

China's rural enterprises, commonly known as township enterprises, are economic entities established by various levels of local government in the countryside, or by the peasants themselves. They may be run by towns (*zhen*), townships (*xiang*), districts (*qu*) and villages (*cun*), or by peasants either as individuals, in partnerships or in co-operation with their village. Their undertakings encompass all types of economic activity, including agriculture, industry, construction, transport, commerce and services.[1] As Chinese statistics provide a breakdown based on ownership of or responsibility for assets, it is possible to distinguish between rural and urban enterprises because rural enterprises are owned by the successors to the commune system and by the peasants, while urban enterprises are owned by the various levels of state government and by urban residents.[2]

Rural enterprises operate outside the state plan and are subject to 'hard budget constraints' in that their owners (the peasants or the townships) do not have any guaranteed budget income from above. They buy inputs and sell outputs in free markets, without having to fulfil plan obligations to the state. Despite this market orientation, their origins in the collective system mean that they commonly have a strong linkage with governments at *zhen* level and below.[3] The origins of this link and its implications are explored below.

Rural enterprise growth

As a result of the rural reforms of 1978, township enterprises experienced an unprecedented phase of rapid development.[4] The total number of enterprises increased from 1.5 million in 1978 to 20.8 million in 1992, more

Table 20.1 *Rural enterprises: numbers, workers and output value, 1978–89[a]*

Year	Number of rural enterprises (million)	Number of workers in rural enterprises (million)	Total output value of rural enterprises (billion yuan)	
			Nominal	Real[b]
1978[a]	1.5242	28.2656	49.3070	49.3070
1979	1.4804	29.0934	54.8410	54.4082
1980	1.4246	29.9967	56.6900	60.7711
1981	1.3375	29.6956	74.5300	67.3446
1982	1.3617	31.1291	85.3080	75.6253
1983	1.3464	32.3464	101.6830	88.8093
1984	6.0652	52.0811	170.9890	145.2338
1985	12.2245	69.7903	272.8390	212.9743
1986	15.1513	79.3714	354.0870	260.1530
1987	17.4464	87.7640	474.3100	325.5491
1988	18.8816	95.4546	649.5660	376.2831
1989	18.6863	93.6678	742.8380	365.2376

Notes:
[a] 1978–83 covers township and village levels only; 1984–89 covers all rural enterprises.
[b] Real output value is derived by dividing nominal value by an index of prices of capital goods and consumer goods.
Sources: SSB, ZTN (1988: 292; 1990: 250, 390–401).

than a tenfold increase (table 20.1). Their total labour force rose from 28.3 million to 105.8 million, an increase of over 70 million, and their total output value grew from 49 billion yuan to 1,769 billion yuan in current year prices.[5] In real terms, output increased 23 per cent a year up to 1988 and then fell by 3 per cent in 1989. The former high growth rates were restored after 1991.

By 1987 the total output value of these enterprises accounted for over 50 per cent of rural social output value (exceeding the total output value of agriculture for the first time), and for 21 per cent of national social output value. These shares were stable for the period 1987 to 1989 and then increased to 70 per cent and 32 per cent respectively in 1992 (table 20.2).

The rapid recovery after 1989 indicates that the austerity policies of 1988–90 did not undermine the momentum of rural enterprise development. The national figures, however, disguise significant regional variations.[6] This trend in the share of rural industries in output is expected to

Table 20.2 *Significance of rural enterprises in the national economy, 1980–9*

Year	Gross output value of rural enterprises (A)	Gross output value of rural society (B)	Gross output value of national society (C)	A/B %	A/C %
1980	65.69	279.212	853.2	23.53	7.70
1983	101.683	412.378	1112.5	24.66	9.14
1984	170.989	503.379	1316.6	33.97	12.99
1985	272.839	634.004	1658.8	43.03	16.45
1986	354.087	755.423	1906.6	46.87	18.57
1987	474.31	943.161	2303.4	50.29	20.59
1988	649.566	1253.469	2980.7	51.82	21.79
1989	742.838	1448.017	3460.4	51.30	21.47

Sources: SSB, ZTN (1988: 37, 214, 294; 1990: 49, 333, 401).

be particularly marked in the coastal provinces with low per capita land ratios, dense populations, better infrastructure and the potential for rural enterprises to build profitable links with existing industries.

Some care must be exercised in interpreting these figures, not only because of the margins of error in Chinese data, especially in respect of the private sector, but also because of the many changes that have taken place in the Chinese statistical system in recent years. Before 1978 enterprises were classified as commune and brigade, and their economic statistics were recorded as part of the collective system. With the reforms of 1978, they were established as a separate statistical category, though until 1983 the official figures still remained limited to those enterprises run by communes and brigades.[7] After the demise of the communes, the category was expanded in 1984 to include co-operative enterprises run by peasants independently and other forms of co-operative or private industrial enterprises in the countryside. In 1985 and 1986, this definition was further adjusted to include other non-industrial enterprises run co-operatively or privately. These changes mean that the figures in table 20.1 must be treated with caution when measuring rates of growth. Nevertheless, the continual adjustment of categories reflects both the changes in ownership and management taking place, and the rapid growth occurring outside the existing categories and thereby forcing the continual changes in statistical methods. It is therefore reasonable to assume that the overall rise in enterprise numbers between 1978 and 1987 closely represents the long-term growth taking place, even though the jumps from 1.4 million in 1983 to 6.1 million in 1984 and again to 12.2 million in 1985 reflect changes in statistical procedures rather than actual growth for the years concerned.

Another issue is that the data refer to output value. In the Chinese statistical system, output value includes the value of intermediate products and therefore possibly presents a distorted picture of the growth of manufacturing activity. A more accurate set of indicators is the volume of other inputs into rural industry (table 20.3).[8] They show that between 1980 and 1991 there was nearly a ninefold increase in the value of assets in these enterprises, a nearly sixfold increase in the wage bill, and a fivefold increase in value-added (defined as payments to capital and labour, plus taxes). The final statistic implies that value-added was increasing by about 16 per cent a year (9 per cent a year in real terms) over that period.

By contrast, financial indicators of state-run enterprises show that their profits and taxes increased nearly two times between 1980 and 1991, an average growth rate of about 13 per cent (omitting 1989, the average growth rate rises to 9 per cent), their wage bill grew at 13 per cent a year (to 1991) and value-added grew at 12 per cent a year (about 6 per cent in real terms) (SSB 1988b). Thus value-added in township and village enterprise was growing over the 1980s faster than that in state enterprises. It accounted for 29 per cent of that in state enterprises in 1984 but rose to 33 per cent in 1991.

While this growth was taking place, the nature of rural enterprise activity was also changing. The proportion engaged in the primary sector (defined as agriculture and mining) declined rapidly (table 20.4). By the end of 1989 the number of enterprises, the labour force and the output value of this sector respectively accounted for only 1.2 per cent, 2.6 per cent and 1.7 per cent of township enterprises as a whole. By contrast, enterprises in the tertiary sector (defined as commerce and services) developed rapidly. By the end of 1989 the number of enterprises, the number of labourers and the output value of such enterprises accounted for 54.4 per cent, 22.4 per cent and 15.8 per cent of the respective totals. Secondary industry (defined as manufacturing) developed steadily. At the end of 1989 the number of enterprises, labour force and output value accounted for 44.4, 75.0 per cent and 82.5 per cent of the respective totals. In other words, the changing nature of rural enterprises illustrated the shift away from primary agricultural production towards secondary industries and services.

The data in table 20.4 refer to all rural enterprises. A more detailed division of activities in the secondary industry for 1980 and 1991 is reported (table 20.5), although these data are only available for enterprises run at township or village level. This evidence indicates that there has been a considerable diversification of activities. Construction materials, textiles and machinery were the top three in both years, followed by metals and chemicals, but over the intervening years their share had fallen from 80 per cent to about 45 per cent.

Table 20.3 *Main financial indicators of enterprises run by townships and villages, 1978–89 (billion yuan)*

Year	Original value of fixed assets	Net value of fixed assets	Circulating funds	State taxes (A)	Net profits (B)	Total wages (C)	Value-added (A+B+C) (D)	Total wages value-added (C/D)*100
1978	22.960	..	..	2.200	8.810	8.660	19.670	32.87
1979	28.920	..	..	2.260	10.450	10.380	23.090	37.38
1980	32.630	..	17.720	2.570	11.840	11.940	26.350	45.31
1981	37.540	..	20.100	3.430	11.280	13.060	27.770	47.03
1982	42.930	..	23.050	4.470	11.550	15.330	31.350	48.90
1983	47.570	37.928	26.250	5.890	11.780	17.580	35.250	49.87
1984	57.500	44.567	39.870	7.910	12.870	23.930	44.710	53.52
1985	75.040	58.975	59.010	10.360	17.130	30.140	58.130	51.85
1986	94.675	74.316	76.981	13.774	16.103	35.551	65.428	54.34
1987	122.665	95.977	113.464	16.808	18.775	42.768	78.351	54.59
1988	158.430	123.450	154.060	23.650	25.920	54.120	103.690	52.19
1989	192.070	148.620	189.010	27.250	24.010	58.070	109.330	53.11

Sources: Yearbook of Rural, Social and Economic Statistics of China 1986, 228; SSB, ZTN (various issues); Ministry of Agriculture (1987: 656); Ministry of Agriculture (1989: 286–9).

Table 20.4 *Distribution of rural enterprises by economic sectors, 1978 and 1989*

Sectors	Number of enterprises (million)			Number of workers (million)			Total output value (billion yuan)		
	1978 (%)	1989 (%)	Growth (%)	1978 (%)	1989 (%)	Growth (%)	1978 (%)	1989 (%)	Growth (%)
Primary[a]	0.4946 (32.45)	0.2268 (1.2)	-45.86	6.0842 (21.53)	2.393 (2.6)	-39.33	3.619 (7.34)	12.603 (1.7)	348.25
Secondary[b]	0.8407 (55.16)	8.2902 (44.4)	986.11	19.6998 (69.69)	70.2783 (75)	356.75	42.006 (85.19)	60.9047 (82.5)	144.99
Tertiary[c]	0.1889 (12.39)	10.1693 (54.4)	5383.43	2.4816 (8.78)	20.9965 (22.4)	846.09	3.682 (7.47)	11.7178 (15.8)	318.25
Total	1.5242	18.6863	1225.97	28.2656	93.6678	331.38	49.307	74.2838	150.66

Notes:
[a] Includes agricultural, forestry, animal husbandry and fisheries.
[b] Includes manufacturing and construction.
[c] Includes social services, transport and communications.
Sources: SSB, ZTN (1988: 292–4; 1989: 399–401).

Table 20.5 *Main sectors of township and village-run rural industrial enterprises, 1980 and 1989*

Industries	1980 output value (billion yuan)	% of total	1989 output value (billion yuan)	Growth % of total	Growth (%)
Construction materials	11.26	22.3	65.011	14.89	577.36
Textiles	5.8	11.5	55.782	12.78	961.76
Machinery	14.25	28.2	44.076	10.10	309.31
Food	4.47	8.9	28.25	6.47	631.99
Chemicals	4.52	9	22.408	5.13	495.75
Metal			28.726	6.58	
Sub-total	40.3	79.9	244.253	55.96	606.09
Total output of rural industries	50.491	100	436.501	100	864.51

Sources: Editorial Board of China Agricultural Yearbook, 1986: 43; State Statistical Bureau (ZTN) 1990: 450–1.

The regional distribution of township enterprises as a whole remains very uneven (table 20.1). In 1991 the output value of township enterprises in the eastern coastal provinces and municipalities accounted for 67 per cent of the total. The same region accounted for 71 per cent of the value of industrial output and, in 1988, 83 per cent of rural enterprise exports. In comparison, the eastern region accounts for just over 40 per cent of China's total population. Industrial enterprises in the eastern regions have also tended to grow faster than these types of enterprises in other regions.

In terms of ownership, the encouragement given to private and new types of co-operative ventures since 1978 has created a much more complex economic system. The most dynamic growth has taken place in individually owned enterprises, even though their labour force and sales revenue reflect their smaller size and lower levels of capital intensity. At the end of 1991 these made up 92 per cent of all enterprises, employed 50 per cent of the total workforce, and produced 34 per cent of total income. Township and village-run enterprises, though only 8 per cent of the total in 1991, were just as important in terms of number of workers (50 per cent) but more important as total income (67 per cent) (SSB, ZTN 1992: 48, 389–90). This demonstrates the major role the collectively owned sector continues to play in this aspect of the rural industrial sector.

The growth of township enterprises has also had a significant effect on government budgets at all levels. In 1987 tax paid by township and village enterprises amounted to 16.8 billion yuan, 7.2 per cent of the total state budget income of 234.7 billion yuan and 12.2 per cent of industrial and commercial tax revenue of 138.1 billion yuan (Chen, Watson and Findlay 1991). Taxes on township enterprises also accounted for considerable shares of revenue at county level. According to information from counties in suburban Shanghai and in southern Jiangsu, industrial and commercial taxes, product taxes and income taxes from rural enterprises generally made up 70–80 per cent of county budget income.[9] Furthermore, from 1980 to 1987 enterprises run by townships and villages have spent 85.4 billion yuan on reinvestment, on supporting agricultural production, and on collective welfare activities (Ministry of Agriculture 1987a: 656). This is 9.8 per cent more than state budget expenditure of 77.8 billion yuan (Chen, Watson and Findlay 1991) on supporting agricultural production and other agricultural activities over the same period. The wealth generated by these enterprises was also important therefore for other aspects of the economy.

Last, but not least, the development of rural enterprises accelerated the development of small towns. From 1981 to 1985 the growth of township enterprises led to the establishment of more than 1,300 small towns annually (Third Bureau, Ministry of Public Security 1985: 101–2). Once again, this figure has to be treated with caution as many of these towns may have existed previously as commune headquarters and their reclassification as towns to some extent merely reflects the administrative reforms taking place. Also, the rules for reclassification were changed in 1984 to allow for a smaller proportion of non-agricultural population in towns (Third Bureau, Ministry of Public Security 1985: 101–2), and there are many perceived advantages to local officials in gaining the new status, including additional budget expenditures and the rights to establish administrative units associated with town status. Nevertheless, the growth of rural industries has been one of the factors enabling the reclassification to take place. As a result of these changes, the proportion of the population classified as urban, under 20 per cent for most of the period since 1949, jumped to 32 per cent in 1984 and reached nearly 47 per cent in 1987 (Chen, Watson and Findlay 1991). The demand for industrial products generated by this growth of town and rural enterprises also had a feedback effect on urban industry. According to one source, in 1987 township enterprises consumed products worth 30 billion yuan from state-run enterprises.[10]

Origins of rural industry development

1949 to 1978

The development of rural enterprises in China has passed through three main stages since 1949. The evolution of these phases saw a shift in the rural development strategy from one which gave primacy to the development of agricultural production and inputs to one which saw rural development as a more complex process of sectoral change in which agricultural production might cease to be the sole or even the main target. In the first stage, such enterprises were mainly engaged in handicraft production and the primary processing of agricultural products. In 1949, the output value of these activities was only 5.2 billion yuan, but with the revival of the rural economy this rose to 8.1 billion yuan in 1952.[11] After 1953, farmers who produced handicrafts to earn a cash income during the slack farming season and professional rural craftsmen were brought within the agricultural co-operatives. At the same time, the output of urban industry could not meet rural demand, so the development of rural handicrafts and primary processing industries was necessary. The Central Committee's 'Resolution on Developing Agricultural Producer Co-operatives' stated therefore that 'agricultural producer co-operatives can use their surplus labour and capital to develop rural sidelines, and make the operation of these sidelines serve to expand agricultural production' (Ministry of Agriculture 1987b). The Party and the State Council subsequently issued a series of documents guiding the development of rural sidelines and, by the end of 1957, the output value of rural sidelines approached nearly 10 billion yuan.

The establishment of the communes in 1958 marked the second phase of growth. The government called for the large-scale development of rural industries. Under this policy, large numbers of peasants were set to work in commune industries and, at the same time, some state-owned commercial and other enterprises located in rural areas were transferred to the communes. In this phase, the industrial nature of the sidelines and their production of inputs for agriculture were stressed. More than 35,000 handicraft co-operatives owned by rural townships were also transformed into commune industries without compensation. As a result, by the end of 1958 there were 2.6 million commune-run industrial enterprises with a total output value of around 10 billion yuan. The economic collapse that followed the Great Leap Forward and the establishment of the communes, however, led to a retrenchment. By the end of 1964 the number of commune enterprises had declined to 1 million, and their output value was only 460 million yuan (Ministry of Agriculture 1987b).

As the economy recovered, and especially after the reassertion of the commune strategy in the Cultural Revolution, communes and brigades once again began to develop their industrial enterprises. To some extent this was done by relying on the workers who had been transferred back to the countryside from cities at the beginning of the 1960s in the wake of the collapse of the Great Leap Forward. Then, in the 1970s, with the aim of speeding up agricultural mechanisation, the government encouraged the development of agricultural machinery workshops and farm machinery manufacturing and repair plants. The emphasis of these industries was again in supporting agricultural production. The returns to light industry could be invested in the production of agricultural inputs, thereby raising agricultural output, rural incomes and the demand for light industrial products (Riskin 1987: 214). As such, they were not oriented towards the market or consumer products and remained embedded in an economic philosophy which gave priority to agricultural production. Nevertheless, they formed a network across the rural areas and became the basis for rural mechanised industry. An additional factor which also helped the growth of these industries was the transfer of educated urban youth to the countryside, who provided a new source of knowledge and skills. Their links with the cities also often enabled communes and brigades to establish enterprises with help from urban industry. As a result of these factors, by the end of 1976 the industrial output value of commune and brigade-run enterprises had risen to 24.3 billion yuan (Ministry of Agriculture 1987a: 2).

The reforms of 1978

When the rural economic reforms began in late 1978, the Central Committee's 'Decision on Some Problems in Accelerating the Development of Agriculture' stressed that the new rural development strategy relied on the comprehensive development of agriculture, industry and commerce. It also pointed out that commune and brigade-run enterprises needed to expand in order to promote the growth of small towns in rural areas (Editorial Committee of China Agricultural Yearbook 1980: 57–63). This decision recognised that rural policy should have a wider perspective than its previous concentration on crop farming. Subsequently, in March 1984 the Central Committee and the State Council approved the 'Report on Creating a New Situation in Commune and Brigade-run Enterprises', which signalled a new phase of development for township enterprises (Ministry of Agriculture 1984: 343–56). This report envisaged that the former collective enterprises, now run by townships and villages, together with the co-operative and private undertakings that had grown up since 1978, would become the focus of a new phase of integrated rural development, providing inputs for agriculture, absorbing rural labour, helping to raise rural incomes and producing for the market. It stressed that the enterprises were responsible for their own profits and losses but that their development should be supported and encouraged by government at all levels.

Fiscal contracting[12]

One of the incentives for local governments to promote rural industry arose from a new set of fiscal arrangements between the central and local governments, fiscal contracting. Experiments with this reform began at the provincial level in 1977 and accelerated after 1979. It was introduced at county level in 1980 in Sichuan and thereafter spread to counties in all provinces.[13] The centralised system whereby all revenue was handed upwards and all expenditure was allocated from above was replaced by a system whereby each level of government makes an agreement with the next level up to meet certain income and expenditure targets (Tian, Zhu and Xiang 1985; Han and Mai 1984; Xiang 1987: 1–9; Editorial Board of China Economic Yearbook 1981: II-130, 1983: VIII-56). If an administrative level is able to generate additional revenue, this is shared with its next superior level according to an agreed ratio set out in the fiscal contract. That contract also stipulates any expenditure subsidy to be provided to the lower level, regardless of changes in its revenue during the contract period. The surplus income retained at the lower level (which may be all such income) can be used to cover new investment or other expenditure at its own discretion.

   One of the major aims of this change was to provide lower levels of government with the incentive to increase revenue and to improve their financial efficiency, thereby reducing the numbers of government units operating with a budget deficit. An important result of the reform, however, was that the central government lost much of the direct control it once had over investment funds. In national terms, state budget expenditure on capital construction investment dropped from 83 per cent of the total in 1978 to 39 per cent in 1985, with the extra-budget investment funds coming from lower levels of government, administrative departments and production units themselves.[14]

   The changes inevitably generated friction between the various levels of administration as each tried to increase the range of their autonomy, maximise the proportion of funds transferred downwards and minimise the amount of revenue controlled within the contract. They also had important implications for behaviour at county level and below. The changes meant that local economic interests were very clearly defined, and gave local governments the independence to achieve their economic goals. In particular, they provided a strong incentive to promote local industrial and enterprise development, and this became a major source of income for local governments.[15]

The changes also stimulated a major surge of investment in rural infrastructure and services. In Wendeng county, Shandong, for example local government investment in fixed assets grew at a rate of 56.4 per cent a year from 1983 to 1985, with the overwhelming proportion going to industry and urban construction (He Daofeng *et al.*, 1987). By contrast, agricultural investment declined as a proportion of total investment. Furthermore, apart from its direct intervention through control of budget and extra-budget investment, the county government was also able to use indirect influence on bank investment to direct economic growth along its preferred lines.[16]

Some further issues

The growth of rural industry in China and its significance in the rural economy was not widely appreciated for many years into the reform period, and is still generally underestimated.

A number of issues associated with the growth of rural industry are beyond the scope of this study but are noted here. One is the question of ownership. The definition of property rights over township and village-run enterprises is not resolved. The reforms have created a situation where the successors to the communes have inherited the ownership of collective assets but the mechanisms of collective economic distribution which once expressed that ownership, however imperfectly, have disappeared. Enterprises have either become subordinate units of local government or have gradually been transformed into semi-private or fully private enterprises. Various solutions have been proposed by Chinese economists. All attempts to solve the problem have involved clarifying ownership in terms of one of the three major actors in the enterprises: the original communal owners, the workers themselves and the local government. The first solution raises problems in defining the economic rights of the peasant owners. The second implies the establishment of a new body of independent owners, though once again the joint nature of ownership may need to be clarified. The third, the practical outcome of the current situation, embodies many of the uncertainties of the commune period. All three solutions serve to underline the legacy of the particular nature of collective ownership under the commune system. This defined ownership of all local assets in terms of a community living within a geographically defined area of administration. The key unifying feature was the geographical boundary, and the basic economic activity for the community was agriculture. The diversification out of agriculture associated with reform and growth, mobility in the use of resources (land, labour, capital and raw materials), and market relationships has placed strains on the geographical definition of ownership. Until this issue is resolved, the administrative mechanisms of the old structure will continue to shape the development of the new.

The pressures to sustain revenue and to meet community goals provide the motives for local government to encourage the establishment of township enterprises. Their contribution to investment in those enterprises is significant. Their control of funds and the allocation of those funds to local activities however, encourages extensive rather than intensive development. This raises issues about the efficiency of the enterprises created in terms of both their scale and their location.

Once an enterprise is established, local governments have strong incentives to intervene directly in its management. At the same time, the combination of inherited rights of collective ownership and the indistinct definition of private property rights make it easy for them to do so. As the centre of power within their communities, township and village governments not only have administrative authority but also assume the functions of owner. By controlling personnel appointments, they can intervene directly in management, decision-making, profit distribution and investment plans.

Other issues arise in the system of the distribution of industrial intermediate products, where the needs of urban industry are guaranteed first. Urban and rural industries then compete in the market for the remainder. The quantity of the surplus is thus influenced by the speed of urban development. When it is slow, the volumes available for market distribution are relatively large, and rural industries have greater opportunities. When urban development is rapid, however, supplies are scarce. The quantity distributed through administrative allocation tends to grow. Rural industries face higher prices, while urban industries obtain more guaranteed supplies at lower plan prices. This situation has two consequences. First, there is a leakage of goods from the planned sector for sale at higher market prices, and the corruption of those with power over distribution tends to increase. Second, local authorities try to restrict the flow of industrial raw materials out of their area in order to ensure supplies go first to their own rural industries on which they depend for income. This incentive to intervene has led to various commodity 'wars' and tensions between rural and urban industry.[17] Ultimately, therefore, the combination of fiscal contracting and the growth of rural enterprises has generated differences in economic interests between the central and local governments. These different sets of interests have important implications for economic behaviour and central–local political relationships.

Notes

1 In the following sections, we sometimes distinguish between rural enterprises in total and those run by townships and villages. The latter are a sub-set of the former, the other sub-set being those enterprises which are run by individuals or co-operatively.

2 This classification of enterprises by type of ownership and control does not always correspond precisely to a classification by location, not all urban enterprises will be within the state plan. In the urban economy, there are some collectively or privately owned enterprises that are outside the plan, but their significance is small in urban economies relative to state enterprises. Furthermore, some rural enterprises may operate in or close to urban areas.

3 There are major issues involved in the ownership and control of these enterprises. Rural enterprises have become very important sources of revenue for basic levels of rural government. (Chen, Watson and Findlay 1991). Aspects of the organisation of the enterprise and their links with local government also affects their behaviour. What is of interest is the use of policy instruments by local governments to promote the interests of enterprises within their region. Examples are given below.

4 See the State Council Research Unit Rural Economy Group and the Rural Development Research Institute of the Chinese Academy of Social Sciences (1990), Byrd and Lin (1990).

5 The figures cited are from the State Statistical Bureau System. Other sources give different figures. The Ministry of Agriculture gave 840 billion yuan for 1989 (see *Jingji ribao*, [Economics Daily] 10 May 1990: 3). Some economists argue that the Ministry of Agriculture series may be more reliable since the Ministry statistical system reaches more deeply into the countryside.

6 In Shandong, for example, the output value of rural industries in the first five months of 1990 accounted for 50 per cent of all industrial output value, up 6 per cent over the same period of the previous year (*Zhongguo xiangzhen qiye bao*, [China Township Enterprise Paper] 25 June 1990: 1). In Guangdong it was anticipated that the output value would account for 30 per cent of provincial industrial output value in 1990 (*Ao-gang xinxi bao*, [Macao-Hong Kong News] 9 October 1990). In Zhejiang the proportion was nearly 51 per cent in 1987 (*Zhongguo xiangzhen qiye* [China Township Enterprise Paper] No.9, 1988: 21–6).

7 The nature and changes in the statistical system are outlined in Ministry of Agriculture 1987b: 416.

8 These data refer only to enterprises run by townships and villages, not to all rural enterprises.

9 Document issued by the Ministry of Finance, 5 November 1988.

10 Document issued by the Ministry of Finance, 5 November 1988.
11 The following discussion of the three periods of development is based on *Zhangguo Xiangzhen Qiye Guanli Baike Quanshu* [Chinese Encyclopedia of Rural Enterprises] (Ministry of Agriculture 1987: 1–2).
12 For more detail of the budget process, see Findlay and Watson (1992b). The following discussion draws on Donnithorne (1981), Oksenberg and Tong (1991: 1–32), and Deng, Yao, Xu and Xie (1990).
13 The Sichuan experiments are discussed in Lu and Yang (1986: 47–50). Much of the following discussion is also based on Gu Xiulin (1986: 67–82), Tian, Zhu and Xiang (1985), Han and Mai (1984), Xiang (1987: 1–9), Editorial Board of the China Economic Yearbook (1981: II-130, 1983: VIII-56), and interviews with the Finance Department of Ling County, Shandong, September 1988. A useful source on the impact of the growth of extra-budget funds during the first half of the 1980s is Deng, Yao, Xu and Xie (1990).
14 For a discussion of the relationship between budget and extra-budget investment, see Ma (1982: 409–11) and Deng, Yao, Xu and Xie (1990).
15 The link between fiscal contraction and rural enterprise growth is stressed by Wong (1992: 197–227).
16 We examine the sources of funding for rural industry in more detail in Chen, Watson and Findlay (1991).
17 See, for example, Zhang Xiaohe *et al.*, Chapter 10. Findlay and Watson (1992a) discuss the long-run development of relationships between rural and urban industry in China.

References

Ahmad, Ehtisham and Yan Wang (1991) 'Inequality and poverty in China: institutional change and public policy, 1978 to 1988', *World Bank Economic Review*, 5(2): 231–57

Almanac of China's Agriculture (1990)

Anderson, Kym (1990) *Changing Comparative Advantage in China: Effects on Food, Feed and Fibre Markets*, Paris: OECD Development Centre

(1992) 'Analytical issues in the Uruguay Round Negotiations on agriculture', *European Economic Review*, 36: 519–26

Anderson, Kym and Yujiro Hayami (1986) *The Political Economy of Agricultural Protectionism: East Asia in International Perspective*, Sydney: Allen & Unwin

Anderson, Kym and Y. I. Park (1988) 'China and the international relocation of world textile and clothing activity', *Weltwirstschaftliches Archiv*, 125(1): 29–48

Aschmoneit, Walter H. (1990) 'Life quality index of China: a manual for development aid', in Jorgen Delman, Clemens Stubbe Ostergaard and Flemming Christiansen (eds), *Remaking Peasant China: Problems of Rural Development and Institutions at the Start of the 1990s*, Aarhus: Aarhus University Press

Ash, Robert F. (1988) 'The evolution of agricultural policy', *The China Quarterly*, 116 (December): 529–55

Aston, Basil, Kenneth Hill, Allan Piazza and Robin Zeitz (1988) 'Famine in China, 1958-61', *Population and Development Review*, 10 (December): 613–45

Atkinson, Anthony B. (1991) 'Comparing poverty rates internationally: lessons from recent studies in developed countries', *The World Bank Economic Review*, 5(1): 3–21

Balassa, Béla (1965) 'Trade liberalization and "revealed" comparative advantage', *Manchester School of Economic and Social Studies*, 33(2): 99–124

Banister, Judith (1987) *China's Changing Population*, Stanford: Stanford University Press

Bian Jibu (1989) 'Strengthening social welfare', *Beijing Review*, 32(5): 27–8

Brandão, A. and Martin, W. (1993) 'Implications of agricultural trade liberalisation for the developing countries', *Agricultural Economics*, 8: 313–43

Buchanan, J. and G. Tullock (1962) *The Calculus of Consent: Logical Foundations of Constitutional Democracy*, Ann Arbor: University of Michigan Press

Buckwell, Allan and Medland, John (1991) 'The effects of trade liberalisation: problems of modelling the effects of liberalising agricultural trade', *European Economic Review*, 35: 552–61

Byrd, W.A. and Lin Qingsong (eds.) (1990) *China's Rural Industry: Structure, Development and Reform*, Oxford: Oxford University Press for the World Bank

Carter, Colin and Zhong Fu-ning (1991) 'China's past and future role in the grain trade', *Economic Development and Cultural Change*, 39: 791–814

Chen, Jiyuan and Deng Yiming (1993) 'On influences of resumption of the GATT membership on grain production and policy response', *Zhongguo nongcun jingji* [China's Rural Economy], 9: 48–51

Chen, L. and A. Buckwell (1991) *Chinese Grain Economy and Policy*, Melksham: Redwood Press Ltd

Chen Chuan (1984) *A Comprehensive History of the Tea Industry*, Beijing: Agricultural Publishers (in Chinese)

Chen Chunlai, Andrew Watson and Christopher Findlay (1991) 'One state – two economies: current issues in China's rural industrialisation', Chinese Economy Research Unit, Working Paper 91/15, University of Adelaide

Cheng Enjiang (1994) 'Comparison of Chinese and international grain prices', Chinese Economy Research Unit, Working Paper 94/12, University of Adelaide

Cheng Guoqiang (1993) 'Agricultural protection and economic development [Nonye baofu yu jinji fazhan]', *Economic Research* [Jinji yanjiu], 4: 27–34

Cheng Zhiping (1989) 'Strive to maintain basic stability in vegetable retail prices this year', *Jiage lilun yu shijian* [Price Theory and Practice], 6: 2–5

China's Rice Research Institute (1987) *Zhongguo shuidao zhongzhi quhua yanjiu* [Research on the Regional Division of Rice Cultivation in China], Beijing: Kexue Chubanshe

Chinese Academy of Agricultural Science (1988) *Zhongguo liangshi zhi yanjiu* [Research on China's Grain Issues], Beijing: Chinese Agricultural Scientific and Technological Publishing House

(1989) *Zhongguo liangshi zhi yanjiu* [Research on China's Grain Issues], Beijing: Chinese Agricultural Scientific and Technological Publishing House

Chinn, Dennis L. (1980) 'Cooperative farming in North China', *Quarterly Journal of Economics*, 95 (March): 279–97

Chiu, T. F. (1991) 'The present status of tea cultivation, manufacture and utilisation in Taiwan', Paper presented at the International Symposium on Tea Science, Shizuoka, Japan, 26–9 August

Chow, Kit and I. Kramer (1990) *All the Tea in China*, San Francisco: China Books and Periodicals

Chu Yijie (1989) 'Liangshi diaochushi de ku zhong [The difficulties of grain transfers are heavy]', *Jingji cankao* [Economic Information], 8 June

Coady, D., Gang Qiao and A. Hussain (1990) 'The production, marketing and pricing of vegetables in China's cities', *STICERD China Program Report*, 6 (May), London School of Economics

Cramer, G., E. Wailes and S. Shui (1993) 'Impacts of liberalising trade in the world rice market', *American Journal of Agricultural Economics*, 75: 219–26

Crook, Frederick W. (1985) 'The *baogan daohu* incentive system: translation and analysis of model contract', *The China Quarterly*, 102 (June): 291–305

—— (1991) 'China's regional grain production 1963 to 1989: a preliminary examination', in CPE Agriculture Report, March/April, Centrally Planned Economies Branch, USDA, Washington, DC

Deng Yingtao, Yao Gang, Xu Xiaobo and Xie Yuwei (1990) *Zhongguo yusuanwai zijin fenxi* [An Analysis of Extra-Budgetary Funds in China], Beijing: Zhongguo Renmin Daxue Chubanshe

Dixit, A. K. and G. M. Grossman (1982) 'Trade and protection with multistage production', *Review of Economic Studies*, 49: 583–94

Dong Fureng (1982) 'Relationship between accumulation and consumption', in Xu Dixin *et al.*, *China's Search for Economic Growth*, Beijing: New World Press

Dong Ying and Cheng Jianhua (1994) 'Dui woguo mianhua zhidu de lishi huigu [A historical review of China's cotton system]', *Zhongguo nongcun jingji* [China's Rural Economy], 6: 28–34

Donnithorne, Audrey (1981) 'Centre-provincial economic relations in China', *Contemporary China Papers*, 16, Contemporary China Centre, The Australian National University

Dreze, J. and A. Sen (eds.) (1989) *Hunger and Public Action*, Oxford: Clarendon Press

—— (1990) *The Political Economy of Hunger*, New York: Oxford University Press

Du Rensheng (1992) 'The rural reform objective: establishing the market economy under the socialism system', *Zhongguo nongcun jingji* [China's Rural Economy], 12: 3–8

Eckstein, Alexander (ed.) (1980) *Quantitative Measures of China's Economic Output*, Ann Arbor: University of Michigan Press

Editorial Board of China Agriculture Yearbook (various issues) *Zhongguo nongye nianjian* [China Agriculture Yearbook], Beijing: China Agriculture Press.

Editorial Board of China Economic Yearbook (1981) *Zhongguo jingji nianjian* [China Economic Yearbook], Beijing: China Agriculture Press

Editorial Board of the Almanac of China's Foreign Economic Relations and Trade (1986) *Almanac of China's Foreign Economic Relations and Trade 1986*, Beijing: Zhongguo Zhanwang Press

Etherington, D. M. (1971) 'Economies of scale and technical efficiency: a case study in tea production', *East African Journal of Rural Development*, 4(1): 72–87

—— (1987) 'Guidelines for bio-economic modelling of tea production and processing in China and establishing effective research producer liaison', Report prepared for the FAO, Rome (August): 72

—— (1990) 'An economic analysis of a plant density experiment for tea in China', *Tropical Agriculture*, 67(3) (July): 248–56

Etherington, D. M. and K. Forster (1989a) 'Visits to the Chinese countryside', *Tea and Coffee Trade Journal*, 161(9) (September): 36–8

—— (1989b) 'The complex case of the Chinese tea industry', *Food Research Institute Studies*, 21(3): 265–308

296   References

(1991) 'Provincial profiles of tea in China: Yunnan province', *Tea and Coffee Trade Journal*, 163(5) (May): 30–40

(1992) 'The structural transformation of Taiwan's tea industry', *World Development*, 20(3) (March): 401–22

(1993) *Green Gold: The Political Economy of China's Post-1949 Tea Industry*, Hong Kong: Oxford University Press

Fan Shenggen (1991) 'Effects of technological change and institutional reform on production growth in Chinese agriculture', *American Journal of Agricultural Economics*, 73 (May): 266–75

Fang Cai (1992) 'Regional comparative advantages and sources of agricultural growth', *Zhongguo nongcun jingji* [China's Rural Economy], 11

(1993) 'China's agricultural comparative advantage and internationalisation', Paper presented to the workshop: China's Rural Reform and Development in the 1990s, Beijing, December

Findlay, Christopher and Andrew Watson (1991) 'The "wool war" in China', in Christopher Findlay (ed.), *Challenges of Economic Reform and Industrial Growth: China's Wool War*, Sydney: Allen & Unwin

(1992a) 'Surrounding the cities from the countryside: China's rural enterprises and their implications for growth, trade and economic reform', in Ross Garnaut and Liu Guoguang (eds), *Economic Reform and Internationalisation: China and the Pacific Region*, Sydney: George Allen & Unwin

(1992b) 'Issues in fiscal contracting in China', Paper presented to the 21st Conference of Economists, University of Melbourne, July

Findlay, Christopher and Li Ze (1991) 'The Chinese wool textile industry', in Christopher Findlay (ed.), *Challenges of Economic Reform and Industrial Growth: China's Wool War*, Sydney: George Allen & Unwin

Food and Agricultural Organisation (1991a) 'Demand prospects for rice and other foodgrains in selected Asian countries', FAO Economic and Social Development Paper 97, Rome

(various years) *FAO Production Yearbook*, Rome

Food Study Group (1991) *A Study of Medium- and Long-Term Strategies of Food Developments in China*, Beijing: China Agricultural Press

Forster, K. (1990) 'Tea types and their processing in China', *Tea and Coffee Trade Journal*, 162(10) (October): 26–32

(1991) 'China's tea war', Chinese Economy Research Unit Working Paper 91/3 (June), University of Adelaide

Forster, K. and D. M. Etherington (1991) 'China's dynamic tea industry', Paper presented at the International Symposium on Tea Science, Shizuoka, Japan, 26–9 August

Foster, James E., J. Greer and E. Thorbecke (1984) 'A class of decomposable poverty measures', *Econometrica*, 52: 761–6

Gaag, J. van der (1984) 'Private household consumption in China: a study of people's livelihood', World Bank Staff Working Paper 701, Washington, DC: World Bank

Gao Xiaomeng and Xiang Ning (1992) *Zhongguo nongye jiange zhence fenxi* [China's Agricultural Price Policy Analysis], Hangzhou: Zhejiang People's Press

Garnaut, Ross and Kym Anderson (1980) 'ASEAN export specialisation and comparative advantage', in Ross Garnaut (ed.), *ASEAN in a Changing Pacific and World Economy*, Sydney: Allen & Unwin

Garnaut, Ross and Ma Guonan (1992a) *Grain in China*, Canberra: Australian Government Publishing Service

(1992b) *China's Grain Economy*, Canberra: Australian Government Publishing Service

(1993a) 'How rich is China?: evidence from the food economy', *The Australian Journal of Chinese Affairs*, 30: 121–46

(1993b) 'Economic growth and stability in China', *Journal of Asian Economics*, 4(1): 5–24

Garnaut, Ross and Huang Yiping (1994a) 'Grain in developing Asia: a comparative overview', Paper presented to the workshop, Grain in Developing Asia, The Australian National University, Canberra, 28 February

(1994b) 'China's agricultural policy at a turning point', Department of Economics, Research School of Pacific and Asian Studies, The Australian National University, Canberra

(1994c) 'How Rich Is China: More Evidence', Research School of Pacific and Asian Studies, The Australian National University, Canberra

Goldin, I. and E. Knudsen (eds.) (1990) *Agricultural Trade Liberation Implications for the Developing Countries*, Paris: OECD/Washington, DC: World Bank

Gu Xiulin (1986) 'Xian-ji jingji tizhi gaige he caizheng bao gan wenti [Reform of the county-level economic system and the question of financial contracting]', *Nongcun fazhan yanjiu* [Rural Development Studies] (January)

Gu Huanzhang and Gu, Haiying (1993) 'The GATT and China's rural economic structural adjustment', *Agricultural Economic Issues*, 3: 23–8

Guangdong Statistical Department (various issues) *Guangdong Statistical Yearbook*, Guangdong: Guangdong Press

Guangdong Statistical Department, Commerce Section (1990) *Statistical Materials of Economic Development of Guangdong*, Guangdong: Guangdong Press

Guangzhou City Prices Bureau (1986) 'A review of vegetable price reform in Guangzhou', *Jiage lilun yu shijian* [Price Theory and Practice], 5: 37–8

Gunasekera, H.D.B.H., G. Rodriques and N. Andrews (1992) *Effects of Domestic Chinese Policies on the World Grain Market: Implications for Australia*, Canberra: Australian Bureau of Agricultural and Resource Economics

Gunasekera, H.D.B.H. *et al.* (1991) 'Agricultural policy reform in china', Discussion Paper 91.4, Australian Bureau of Agricultural and Resource Economics, Canberra

Guo Shutian *et al.* (1993) 'GATT membership and China's agriculture', *Zhongguo nongcun jingji* [China's Rural Economy], 8: 8–12

Guo Shutian, Ma Xiaohe, Cai Fang and Zhong Fu-ning (1993) 'An analysis of the current situation of China's agricultural protection', *Zhongguo nongcun jingji* [China's Rural Economy], 3: 11–14

Guo, W. F., K. Sakata, A. Yagi, K. Ina and S. J. Luo (1991) 'A new venture to prepare Chinese black tea from stale green tea', Paper presented at the

International Symposium on Tea Science Shizuoka, Japan, 26–9 August
Han Bi and Mai Fukang (eds) (1984) *Guojia yusuan cankao ziliao* [Reference Materials on the National Budget], Beijing: Zhongyang Guangbo Dianshi Daxue Chubanshe
Hayami, Yujiro (1988) *Japanese Agriculture under Siege – The Political Economy of Agricultural Policies*, New York: St Martin Press
He Daofeng *et al.* (1987) 'Dui xian-ji zhengfu xingwei de chuba fenxi [A preliminary analysis of country-level government behaviour]', *Nongye jingi wenti* [Issues of Agricultural Economy], 4: 19
He Yaoceng and Qian Liang (1990) 'Notes on a trip to tea areas in Yixing', *Chaye tongxua* [Tea Report], 3: 33–9
Hu Changnuan (1988) 'Comments on the successes and failure in agricultural price policy for the last nine years', *Nongye jingji wenti* [Issues of Agricultural Economy], 6: 7–11
Hu Ping (1980) 'A brief introduction to the survey of tea fields in Zhejiang Province', *Zhongguo chaye* [China Tea], 6: 18–19
—— (1987) 'A new type of specialist contract household – the family state farm', *Zhongguo chaye* [China Tea], 5: 9–10
Huang Lixun (1987) 'An inquiry into several policy questions concerning the development of tea production in Zhejiang', *Zhongguo chaye* [China Tea], 3: 5–7
Huang Shihong (1993) 'Influences of the resumption of the GATT membership on China's agricultural trade', *Zhongguo nongcun jingji* [China's Rural Economy], 3: 19–24
Huang Yanxin (1993) 'Effects of the resumption of the GATT membership on China's agriculture and trade of agricultural products and policy responses', *Zhongguo nongcun jingji* [China's Rural Economy], 4: 30–2
Huang Yiping (1993) 'Government intervention and agricultural performance in China', Ph.D. dissertation submitted to The Australian National University, Canberra
—— (1994a) 'The Uruguay Round and China's agricultural policy choices', Paper presented to the workshop, China and East Asian Trade Policy, Australian National University, 1–2 September 1994
—— (1994b) 'China's grains and oilseeds sectors: a review of major changes underway', A report prepared for the Directorate for Food, Agriculture and Fisheries, OECD, Paris
—— (1994c) 'The Uruguay Round and China's agricultural policy choices', Paper presented to the International Workshop China and East Asian Trade Policy, Australia–Japan Research Centre, The Australian National University, Canberra, 1–2 September
International Monetary Fund (various issues) *International Financial Statistics*, IMF, Washington, DC
Ito, S., E. Wesley, F. Peterson and W. Grant (1989) 'Rice in Asia: is it becoming an inferior good?', *American Journal of Agricultural Economics*, 71 (1): 32–42
—— (1991) 'An economic analysis of rice consumption in the People's Republic of China', *Agricultural Economics*, 6: 67–78

Jamison, D. T. *et al.* (1984) *China: The Health Sector*, Washington, DC: World Bank

Jamison, D. T., F. R. Trowbridge and T. J. Ho (1981) 'Food availability and the nutritional status of children in China', China: Socialist Economic Development Supplementary Paper III of Annex B, Washington, DC: World Bank

Jiang, J., and X. Luo (1989) 'Changes in Income of Chinese Peasants since 1978', in J. Longworth (eds.), *China's Rural Development Miracle: With International Comparisons*, Queensland: University of Queensland Press

Jiang Yaping (1988) 'Wo men bu gou yao zhong di: beijing shunyixian yiqi chengbao tudi hetong jiufeng jishi [All we want is to cultivate land: an on the spot report of a dispute of land contract in Shunyi county, Beijing]', *Renmin ribao* [People's Daily], 26 October

Johnson, D. Gale (1991) 'Agriculture in the liberalization process', in Lawrence B. Krause and Kim Kihwan (eds.), *Liberalization in the Process of Economic Development*, Berkeley: University of California Press

Ke Bingsheng (1993) 'China's grain trade protection coefficients and policy implications', *Zhongguo nongcun jingji* [China's Rural Economy], 3: 25–8

Khan, A. R., K. Griffin, C. Riskin and Zhao Renwei (1992) 'Household income and its distribution in China', Unpublished paper, Economic Research Institute, Chinese Academy of Social Sciences, Beijing

Kojima, Reeitsu (1988) 'Agricultural organization: new forms, new contradictions', *The China Quarterly*, 116 (December): 706–35

Kong Xianqin and Shi Zhisheng (1989) 'Mian liang guo cai bijia wenti ji dai jiejue [The problem of relative prices between cotton, grain, fruit and vegetables urgently needs to be solved]', *Nongye jingji wenti* [Issues of Agricultural Economy], 8: 55–7

Kueh Yak-Yeow (1985) 'The economics of the "second land reform" in China', *The China Quarterly*, 101 (March): 122–31

(1988) 'Food consumption and peasant incomes in the post-Mao era', *The China Quarterly*, 116 (December): 634–70

Lardy, N. (1983a) 'Agricultural prices in China', World Bank Working Paper 606, Washington, DC: World Bank

(1983b) *Agriculture in China's modern economic development*, Cambridge: Cambridge University Press

(1984) 'Prices, markets and the China peasantry', in Carl K. Eicher and John M. Staatz (eds), *Agricultural Development in the Third World*, Baltimore: Johns Hopkins University Press

(1986) 'Prospects and some policy problems of agricultural development in China', *American Journal of Agricultural Economics*, 68(2) (May): 451–7

(1990) 'China's Interprovincial Grain Marketing and Import Demand', US Department of Agriculture, Agriculture and Trade Analysis Division, Economic Research Service, Staff Report No. AGES 9059, September

(1992a) 'Chinese foreign trade', *The China Quarterly*, 131 (September)

(1992b) *Foreign Trade and Economic Reform in China, 1978–1990*, Cambridge: Cambridge University Press

Latham, Richard J. (1985) 'The implications of rural reforms for grass roots cadres', in E. J. Perry and C. Wong (eds), *The Political Economy of Reform in Post Mao China*, Cambridge, Mass: Harvard University Press

Lee, Yok-shiu F. (1989) 'Small towns and China's urbanization level', *The China Quarterly*, 120 (December)

Lewis, P. and N. Andrews (1989) 'Household demand in China', *Applied Economics*, 21: 793–807

Li Ji (1989) 'A study of vegetable wholesale marketing in Beijing', *Beijing shangxueyuan xuebao* [Bulletin of the Beijing Commercial Institute], 2: 56–61

Li Laiyu (1988) 'Contract purchase is the main way of realising the policy of linking grain and vegetables', *Jingji wenti tansuo* [Exploration of Economic Issues], 7: 48–51

Li Maolin, Chen Jianmin and Diao Limin (1989) 'Guanyu wending mianhua shengchan wentide tantao [On the issue of stabilizing cotton production]', *Zhongguo nongcun jingji* [China's Rural Economy], 8: 20–5

Li Peng (1988) 'The basic way to improve urban vegetable supplies lies in reform', Speech on 1 May 1988, *Zhongguo jingji tizhi gaige* [China Economy System Reform], 6: 6–11

Li Qingzeng (1991) 'Government control over grain production in China', Chinese Economy Research Unit Working Paper 91/7, University of Adelaide

Li Qingzeng, Zhou Binbin and Gao Hongbin (1988) 'Nongcun gaige shinian: xianzhen yu weilai [Ten years of rural reform: the current situation and the future]', *Jingjixue zhoubao* [Economics Weekly], 7 February

Li Zhensun *et al.* (1988) 'The target model for reform of the vegetable production and sales system: a study of "two systems in one line"', *Shangye jingji wenhui* [Commercial Economics Bulletin], 4: 15–19

Li Zhiqiang (1994) '1994 nian mianhua shengchan xingshi fenxi [Analysis of the situation in cotton production in 1994]', *Zhongguo nongeun jingji* [China's Rural Economy], 6: 25–7

Li Zuoyan (1989) 'Shi lun mianhua fazhan zhong de zhengce wenti [Policy issues in the development of cotton]', *Nongye jingji wenti* [Issues of Agricultural Economy], 9

Lim, Steven and R. Harris (1991) 'Work incentives, communes and the responsibility system in China', Paper presented at the 20th Conference of Economists, held by the Economic Society of Australia, Hobart, 30 September to 3 October

Lin Justin Yifu (1987) 'The household responsibility system reform in China: a peasant's institutional choice', *American Journal of Agricultural Economics*, 69 (May): 410–15

(1988) 'The household responsibility system in China's agricultural reform: a theoretical and empirical study', *Economic Development and Cultural Change*, 36 (April): S199–S224

(1989a) 'Rural reforms and agricultural productivity growth in China', UCLA Working Paper 576 (December)

(1989b) 'Rural factor markets in China after the household responsibility reform', in Bruce Reynolds (ed.), *Chinese Economic Policy*, New York: Paragon

(1991a) 'Collectivization and China's agricultural crisis in 1959–1961', *Journal of Political Economy*, 98 (December): 1228–52

(1991b) 'The household responsibility system reform and the adoption of hybrid rice in China', *Journal of Development Economics*, 37 (July): 353–72

(1992a) 'Rural reforms and agricultural growth in China', *American Economic Review*, 82 (1) (March): 34–51

(1992b) 'Rural reform and development', in Ross Garnaut and Liu Guoguang (eds), *Economic Reform and Internationalisation: China and the Pacific Region*, Sydney: Allen & Unwin

Lin Justin Yifu, Cai, Fang and Li, Zhou (1994) 'China's economic reforms: pointers for other economies in transition?', Policy Research Working Paper 1310, Agricultural Policies Division, Agriculture and Natural Resources Department, Washington DC: World Bank

Lin Wenyi (1988) 'The nature of problems in China's vegetable marketing and the appropriate policies', *Guangxi shangye jingji* [Guangxi Commercial Economics], 3: 9–16

Lin Xiangjin (1991) 'Woguo chan–xiao xingshi fenxi ji zhengcexing jianyi [An analysis of the situation in China's wool production and marketing and some policy proposals]', *Nongye jingji wenti* [Issues of Agricultural Economy], 12: 15–19

Liu Jiang (1988a) 'Thoughts on aims and methods of achieving the "vegetable basket project"', *Keji ribao*, 7 August, p. 2

(1988b) 'Realise the "vegetable basket project" in order to solve the problem of urban food supplies', *Zhongguo nongcun jingji* [China's Rural Economy], 10: 9–10, 36

Liu Suinian and Wu Qunmin (eds.) (1986) *The National Economy during the 'Cultural Revolution', 1966–1976*, Harbin: Heilongjiang People's Publishers (in Chinese)

Liu Xiaowen (1990) 'Woguo mianhua chan–xu de Kunjing yu duice [The problems and possible counter-measures of China's cotton supply and demand]', *Jihua yu shichang* [Planning and Market], 6: 30–2

Longworth, J. W., 1989, *China's Rural Development Miracle: With International Comparisons*, Queensland: University of Queensland Press

Lu Anhe and Yang Xueyi (1986) 'Gaishan shou bu di zhi xian caizheng zhuangkuang de tantao [An Exploration of the Improvement of Financial Administration in Deficit Counties]', *Nongye jingji congkan* [Agricultural Economics Series] (March)

Lu Weiguo (1991) 'A review of recent developments in the Chinese textile industry', Paper presented at the conference 'Wool in Japan', held by the Australian–Japan Research Centre, The Australian National University, Canberra, 12 September

Luo Hanxian (1985) *Economic Changes in Rural China*, Beijing: New World Press

Ma Hong (1982) *Xiandai Zhongguo jingji shidian* [An Encyclopedia of the Contemporary Chinese Economy], Beijing: Zhongguo Shehui Kexue Chubanshe

302   References

Ma Xiaohe (1993a) 'Resumed GATT status of China and agricultural production: an analysis', *Nongye jingji wenti* [Issues of Agricultural Economy], 11

(1993b) 'Analysing the influences of the resumption of the GATT membership on China's agricultural production', *Agricultural Economic Issues*, 1: 27–30

Mao Zhibin (1984) 'An inquiry into several issues concerning the responsibility system in tea fields', *Zhongguo chaye* [China Tea], 6: 6–7 (in Chinese)

Martin, Will (1991) 'Effects of foreign exchange reform in raw wool demand: a quantitative analysis', in Christopher Findlay (ed.), *Challenges of Economic Reform and Industrial Growth: China's Wool War*, Sydney: George Allen & Unwin

Martin, Will and Peter Warr (1991) 'Explaining agriculture's relative decline: a supply side analysis for Indonesia' (mimeo), The Australian National University, Canberra

McMillan, John, John Whalley and Li Jing Zhu (1989) 'The impact of China's economic reforms on agricultural productivity growth', *Journal of Political Economy*, 97 (4)

Ministry of Agriculture (1984) *China Rural Laws*, Beijing: China Agricultural Press

(1987a) *Zhongguo xiangzhen qiye guanli baike quanshu* [Chinese Encyclopedia of Township Enterprises], Beijing: China Agricultural Press

(1987b) *Zhongguo xiangzhen qiye guanli baike quanshu* [Chinese Encyclopedia of Township Enterprises], Beijing: China Agricultural Press

(1989a) *Zhongguo nongcun: zhengce yanjiu beiwanglu* [Rural China: Memorandum on Policy Research], Beijing: Nongye Chubanshe

(1989b) *Zhongguo nongcun sishi nian* [Forty Years in Rural China], Beijing: Zhongguan Nongmin Chubanshe

(1989c) *The Vegetable Basket Plan*, Beijing: China Agricultural Press

(1989d) *Zhongguo nongye tongji ziliao, 1987* [China Agriculture Statistical Material, 1987], Beijing: China Agricultural Press

(1991) *Zhongguo nongye tongji ziliao, 1989* [China Agricultural Statistical Material, 1989], Beijing: China Agricultural Press

(various issues) *Zhongguo nongye nianjian* [China Agricultural Yearbook], Beijing: Agricultural Press

Ministry of Agriculture, Planning Bureau (1989) *Zhongguo nongcun jingji tongji ziliao daquan, 1949–1986* [A Comprehensive Book of China's Rural Economic Statistics, 1949–1986], Beijing: China Agricultural Press

Ministry of Agriculture, Policy and Law Department (1989) *Zhongguo hongcun sishi nian* [China's Countryside over Forty Years], Henan: Zhongguan Nongmin Chubanshe

Ministry of Agriculture, Rural Research Centre, Agricultural Products Wholesale Markets Research Team (1992) 'Wo guo shucai pifa shichang gaikuang [An Outline of China's Wholesale Vegetable Markets]', *Zhongguo wujia* [China Prices], 3: 10–14

Niu, R. and P. Calkins (1986) 'Towards an agricultural economy for China in a new age: progress, problems, response, and prospects', *American Journal of Agricultural Economics*, 68 (2): 445–50

Niu Xiaofeng and Zhao Yipu (1989) 'Xieran yuanliang lu [The Grain Transport Road Dyed with Blood]', *Nongmin ribao* [Peasant's Daily], 17 January

Office of the Leading Group (of Economic Development in Poor Areas under the State Council) (1989) *Outlines of Economic Development in China's Poor Areas*, Beijing: Agricultural Publishing House (in Chinese)

Oksenberg, Michael and James Tong (1991) 'The evolution of central-provincial fiscal relations in China 1971–1984: the formal system', *The China Quarterly*, 125 (March): 1–32

Park, Young Il (1988) 'The changing pattern of textile trade in Northeast Asia', *Pacific Economic Papers*, 157, Australia–Japan Research Centre, The Australian National University, Canberra

Park, Young Il and K. Anderson (1988) 'The rise and demise of textiles and clothing in economic development: the case of Japan', *Pacific Economic Papers*, 163, Australia–Japan Research Centre, The Australian National University, Canberra

Perkins, D. W. (1969) *Agricultural Development in China, 1368–1968*, Chicago: Aldine Press

 (1988) 'Reforming China's economic system', *Journal of Economic Literature* (June): 601–45

Piazza, Alan (1983) 'Trends in food and nutrient availability in China, 1950–81', World Bank Staff Working Paper, Washington, DC: World Bank

Pudney, S. and L. Wang (1991) 'Rationing and consumer demand in China: simulating effects of a reform of the urban food pricing system', The Development Economics Research Program Working Paper No. 15, London School of Economics

Qian Yaonan (1989) 'Case studies on the Chinese textile industry' (mimeo), Academy of Ministry of Textile Industry (July)

Qu Yuxing (1991) 'Tea production estimates', *Chaye zhazhi* [Tea Industry Journal], 13 (3): 6–9

Ravallion, Martin and Monika Huppi (1991) 'Measuring changes in poverty: a methodological case study of Indonesia during an adjustment period', *The World Bank Economic Review*, 5 (1): 57–82

Research Centre of Guangdong Provincial Government (1988) *Research Materials of Guangdong Social and Economic Development Strategy*, Guangdong Provincial Government, Guangdong (in Chinese)

Research Office, CCP Shaanxi Provincial Committee and Shaanxi Bureau of Statistics (1986) *The Affairs of Shaanxi's Counties*, Xian: Shaanxi People's Publishers (in Chinese)

Ringen, Stein (1991) 'Households, standards of living and inequality', *Review of Income and Wealth*, 37 (1), March

Riskin, C. (1987) *China's Political Economy*, Oxford: Oxford University Press

 (1991) 'Income distribution and poverty in rural China: some results of the China household income project', Paper prepared for the conference on Distribution of Household Income in China, Xi'an, 28–30 December

Sadoulet, Elisabeth and de Janvry, Alain (1992) 'Agricultural trade liberalisation and low income countries: a general equilibrium-multimarket approach', *American Journal of Agricultural Economics*, 74: 268–80

Scandizzo, Pasquale Lucio (1992) 'Trade liberalisation and agricultural prices', *Journal of Policy Modelling*, 14 (5): 561–82

Schultz, Theodore W. (1964) *Transforming Traditional Agriculture*, New Haven: Yale University Press

Sen, Amartya (1979) 'Issues in the measurement of poverty', *Scandinavian Journal of Economics*, 81: 285–307

Shen Kedi and Wang Liming (1987) 'Estimates of China's tea production and sales for the period of the Seventh Five-Year Plan', *Zhongguo chaye* [China Tea], 5: 6–9

Shi, W. (1990) *The Problems of Fiscal Subsidies: Challenges and Options*, Beijing: Beijing Science and Technology Press

Sicular, Terry (1988a) 'Agricultural planning and pricing in the post-Mao period', *The China Quarterly*, 116 (December): 671–705

    (1988b) 'Plan and market in China's agricultural commerce', *Journal of Political Economy*, 96 (2): 283–307

Skinner, G. William (1978) 'Vegetable supply and marketing in Chinese cities', *The China Quarterly*, 76 (December): 733–93

Small Group (on Chinese Rural Poverty) (1989) 'Chinese rural poverty standard', *Research Report on the Poverty Standard for Rural China*, Beijing

Song Guoqing (1987) 'Cong tongguo tongxiao dao tudishui [From Unified Purchase and Supply to Land Taxation]', in Gao Xiaomen *et al.*, *Zhongguo liangshi wenti yanjiu* [Research into China's Grain Problems], Beijing: Jingji Guanli Chubanshe

Song, Q. (1990) 'The feedback of relative prices mechanism between grain and cotton', *Jingji ribao* [Economic Daily], 17 August

State Council Research Unit Rural Economy Group and the Rural Development Research Institute of the Chinese Academy of Social Sciences (eds.) (1990) *Bie wu xuanze – xiangzhen qiye yu guomin jingji de xietiao fazhan* [There is No Other Choice – The Co-ordinated Development of Rural Enterprises and the National Economy], Beijing: Gaige Chubanshe

SSB (State Statistical Bureau) (1984) *Quanguo nongye tongji ziliao (xubian), 1978 1983* [National Agricultural Statistics (Continuation), 1978, 1983], Beijing: China Statistical Publishing House

    (1987) *Guominshouru tongji ziliao huibian* [A Compilation of National Income Statistics Data], Beijing: China Statistical Publishing House

    (1988a) *Zhongguo nongcum tongji nianjian* [Rural Statistical Yearbook of China 1988], Beijing: China Statistical Publishing House

    (1988b) *Zhongguo gongye jingi tongji nianjian* [Chinese Industrial Statistical Yearbook], 27: 48

    (1989a) *China Price Yearbook 1989*, Beijing: China Statistical Publishing House

    (1989b) *Zhongguo nongcum tongji nianjian* [Rural Statistical Yearbook of China 1989], Beijing: China Statistical Publishing House

(1990a) *China Statistical Yearbook 1990*, Beijing: China Statistical Publishing House

(1990b) *Zhongguo nongcum tongji nianjian* [Rural Statistical Yearbook of China 1990], Beijing: China Statistical Publishing House

(1990c) *China Agricultural Yearbook*, Beijing: China Statistics Press

(1991a) *Zhongguo tongji zhaiyao* [Statistical Abstract of China], Beijing: China Statistical Publishing House

(1991b) *China Price Yearbook 1991*, Beijing: China Statistical Publishing House

(1991c) *Statistical Yearbook of Township Enterprise 1991*, Beijing: China Statistical Publishing House

(1992) *Zhongguo nongcum tongji nianjian* [Rural Statistical Yearbook of China 1992], Beijing: China Statistical Publishing House

(1994) *A Statistical Survey of China 1994*, Beijing: China Statistical Publishing House

(various issues) *Zhougguo tongji nianjin* (ZTN) [China Statistical Yearbook], Beijing: China Statistical Press

(various issues) *Statistics of China's Domestic and Foreign Trade*, Beijing: China Statistical Publishing House

(various issues) *Statistical Yearbook of China's Domestic Market*, Beijing: China Statistical Publishing House

SSB, Fixed Capital Investment Statistics Division (1987) *Zhongguo guding zichan tongji ziliao, 1950–1985* [China Fixed Capital Investment Statistics, 1950–1985), Beijing: China Statistical Publishing House

SSB, Trade and Price Statistical Division (1986) *Zhongguo maoyi wujia tongji ziliao 1952–1983* [China Trade and Price Statistics, 1952–1983], Beijing: China Statistical Publishing House

SSB, Urban Sampling Survey Team (1988) *Wujia tongji wenjian huibian* [A Compilation of Price and Statistics Documents], Beijing: China Statistical Publishing House

Stone, Bruce *et al.* (1991) 'Commercialization of agriculture in China: income growth and structural change in poor areas', Unpublished paper

Summary of World Broadcasts, Part 3, The Far East: FE/0148/B2/1, 11 May 1988; FE/0153/B2/1–2, 17 May 1988; FE/0627/B2/3, 30 November 1989; FE/0820/B2/1–4, 19 July 1990; FE/0866/B2/1–2, 11 September 1990

Sun Keliang (1991) 'Crisis and adjustment: what is happening in the Chinese textile industry?' (mimeo), Australia–Japan Research Centre, The Australian National University, Canberra

Sun Yun-Wing (1985) 'The role of Hong Kong and Macau in China's export drive', National Centre for Development Studies Working Paper 85/11, The Australian National University, Canberra

Suzuki, N. (1987) 'Rice demand and supply in China and other countries', in K. Ogha (ed.), *International Rice Market and the Impact of Japanese Rice Liberalisation*, Kenkyu Sosho, No. 107

SWB, BBC *Summary of World Broadcasts*, Part 3, The Far East (various issues)

Tan Liuming (1989) 'A cursory discussion of the appropriate business scale for tea

Tangshan Government, Hebei (1989) 'Follow the laws, unite relaxation with control and move smoothly to a new system', *Nongye jingji wenti* [Issues of Agricultural Economy], 5: 33–5

Tea Research Institute of China (TRI) (1986) *Tea Culture of China*, Shanghai: TRI (in Chinese)

Telser L. G. (1980) 'A theory of self-enforcing agreements', *Journal of Business*, 53: 27–44

Third Bureau, Ministry of Public Security (1985) *Zhongguo xiangzhen renkou ziliao shouce* [China Township Population Materials Handbook], Beijing: Ditu Chubanshe

Tian Yinong, Zhu Fulin and Xiang Huaicheng (1985) *Lun zhongguo caizheng guanli tizhi de gaige* [On the Reform of China's System of Financial Administration], Beijing: Jingji Kexue Chubanshe

Tian Yuan *et al.* (1988) 'A survey of and proposals for the relationship between vegetable production and sales in the Beijing-Hebei area and the development of base production areas', *Jingji cankao* [Economic Reference News], 27 April, p. 1 and 28 April, p. 1

Tyers, R. and K. Anderson (1992) *Disarray in World Food Markets*, Cambridge: Cambridge University Press

UNIDO Secretariat (1989) 'Textile policy issues for developing countries', *Industry and Development*, 25: 93–155

Urban Social Economy Investigation Group, State Statistical Bureau (1989) *China Yearbook of Price Statistics*, Beijing: China Statistics Publishing House

Vogel, E. (1989) *One Step Ahead in China: Guangdong Under Reform*, Cambridge, Mass: Harvard University Press

Vousden, N. (1990) *The Economics of Trade Protection*, Cambridge: Cambridge University Press

Wang Huimin (1994) 'Debate on agricultural protection issues in China', *Rural Economy and Society*, 4: 43–6

Wang Jun (1989) 'Thoughts on transforming the hidden subsidies on the prices of four foodstuffs into open subsidies', *Jihua yu shichang tansuo* [Explorations of the Plan and the Market], 5: 5–8

Wang, Y. (1991) 'Estimation and implications of urban housing welfare benefits', *Reform*, 3: 106–12

Wang, Z. (1989) 'The rationing effects on consumption structure change of Chinese urban households during 1981–1987', Paper presented at the Fifth Annual Conference of Chinese Young Economists Society, University of Pittsburgh, July

Watson, A. (1987) 'The family farm, land use, and accumulation in agriculture', *The Australian Journal of Chinese Affairs*, 17 (January): 1–17

—— (1988) 'The reform of agricultural marketing in China since 1978', *The China Quarterly*, 113 (March): 1–28

—— (1989) 'Investment issues in the Chinese countryside', *The Australian Journal of Chinese Affairs*, 22 (July): 85–126

Watson, A., C. Findlay and Yintang Du (1989) 'Who won the "wool war"?: a case study in rural product marketing in China', *The China Quarterly*, 118 (June): 213–41

Wen Guanzhong James (1989) 'The current land tenure and its impact on the long term performance of the fanning sector: the case of modern China', Unpublished dissertation, Department of Economics, University of Chicago

Wong, Christine P.W. (1992) 'Fiscal reform and local industrialization', *Modern China*, 18(2) (April): 197–227

World Bank (1984) *China: The Health Sector*, Washington, DC: World Bank

(1988) *China: External Trade and Capital*, Washington, DC: World Bank

(1990a) 'Grain marketing, price policy and foreign trade', China Department Working Paper 7, Agricultural Operations Division, Asia Regional Office, Washington, DC

(1990b) *World Development Report, 1990*, Washington, DC: World Bank

(1991a) *China: Options for Reform in the Grain Sector* (World Bank Country Study), Washington, DC: World Bank

(1991b) 'China: Managing an Agricultural Transformation', World Bank Report No. 8652–CHA, April, p. 154

Wu Hui (1985) *Zhongguo lidai liangshi muchan yanjiu* [Studies on the History of Grain Output per Mu in China], Beijing: Nongye Chubanshe

Xiang Huaicheng (1987) 'Zai gaige zhong qianjin de Zhongguo caizheng [China's financial administration advancing through reform]', *Caizheng yanjiu* [Financial Research], 2 (February): 1–9

Xie Zhaochuan (1989) 'An inquiry into the forms of production responsibility systems in tea field management', *Zhongguo chaye* [China Tea], 2: 34–5

Xu Yicai *et al.* (1988) 'Vegetable price reform and subsidies', *Jingji cankao* [Economic Reference News], 3 May, p. 2

Xu Yuanming *et al.* (1989) 'Some thoughts on balancing supply of urban food-stuffs in Jiangsu', *Nongye jingji wenti* [Issues of Agricultural Economy], 5: 29–32

Yan Zhenguo (1988) 'Where is the way out for reform of vegetable management in Beijing', *Renmin ribao* [People's Daily], 27 October, p. 2

Yang Yongzhe (1990a) 'Fighting poverty: the efforts of the Chinese government', *Development and Prosperity*, 2 (in Chinese)

(1990b) 'Experience and lessons of the implementation of China's anti-poverty plan', *Development and Prosperity*, 2 (in Chinese)

(1991) 'Are China's clothing and textile exports demand or supply constrained?' (mimeo), National Centre for Development Studies, The Australian National University, Canberra

Yang Yongzheng and Rod Tyers (1989) 'The economic costs of food self-sufficiency in China', *World Development*, 17 (2) (February)

Zhang Xiaohe (1990) 'The classification of the industries by factor intensity and the corresponding trade pattern of China', Chinese Economy Research Unit Working Paper 1/91, University of Adelaide (also in Chinese Students' Society for Economic Studies (ed.), *China: Trade and Reform*, National Centre for Development Studies, The Australian National University, Canberra

(1991) 'China's textile industry and cotton production' (mimeo), Chinese Economy Research Unit, University of Adelaide

(1992) 'Rural–urban isolation and its impact on China's production and trade pattern', *China Economic Review*, 3 (1): 85–105

(1994) 'Rural–urban migration restriction versus rural industrialization', in Wu Yanrui and Zhang Xiaohi (eds), *Chinese Economy in Transition*, National Centre for Development Studies, The Australian National University, Canberra

Zhejiang Provincial Government (1989) *Zhejizng tongji nianjian 1989* [Zhejiang Statistical Yearbook 1989], Hangzhou: Zhejiang People's Publishers

Zheng Chunfeng (1993) 'Challenges of the GATT to China's agricultural products and policy responses', *Agricultural Economic Issues*, 1: 22–6

Zhongguo fangzhi gongye nianjian [Almanac of China's Textile Industry] (various issues), Beijing: Fangzhi Gongye Chubanshe [China Textile Publishing House]

Zhongguo xiangzhen qiye guanli baike quanshu [Chinese Encyclopedia of Township Enterprises (1987) Beijing: China Agricultural Press

Zhong Fu-ning (1994) 'China's grain trade after the Uruguay Round', *Zhongguo nongcun jingji* [China's Rural Economy], 3: 21–6

Zhou Haichun (1994) 'An analysis of impact of grain prices on overall retail prices', *Zhongguo nongcun jingjj* [China's Rural Economy], 9: 42–7

Zhu *et al.* (1991) 'Food consumption and food acquisition behaviour among rural households in China', in *Proceedings of International Conference on Food, Nutrition, and Social-Economic Development*, Beijing: Science and Technology Publishing House

Zhu Rongji (1994), Speech at State Council National Conference on Cotton, SWB, FE/2094/G/7–8, 7 September

Zhu Shan and Zhou Jiarang (1987) 'Vegetable pricing', *Jiage lilun yu shijian* [Price Theory and Practice], 4: 61–3

Zhu Songhua (1989) 'The basic ways for Shanghai to establish the "vegetable basket project" and the problems to be solved', *Shanghai jingji* [Shanghai Economy], 4: 11–14

Zhu Xigang and Tian Weiming (1989), 'The system of decision making for agriculture in China', *The Australian Journal of Chinese Affairs*, 21 (January): 161–70

Index

to agricultural inputs, 92
urban housing, 46

Tea war, 272–4
Tea
black, 269, 274
compressed, 269
domestic marketing of, 271
green, 269
Oolong, 269
output, 265
planted area, 265–6
plucked area, 265–6
scented, 269
the reformation and transformation of
the industry, 265–76
Third Bureau, Ministry of Public Security,
285
Third revolution, 1–9, 27–37
Total factor productivity, 23–4
Township and village enterprises, 263–4
Turning point in agriculture, 185–98
Two-tier price system for agricultural
products, 82, 94

UNIDO Secretariat, 120
Unified purchase and marketing system for
agricultural products, 28–9
Unification of the swap and official foreign
exchange markets, 2
Urban population, 14
Urban–rural income disparity, 252
Urbanisation and industrialisation, 47–8,
255

Vegetable basket plan, 159–60
Vote trading, 179

Welfare loss due to agricultural protection,
177–9
Western location, 75
Wholesale markets
agricultural, 113–19
Beijing's Dazhongshi Agricultural, 114,
118, 161
Chengdu Hehuaci Agricultural, 114
Chengdu meat, 114, 119
Chongqing fruit, 119
Dazhongshi vegetable, 119
first central meat, 113
first grain, 113
first sugar, 113
official, 115
reform, *see* Reforms
Shandong's shouguang vegetable, 119
Shanghai meat, 114, 119
Shazikou, 161
Shoiguang Vegetable, 113
Shui Duizi and Beitaipingzhuang, 160
spontaneous, 115
Zhenzhou grain, 117
Wool
end of war, 140–1
processing centres, 139
purchases, 135
secondary market in, 138
state marketing system for, 138
war, 120, 135–41
World Trade Organization (WTO), 85
and agricultural development, 167–72
China's entry into the, 7
membership, 2, 167–9, 197

Zhenzhou wholesale grain market, 116–19

Printed in the United States
By Bookmasters

Printed in the United States
By Bookmasters